Lancaster's Good Man,
John Piersol McCaskey

A Biography by
Dolores Parsil

Lancaster's Good Man, John Piersol McCaskey

by Dolores Parsil

Library of Congress Number: 2015917447
International Standard Book Number: 978-1-60126-475-6

Published 2016 by
Masthof Press
219 Mill Road
Morgantown, PA 19543-9516

Table of Contents

To

WAYNE, my husband, and

ROBERT, my editor of first resort,

with gratitude beyond measure

and great love

ACKNOWLEDGEMENTS

Katharine "Kay" McCaskey Adelman lived with J. P. McCaskey, her great-grandfather, until his death in 1935 when she was eight years old. It was she, my witty and wonderful neighbor, whose memories and stories set me on a path I had not anticipated but came to love in my retirement. It was she who entrusted me with her papers, materials, and hours and who connected me to other relatives, all so very generous as well.

This book would not have been possible without Kay and these McCaskey descendants: Kay's brother James "Jim" McCaskey, their cousin Joanne McCaskey Kersch, great-grandnephew Henry "Hank" Chapman, and great-great-grandchildren Philip McCaskey, Ned McCaskey, Patrick H. McCaskey, Michael Adelman, and Megan McCaskey Johnson. Megan's enthusiastic support was particularly important during a time when my belief in the project was faltering.

I am sorry that neither Jim nor Hank lived to see this book in print. Jim's advice to me to "find the *Journal*" proved invaluable, and Hank, who rescued his great-grandfather Will's remarkable story from obscurity, sent me everything he had involving J.P. from those trunks that had been consigned to the trash. Hank was a gentle, kind man, and I will always treasure our brief meeting in California.

I am deeply indebted to my trio of readers, Katherine Parsil Manzanares, Megan McCaskey Johnson, and Alison Ortiz, busy women who found time to read and critique each chapter. I am also grateful to Frank Gray and Dan Missildine for their suggestions and support along the way. Mary Alice Gerfin and B. David Wagner were excellent go-to picture people.

I am enormously thankful to so many family members and friends for their encouragement, interest, and patience. I wish I could name them all here.

My resource venues and people provided places to dig and mine, and for such repositories of and access to the past I am inordinately thankful: Marjorie Bardeen and LancasterHistory.org and its competent and professional staff; Lancaster Public Library and its most helpful librarians; Leo Shelley at St. James'; Richard Gilfillan at St. John's Episcopal Church, Compass; the staff for Old Leacock Presbyterian; Lancaster City Hall, particularly Janet Spleen and Jim Bowers; Millersville University and Franklin & Marshall College; and Vince Slaugh and Rick Abel.

I thank Dan Mast at Masthof Press for embracing this book and providing a competent editor and designer to give it life. My trips there seemed always to be on beautiful blue-sky days.

I want to commend Thomas Goodhart, a J. P. McCaskey High School Class of 1980 graduate, for his abiding interest in McCaskey, his faithful tending of the once-neglected McCaskey gravesites, and his successful effort to have a John Piersol McCaskey week declared for the anniversary of McCaskey's 175th birthday in October 2012, which included proclamations issued by Mayor Rick Gray, State Representative Michael Sturla, and the Lancaster County Commissioners.

Finally, I thank Sherma Woolstenhulme, recently retired director of the McCaskey Alumni Association, for her enthusiasm and encouragement. I appreciate the work of the association in preserving McCaskey memorabilia and the history of the high school as it services thousands of graduates from a public high school of which McCaskey most assuredly would be very proud.

A Question

The new high school for the city of Lancaster, Pennsylvania, opened February 7, 1938. Expensive, grand, luxurious, marbled and gilded, the Art Deco building welcomed both young men and women into its co-educational classrooms and state-of-the-art facilities. At the dedication ceremony that May, eight-year-old James Douglas McCaskey unveiled a picture of his great-grandfather John Piersol McCaskey, the man for whom the building was named.

What had this John Piersol McCaskey done to deserve such an honor, to merit such distinction? After all, other Lancastrians had done great things for education. Thaddeus Stevens, far more well-known, had kept the law mandating public education in Pennsylvania from repeal. Thomas Burrowes had been the one to shape the system in its complicated incubation, serving as Secretary of the Commonwealth and then as the first Pennsylvania Superintendent of Common Schools.

Lancaster had other famous sons, as well. General John Reynolds was the city's Civil War hero, Robert Fulton her acclaimed inventor. James Buchanan, while not the most highly regarded President of the United States, had resided in Lancaster and was (and still is) the only president from Pennsylvania.

Ask Lancastrians why the school is named for J. P. McCaskey, and most don't know. The common response is, "Well, he must have done something important."

McCaskey's son Walter Bogardus McCaskey and great-grandson James Douglas McCaskey unveiling McCaskey's portrait at the dedication of the John Piersol McCaskey High School, May 1938. (Photo courtesy of the family.)

Chapter 1

As the Years Pass His Memory Grows in Fragrance

McCaskey named a textbook *Lincoln Literary Collection* "in honor of Abraham Lincoln . . . As the years pass his memory grows in fragrance, redolent of the sweet spirit of good-will to men."[1]

In 1861 Abraham Lincoln's inaugural train paused in Lancaster, Pennsylvania, on its way to Washington, D.C. In 1865 his funeral train pulled into the Lancaster station on its somber passage through the country to Springfield, Illinois. Among the thousands of citizens who were present on both occasions was local teacher and reporter John Piersol McCaskey, who esteemed the President as the greatest public figure in American history.

In February 1861 President-elect Lincoln traveled to his inauguration from Springfield, Illinois, to Washington, D.C. Millions lined the tracks in cities, towns, and countryside through which his train journeyed. After Philadelphia, Lincoln and his entourage were slated to travel to Harrisburg on February 22, 1861, without stopping in Lancaster, despite the town's location on the line between the two cities. A delegation of determined Lancaster citizens traveled to Philadelphia and convinced Colonel W. S. Woods, Lincoln's manager, to add a brief interlude in their city.[2]

Excitement about Lincoln was tainted by fear, hatred, and anger. The country had already begun to unravel; in this same month, the Confederate States of America was established in Montgomery, Alabama. Dissent and the threat of assassination followed Lincoln everywhere. According to one Lancaster observer, before the President-elect departed from Philadelphia that winter morning, he stood in front of Independence Hall beneath an American flag, spoke of the great principle that united the country, the principle of liberty for all, and of "the weights [that] should be lifted from the shoulders of all men, and that *all* should have an equal chance." Then he slapped his knee and almost shouted that he would rather be assassinated on the spot than give up anything the flag stood for.[3]

While Lincoln was speaking in Philadelphia, Lancastrians thronged the newly-constructed train station at Chestnut and Queen Streets. Firefighters, military units, and bands were leaving to go to Harrisburg to greet Lincoln there, as previously scheduled. McCaskey, 23, was in that early morning crowd to cheer on his brother William ("Will") S. McCaskey and the Fencibles, one of the militias boarding the train. Also, he was covering the events of the day for a local paper, the *Daily Evening Express.* He described the groups' departure, enhanced by music, on a crisp winter morning: "A more glorious February morning never dawned than that of today. When the sun uprose not a single cloud floated under the deep blue sky. The air was sharp and bracing, and at the early hour we refer to there was every indication of a pleasant and beautiful day." The bands performed a number of "popular and patriotic airs in the depot" prior to departure.[4]

As Lincoln's train chugged westward, more people came to the depot. Schools and stores were closed. "For two hours previous to the arrival of the special train the neighborhood of the Depot presented a most animated scene. The streets, the windows, and the balconies were crowded with men, women and children—many of whom stood in the cold all this time in order not to be deprived of their positions. The Cadwell House was the great centre of attraction, and every window and available standing room was occupied."[5]

McCaskey, who had cast his first presidential ballot for the candidate from Illinois and remained a Republican all his life, expected a "hearty welcome of the 'rising sun' of the Nation."[6] All were not so ecstatic, however.

An undercurrent of fear and dread played out in "rebel sentiment," that erupted into a fight in front of the Hubley House in Center Square, "in which some prominent man hit one of the bullies over his head."[7]

Shortly before noon, the train approached the city, and a "national salute . . . [was] fired from cannon stationed near the automotive works."[8] Bands played, drumbeats filled the air, and the people cheered and waved hats and handkerchiefs. Flags above the streets fluttered over the crowds. When "Locomotive No. 161 decorated with evergreen boughs and red, white and blue bunting,"[9] pulled the train into the station, the music stopped and the crowd grew quiet. McCaskey recalled where he was standing at that moment, watching as the "Jackson Rifles, under Colonel Henry A. Hambright, were thrown across the street . . . from the train to the hotel entrance. They opened files and pressed back the dense crowd, giving passage way to those of the distinguished party who left the train. I happened to be in the press near the soldiers—"[10]

Abraham Lincoln was in Lancaster. Wearing a black stovepipe hat that made him even more conspicuous, given his height, he walked through the soldiers from the station to the hotel.[11] General Sumner[12]

The Lancaster train station at Queen and Chestnut Streets, circa 1900. (Photo courtesy of LancasterHistory.org.)

was on one side of Lincoln and Peter B. Fordney, chief of the Lancaster escort guard, on the other. McCaskey observed that Fordney was "our [Lancaster's] genial townsman . . . not yet 20 years of age, but standing 'six feet six' to escort Mr. Lincoln's 'six feet four.' The high silk hat of the president-elect measured up well with our good-natured son of Anak [an Old Testament allusion to a race of giant people] and both appreciated the humor of the situation."[13]

Lincoln entered the Cadwell House and spoke briefly from a second-floor balcony, his remarks punctuated by both humor and solemnity. He greeted the people: "'Ladies and Gentlemen of Lancaster County: I am happy to meet the citizens of this great county face to face; but I do not feel prepared to make a speech to you today. I have not the time now nor the strength, and, what is more, have no speech to make. I have come more to see you and let you see me.'" Then, McCaskey reported, Lincoln "complimented the ladies, and said in this respect he had the advantage of seeing them, and therefore [had the] best of the bargain. As regards the gentlemen he could not say so much."[14]

More seriously, Lincoln continued, "I might make a long speech, as there is plenty of matter in the conditions that exist, but I think the more a man speaks in these days, the less he is understood. As Solomon says, there is a time for all things, and I think the present is a time for silence. In a few days the time will be here for me to speak officially and I will then endeavor to speak plainly in regard to the Constitution and the liberties of the American people."[15]

Returning to his train, the President received a "handsome bouquet,"[16] shook hands along the way, and lifted up a "very beautiful little girl in his arms" to kiss.[17] Personal recollections from the townspeople included the following: Thomas J. Davis, a Franklin & Marshall student, commented that Lincoln seemed ill at ease with his tall silk hat. Harry Musselman observed that, although Mr. Lincoln's voice was plain, he spoke with emphasis and was a good orator and "[he] spoke the honest truth." Mr. Simon Raub, who had closed up his tailor shop for the occasion, was relieved, perhaps, that he did not have to be Mr. Lincoln's personal clothier, for he noted that Lincoln was "very tall, ungainly, and walked somewhat slouchy." Mary Baumgardner said Mr. Lincoln was "adept not only in terse argument, but very gracious in his compliments to the ladies, which seemed somewhat a surprise, owing to his general awkwardness."[18]

The entire visit lasted a mere 18 minutes. Lincoln's appearance, McCaskey wrote, "seemed like the shifting scenes of a panorama, to be remembered like a dream. . . . As the cars moved off, Mr. Lincoln bowed adieu from the rear platform, while the assembled crowd sent up the wildest applause."[19] Perhaps the awe of the moment transfixed the people as the train disappeared from view; McCaskey reported that the "crowd *gradually* [author's emphasis] dispersed, and our streets resumed their wonted aspect."[20]

Forty-eight years later, the citizens of Lancaster and their mayor, John Piersol McCaskey, commemorated Lincoln's visit and joined in a national celebration of the centenary of his birth. Festivities throughout the day and evening of February 12, 1909, mirrored those of the 1861 stop. Stores and banks were closed. Crowds filled the streets. Bunting and flags adorned

Mayor McCaskey, just above the letters A-B-R-A, addressing the citizens of Lancaster February 1909 in celebration of the anniversary of Lincoln's birth. (Photo courtesy of LancasterHistory.org.)

buildings, the Sailors' and Soldiers' Monument in Center Square, and even streetcars. At 3 p.m., city officials, the mayor among them, walked the two blocks from City Hall to the Imperial Hotel (the former Cadwell Hotel and current site of The Hotel Lancaster). The dignitaries were accompanied by a military unit of the National Guard, the Patriotic Order Sons of America, and the Junior Order United American Mechanics.[21]

A tablet commemorating Mr. Lincoln's appearance had been placed on the side of the hotel by its owner, Paul Heine,[22] and a banner above the balcony proclaimed that "Abraham Lincoln addressed the citizens of Lancaster on February 22, 1861," from that location. The program began with patriotic music performed by a choral group from the high school and several bands. This was followed by a benediction and the singing of Lincoln's favorite hymn, "Your Mission," by 500 schoolchildren under the direction of Miss Margaret L. Humphreville.[23]

Then it was the mayor's turn. McCaskey, 71 years old, stood where Lincoln had nearly a half-century earlier. He began his speech to the hundreds below him not with his own words, but with Lincoln's "Gettysburg Address." McCaskey lauded its excellence, saying: "[Lincoln read] from a page or two of note paper. There was no murmur of applause. It was a matchless funeral address above the newly made graves of thousands who had died that a nation dedicated to freedom might live." Those who heard it that November day in 1863 responded in a "perfect tribute of silence."[24]

McCaskey linked the Battle of Gettysburg and Lincoln's rhetoric in the address metaphorically, saying: "The top wave of the Rebellion broke on the heights of Gettysburg, and here, too, the eloquence of Abraham Lincoln reached its high water mark."[25] Lincoln's words, he noted, had been memorized by myriads: "Hundreds of thousands—millions, it may be, in the schools and outside of them—repeat these words today from memory. So it must be through the generations."[26] McCaskey had been among those teachers who required their students to do so.

A year after the Civil War ended, the Pennsylvania State Teachers' Association convened in Gettysburg. McCaskey and other educators attended an evening ceremony in the cemetery where Major Harry T. Lee, a teacher who had fought in the Battle of Gettysburg and been present at the cemetery's dedication in November 1863, recited Lincoln's speech. Lee told those gathered that the lengthy speech given by Edward Everett prior to President Lincoln's was technically perfect but lacking in emotion, while the President's touched many hearts and moved many to tears. After a closing prayer, the "national hymn," and a benediction, the educators departed quietly.[27]

The association report, published in *The Pennsylvania School Journal*, suggested that Lincoln was wrong when he said the world would not remember what he had said that day, countering that his words "will live as long as Cemetery Hill endures, as long as the world shall tell the deeds that have made Gettysburg immortal in story." It issued a directive to the readers of the *Journal*: "To the teacher who may chance to read these paragraphs, we would say: Encourage your pupils to commit this Address to memory—never to be forgotten. Let the noble sentiment which breathes become their life-long patriotic creed."[28]

"Declamation exercises [a common pedagogical practice of memorizing and reciting poetry and prose]," the report asserted, "do much to mould the taste and determine the style of the man." Only the best models, such as this address, were to be chosen, and each should exhibit "brevity, pathos, simplicity of style, and a presence of power which even the boy must feel, although he may not be able to understand or analyze it."[29]

McCaskey believed that the value of memorizing the address lay not only in its brilliance as a piece of literature but also in its ability to teach history. "Lincoln's 'Address at Gettysburg,' committed to memory," he wrote, "and the spirit of this gem of literature impressed upon the mind of the pupil is worth more for its historic setting and suggestiveness, worth more for its enduring grip upon the fancy of the boy or girl, than months of ordinary text-book work in history in many a school room."[30]

In 1905, McCaskey took students to Gettysburg after he had found out that many had never been to "this Mecca of freedom to the human race."[31] Willis A. Schindle, a participant, wrote this account of the trip:

"The eighteen High School boys who went to Gettysburg on Friday, October 6th, 1905, had a red-letter day. Dr. McCaskey was in charge of the party. Talking to the boys, a few days before, about the battle—which happened to be suggested by the address of Abraham Lincoln at Gettysburg, that had just been given to us as part of our 'good memory work' for the week—he found that not more than a half-dozen of us had ever been over the field. When we had recited the address in concert he went on to give us an idea of what a wonderful place this battlefield is, and what a great part it has played in the history of the United States and of the world. After an impressive talk, he said, 'Gettysburg is little more than a stone's throw from Lancaster and not more than a half-dozen of you have been there! People from all over the civilized world visit this field with deepest interest. You live near it; but think little of it, and care little for it. Many of you have bicycles. Put a few sandwiches into your pockets some Saturday morning, if you have no money and get there! How many of you would like to see Gettysburg?' Every hand went up, for the boys were stirred with enthusiasm as he talked, and that afternoon we asked him if he would go with us in case we got up a party. He named eighteen as the smallest number he was willing to take.

"We reached his figure, and left on Friday morning by the earliest train. The party changed cars at Hanover, with a delay of forty minutes, during which we had time to see the fine equestrian statue dedicated there on Thursday of the preceding week, in the presence of many thousand people, the largest number ever assembled in this old town. The statue The Picket *stands in the open square and faces Frederick street down which came the retreating rebels in the cavalry skirmish of June 30th, 1863. At Hanover also we had a chance to buy Charley Shue a new hat to replace the one he didn't go after when the wind blew it away as he was passing from one car to another, on the way through York county. The boys were a jolly 'Committee of the Whole' on the purchase of that hat, and we got him a good one. Here also we found a book-store with patriotic souvenir postal cards, and in five minutes we had them all bought up, no more to be had for love or money. Everybody wanted them.*

"Reaching Gettysburg at 10:30 we took two carriages, each seating comfortably ten or twelve persons. Mr. Pitzer, the proprietor of one of the hotels, who is an excellent guide, drove one of them. We went first to the Theological Seminary, from the cupola of which General Robert E. Lee made his observations of the field, and from which we had the same broad view of the surround-

ing country in which the battle was fought. Here Mr. Pitzer showed us on the maps, and overlooking the country, the movements of the armies during the three days' fighting. Then we started for a four-hours' drive of historic interest over the perfect roads of this great battlefield, on which more noble and costly memorials have been erected than upon any other in ancient or modern times. We left the carriages often to inspect more closely one memorial and another. At the foot of a noble statue we all touched the gun that fired the first shot in that tremendous battle.

"Before the great monument in National Cemetery we lined up, with uncovered heads, and repeated President Lincoln's well-known 'Address at Gettysburg,' on the spot where it was delivered more than forty years ago. Our guide, who had stood near Mr. Lincoln and heard him deliver this speech, congratulated the boys and told us we did it 'better than the President!' In the region of the 'Devil's Den' we came across a photographer who was out on a business trip, and

McCaskey and his students at Devil's Den. (Photo from High School News 1906.*)*

we posed for a picture, of which some of the boys ordered copies at fifty cents each. We got back to dinner shortly after three o'clock and were at the depot ready for our train at 3:45, reaching home at 7 o'clock. As Dr. McCaskey got off the train he found the boys awaiting him, and I had the honor of speaking their hearty thanks for a very pleasant and profitable day . . .

"Dr. McCaskey, referring to this excursion a few weeks since, told the boys that the time would come in the lives of some of them when, 'if they could sell the memories of that day's trip for a thousand dollars, they wouldn't take the money.' Such school parties should often be made up, and tens of thousands of boys and girls in the schools of Pennsylvania should visit Gettysburg every year."[32]

McCaskey's suggestion has certainly been heeded; school buses by the hundreds descend upon Gettysburg every spring.

McCaskey wanted to keep the 16th President forever present in the minds of Pennsylvania's schoolchildren and so named an art series and a textbook in his honor. The *Lincoln Art Series* was a collection of lithographs of famous artworks he published for display in the schools. He also selected and compiled poetry and prose pieces for his memory work textbook, the *Lincoln Literary Collection*. Memorization was a habit of the President's, McCaskey explained in his foreword: "This book is named in honor of Abraham Lincoln, in the desire to aid in extending and perpetuating the habit for which our best-loved President is widely known, that of committing to memory poems that he enjoyed. . . . As the years pass his memory grows in fragrance, redolent of the sweet spirit of good-will to men. Let it be kept green in the schools by following his good example, and adopting—knowing it to be his, and speaking of it as his—this wholesome Lincoln habit of committing to memory."[33]

The foreword also extolled Lincoln's virtues and greatness: "He was a unique man, who did many things that are unusual, but seem very human and natural for gracious and tender souls like himself. . . . He was a great man, raised up by Providence at a time when the nation sorely needed so pure a patriot, so far-sighted a leader, so wise a statesman. He was essentially religious, with a deep conviction of the abiding presence and overruling power of God; but at times a sense of the tremendous responsibility upon him made him know profoundly the meaning of his favorite poem, 'Oh, Why Should the Spirit of Mortal Be Proud?'"[34]

"Oh, Why Should the Spirit of Mortal Be Proud?" by William Knox tells of the transitory and inconsequential nature of human existence. Whether one's station in life is high or low, young or old, whether one is a king or a peasant, mother, husband, maiden or lover, saint or sinner, herdsman or beggar, wise man or fool, all fade away, and the next generation comes, only to repeat the same experiences and think the same thoughts as those over whose graves they walk. The joys and sorrows of life are gone in the blink of an eye.

The joys and sorrows of life
are gone in the blink of an eye. . .

Lincoln's funeral train left Washington, D.C., Friday, April 21, 1865, and began its journey to Illinois through countryside, cities, and towns past sobbing, disconsolate citizens. From Harrisburg where rain had poured down all night, the train moved under a clear morning sky on April 22 towards Lancaster. In Middletown, it passed laborers and farmers standing silently on boulders near the tracks. In Elizabethtown, people scrambled over woodpiles to catch a glimpse of the train. It sped through the countryside, past men and women removing hats and bonnets, and through Mount Joy, Landisville, and Dillerville.[35] Former President Buchanan sat in his carriage along the tracks just outside the city and, as the train passed, removed his hat and placed it over his heart.[36] Thaddeus Stevens, standing on a rock along the tracks, "seemed absorbed in silent meditation, unconscious that he was observed." He also uncovered his head as the hearse car went by.[37]

Shortly after 1 p.m., the train arrived in Lancaster. The streets near the station were thick with thirty to forty thousand people.[38] Businesses and schools were closed. Churches and buildings were draped in mourning. The bells were "sadly tolling, and everything betoken[ed] the grief and gloom of the people in this dark hour of our country's history."[39] The funeral engine, decorated in black, pulled nine cars[40] into the same passenger depot that Lincoln's inaugural train had entered four years earlier. Dark drapery and American flags were intertwined and festooned from columns and over office doorways. A U.S. and a Pennsylvania state flag, "large, beautiful silk flags,"[41] were crossed below a portrait of the President, which was wreathed with boxwood and mourning cloths.[42] A large placard proclaimed: "ABRAHAM LINCOLN, THE ILLUSTRIOUS MARTYR OF LIBERTY! THE NATION MOURNS HIS LOSS, BUT THOUGH DEAD HE YET LIVETH!"[43]

"All uncovered their heads when [the train] came into the station and stopped for a minute . . . and they remained uncovered until it pulled out; . . . many of the strong men wept."[44] The crowd surged and pressed in around the train. A woman fainted, but no one moved aside. Near panic broke out as someone yelled that Ulysses S. Grant was on board (he wasn't) and thousands shouted, "Where is he?" Finally, a member of the funeral party on board called for calm,[45] and some members of the Patriot Daughters of Lancaster were able to move through the masses, step into the funeral car, and place an arrangement of camellias and white roses on the flag-draped casket.[46] Five minutes later, the train left the depot. It passed the Lancaster Locomotive Works, where 500-600 people, workmen and their families, stood on railroad cars, on tenders, or on the ground, many wearing mourning badges.[47]

And then it was gone.

By the February 1909 centennial celebration, McCaskey's veneration for Lincoln had grown beyond all proportion. "I little thought that day [in 1861]," McCaskey said at the end of his speech from the hotel balcony, "when I saw this man and heard him speak, that I should come to love him more than any other public man in our national history." The mayor spoke for a multitude of others: "His personality was so attractive that millions came to regard him with a feeling of personal affection, and his integrity and good sense so manifest that their trust in him was boundless."[48]

McCaskey then acknowledged Lincoln's humility, saying that the President would not have anticipated such celebrations as these: "Nothing on that day was farther from his thought than that the people of Lancaster would assemble here nearly 48 years later—as we do now—to celebrate the hundredth anniversary of his birth in a rude log cabin in the wilds of Kentucky." He saluted Lincoln as a mere mortal through whom God had wrought great things: "On this day the nation would rise in gratitude . . . in recognition, to hail him as the Saviour of his country! Verily, indeed, hath God chosen the weak things of the world to confound the things that are mighty."[49]

In his speech, McCaskey also mentioned a proposed "Lincoln Way": The "'Lincoln Way' from Washington to the great [Gettysburg] battlefield is the latest suggestion which commends itself to public favor. By all means let the United States Congress make early provision for such fitting memorial."[50] The project was never completed. (The first transcontinental highway, begun in 1912, connects Philadelphia, Lancaster, and Gettysburg. Now U.S. Route 30, it was named the "Lincoln Highway," and Lancastrians still refer to it that way.) Construction on the Lincoln Memorial in the nation's capital began in 1914, and the site was opened to the public in 1922. The exterior columns are made of marble from the Colorado Yule Marble company, a company in which McCaskey was a stockholder.

Surely he took satisfaction in knowing of this final connection between Lincoln and himself.

Chapter 2

A Dog, a Cane, an Education

Grandfather John McCaskey "used to say that he was going to give me a good college education. He left me . . . his staff [cane] and his favorite dog. The dog died soon, 'Sport' his name, but the staff is here yet. The education I never got in the way he used to think of it, and perhaps it is far better *not*. At all events I am content."[1]

John Piersol McCaskey never graduated from any school. His first teacher was his mother, his first book the Bible. His formal education began in 1844 at a one-room common school and ended in 1855 in Lancaster, several months before he would have graduated from Boys' High School.

Born on October 9, 1837, McCaskey was among the first to benefit from the 1834 Pennsylvania Common School Law. The law mandated free, public education for all children, a goal that had been dreamt of, fought for, and defended by Pennsylvania leaders from the state's earliest days, even when it was a colony. Without free education, McCaskey may well have been relegated to work on the family farm or elsewhere because his parents could not afford to pay for private academies.

In the fall of 1855, McCaskey became a teacher at Boys' High where he remained for 50 years. By the time he retired in 1906, he had become one of the foremost educators in the state, and he had exerted enormous influence on public instruction. Beneficiary had become benefactor.

When he died on September 19, 1935, a newspaper account noted his importance: "Pneumonia closed the amazing career of Dr. John Piersol McCaskey, dean of Pennsylvania educators and a nationally significant figure, on Thursday night, scarcely two years short of his 100th birthday. The white-haired scholar, philosopher and philanthropist died quietly at the old McCaskey homestead, 304 W. King, at about 9 p.m. with his family gathered by his bedside."[2]

In 1681 William Penn inherited vast tracts of land in the New World as a result of debts owed to his father by King Charles II. Persecuted in England for his religious beliefs as a Quaker, Penn offered his land as a haven to people similarly treated, and Penn's Woods became a destination for those seeking freedom of worship. He also held clear views on education, views which then resonated across several centuries of Pennsylvania's history. An educated citizenry was imperative for good government, he believed: "Governments depend more upon men than men upon governments. If men are wise and virtuous, the governments under which they live must also be wise and virtuous! It is, therefore, essential to the stability of a State that people be educated in noble thoughts and virtuous actions." Consequently, the first General Assembly of Pennsylvania decreed in 1682 that the provincial laws were to be taught in the schools.[3]

Acquiring wisdom and virtue did not occur naturally, Penn maintained; rather, they must be inculcated in children: "That which makes a good constitution must keep it, viz [namely]: Men of wisdom and virtue: Qualities that because they descend not with worldly inheritance, must be carefully propagated by a virtuous education of youth." This motto was printed on the title page of every volume of *The Pennsylvania School Journal* from 1852 to 1921, reflecting enduring adherence to William Penn's convictions. Building men of wisdom and virtue, men of character, would also become the hallmark of J. P. McCaskey's teaching.

Less lofty and more pragmatic, reading and writing were added to the education goals by Penn's second General Assembly. Reading was to be taught specifically so that "[children] may be able to read the Scriptures."[4] One hundred fifty years later, when McCaskey's mother, Margaret, taught her brood of children to read using the Bible as primer, she was simply following the precedent.

That same Assembly required compulsory education for all. However, lack of funds for schools stymied this goal, as did other more pressing issues such as hostile Native Americans, financial support for the colony, and involvement in the French and Indian War. Schools were available only to those who could afford to pay for teachers' salaries, books, and other essentials. The Assembly's resolve to educate all would be forgotten.[5]

In the 1700s and early 1800s, providing education in Lancaster City and County fell to the churches and private schools. The Assembly in 1712 and 1730 placed education in the hands of the Protestant churches,[6] ensuring the commingling of religion and education. In that era, "the terms religion and education were synonymous. If the former was the main pillar upon which the Spiritual was to rest, the latter was just as indispensable to the worship of Almighty God; for, to fully comprehend the Scriptures required at least a knowledge of the elements of an education."[7] The Mennonites, Seventh Day Baptists, Moravians, Quakers, Episcopalians, Presbyterians, Reformed, and Lutherans all set up schools.[8]

Private schools in Lancaster included, among others, a morning school for girls, a day school for boys, a night school, and a children's school. Subjects included needlework, sewing, French, English, the classics, and dancing. "Everything from the A B C's to the dead languages" was offered at the Lancaster "Tyrocinium."[9] By the early 1800s, there were many such institutions in Lancaster; however, "there was *not one free* to the average boy or girl whose parents could not afford to pay for their education. They were all intended especially for the well-to-do, who could easily afford the expense of providing their children with the best educational training."[10]

In the sparsely populated areas of the county, "neighborhood schools" were formed, for which one or more families would hire a teacher and provide a building. These were called "pay" or "subscription" schools.[11] Several existed in Leacock Township,[12] where the McCaskeys lived. One, a log cabin, dated back to the 1730s. Another, Zook School, which eventually became the common school McCaskey attended, was established in 1820.[13]

William, McCaskey's father, most likely attended Zook and then, perhaps, an academy. He was on his way into Lancaster from that school to deliver a letter to a relative, an errand most important for William because it was then that he saw his future wife, Margaret Piersol, for the first time.[14]

No records exist to certify whether Margaret attended any school, although she lived in Lancaster where academies and church schools abounded. She came from a line of prominent ancestors, among them Scottish aristocrats, Lancaster judges and justices, and assemblymen. The McCaskey and Piersol families were financially well-off enough to pay for schooling, and William and Margaret were literate. On the 1880 United States Federal Census, the "cannot read" and "cannot write" boxes, first introduced with that census, were left unchecked for both.[15]

So, what about the poor? Penn's Assembly had wanted to educate everyone, from the wealthy to the destitute: "That, to the end that the poor as well as the rich may be instructed in good and commendable learning, which is to be preferred before wealth, *be it enacted*, . . ."[16] but could not effect it. Church and neighborhood schools were not uncharitable; both admitted poor students gratuitously. However, parents responded as might be expected: rather than having their children labeled as needy, they kept them at home.[17]

The 1790 Pennsylvania Constitution provided "for the establishment of schools throughout the State, in such a manner that the poor may be taught gratis," and the Act of 1809 also called for the education of all, the county treasuries paying for supplies and tuition of children whose families could not do so.[18] The act was implemented in the county, including Leacock Township.[19] Under it, pupils were labeled either "pay" or "pauper" scholars.[20] However, only the names of "pauper scholars" were public record.[21] As before, many of the poor children were kept at home rather than having to "suffer the humiliation to which they were subjected by those [children] whose parents could afford the expense of educating them privately."[22]

"The Pauper Act," as it came to be known, was egregious because it "separated the poor from the rich, and hence failed; for in a republic, no system of education, which makes a distinction on account of wealth or birth, can have the support of the people."[23] Nonetheless, no matter how flawed the law was, it helped lead to free public schools for all in the Commonwealth.[24]

The Act of 1809 was eventually modified, and by 1818 the "First School District" of Pennsylvania was set up in Philadelphia to provide *free public* education for all. When a young William Augustus Muhlenberg, one of the directors of the Philadelphia District, came to Lancaster in 1820 to serve as rector of St. James' Episcopal Church, he brought his zeal for education with him: "A better church and a better community could come only from the proper training of young people." He cited education, both religious and secular, as his most important work. [25]

Muhlenberg also imported the Lancasterian system to Lancaster. Named for its originator, Englishman Joseph Lancaster, the method involved older students monitoring younger ones, so that large numbers could be educated without the expense of many teachers.[26] McCaskey called it "Mr. Lancaster's peculiar system," which went, he said, "the way of a thousand other educational fads and fancies."[27]

Lancaster became Pennsylvania's "Second School District" and owes "its first system of public education to [Muhlenberg],"[28] who introduced the Lancasterian methodology to the city. School was conducted in a building erected at Prince and Chestnut Streets in 1823. With both yea and naysayers,[29] Joseph Lancaster's system prevailed for 15 years. In 1838, the

Lancaster school board kept the building but replaced the system, noting that it must "consider the *quality* rather than the *cheapness* of the schools which they [were] about to establish."[30]

Finally, in 1834 a free school system *for all* Pennsylvania children was adopted under the Common School Law, which was written by Samuel Breck. One hundred fifty years in the making, it came about due to the efforts of many legislators and governors such as Thomas Mifflin and George Wolf. Opposition to the law sprang up immediately, and repeal nipped at its heels. Governor Joseph Ritner was an important force in fighting to preserve the act, as was Lancastrian Thomas H. Burrowes, who served as Ritner's Secretary of the Commonwealth.

The very next year, 1835, "The Great Commoner" Thaddeus Stevens, representing Adams County in the state legislature, surprised fellow representatives when he rose from his seat and extemporaneously "delivered what he himself afterwards considered the greatest speech of his life."[31] Stevens convinced angry legislators that the common schools actually saved the Commonwealth money.[32] He had done the math. He echoed William Penn's notion that a wise government can only exist if its citizens are educated to be wise: "If an elective republic is to endure for any great length of time, every elector must have sufficient information to direct wisely the legislatures, the ambassadors, and the executive of the nation; for some part of all these things, some agency in approving or disapproving of them, falls to every freeman."[33] Stevens successfully argued against rescinding the Common School Law, and his words were so impressive that women from Reading, Pennsylvania, had the entire speech printed on a silk banner, which they presented to him. Later in his life, Stevens pronounced this "his most precious possession."[34]

And so, the stage was being set for
McCaskey's first day of public school.

Meanwhile, McCaskey was subject to instruction and example at home. Literacy in the McCaskey household had everything to do with religion, just as it had for the Pennsylvania leaders from the past. Margaret was the teacher, and husband William was the enforcer. McCaskey wrote: "My parents were fortunately not wise enough to know that it is not good to teach children too early to read. I was put at it almost as soon as I could talk—and the Bible was the reading-book. We had but three or four books in those days, and my father's will and my mother's influence kept me at it, so that when I left home at eleven years of age . . ., I was thoroughly saturated with Bible truth and Bible story. . . . I would not now exchange that experience for a knowledge of all other books in the Congressional Library at Washington."[35] The other books in the home library were *Pilgrim's Progress*, *Fox's Book of Martyrs*, *Lives of the Reformers*, and a *Descriptive Geography of the World*.[36]

McCaskey's grandfather, John McCaskey, had come from Ireland in 1795 and settled in Leacock Township, where he made a prosperous living as a farmer and drover. He was, McCaskey wrote, regarded as one of the "most honest men in his community, respected by everyone as a generous man of staunch integrity, undaunted courage, and marked force of character." Illiterate, he kept all his business dealings in his head. He valued education and had young McCaskey read aloud to him about "the war with Mexico, the Congressional debates, the messages of the President and much besides, as given in the weekly issues" of the *Dollar Newspaper*.[37]

In an 1895 letter, McCaskey remembered his grandfather as an old man, treating his grandchildren to candy and making promises: "I was about ten years old when he died. I used to read the newspapers, etc. to him and recall him as a venerable old man, large of size, tall, and blind, who felt his way with a cane that stands over yonder in the closet, who always had licorice in his pocket for us youngsters, who used to give me pennies (big copper cents) for reading to him, and who used to say that he was going to give me a good college education. He left me . . . his staff [cane] and his favorite dog. The dog died soon, 'Sport' his name, but the staff is here yet. The education I never got in the way he used to think of it, and perhaps it is far better *not*. At all events I am content."[38]

McCaskey was born on one of his grandfather's two farms in Gordonville, which is near Paradise in Leacock Township, Lancaster County. He was the oldest of seven children; his siblings were Joseph ("Joe") Barr, Catherine ("Kate") Wilson, William ("Will") Spencer, Cyrus ("Cye") Davis, Margaret ("Cis") Salome, and James ("Newt") Newton. McCaskey entered Zook School in 1844, among the first pupils in the Common School system, under a teacher named Daniel Lefever.[39] The schoolhouse was located near the intersection of Harvest and Old Leacock Roads, less than half a mile through woods from the McCaskey home.

Even as a child, McCaskey exhibited a propensity to help others learn. In 1926, he ran into a Zook classmate and said of the encounter: "[I] greeted gladly an old friend whom I had not seen for nearly 80 years. . . . We went to the old Zook's school house, by the woods, when we were children and she says I used to help her in her arithmetic. I don't remember that, but I know I used to think her 'the nicest girl in school.' She was then Ann Lightner . . . We two are probably the last of those now living who attended [Zook] school in 1847 and 1848."[40]

In writing about the subjects he studied at Zook, McCaskey revealed a competitive nature and conformity to classroom procedures: He "read in the Testament class, kept a 'setting-down book,' learned Comly's speller under pressure as to be 'up' in the spelling classes and matches, ciphered in Pike's arithmetic, with all the rest carried his goose quill to the master to be mended."[41] Besides Comly's and Pike's books, there were two others. One was *The State-Book of Pennsylvania*, written by a future mentor, Dr. Thomas Burrowes, and published in 1847, McCaskey's third school year. It was "a favorite reading book in the country school."[42] A small brown volume, 4½" by 7½", with over 300 pages including illustrations, it is filled with a profusion of facts and figures about the state, such as geography, history, government, climate, agriculture, manufacturing, animals, and counties.[43]

The second was a geography book, which brought Lancaster into sharp focus for the young lad: "In the old copy of Mitchell's Geography at [Zook's] school house, in 1845, we were told that Lancaster was 'the largest inland town in the United States.' It was a thin book, and may have been an old edition even in that day. I remember well the brief paragraph, can see it yet. To my childhood fancy it was a great city—the greatest in the world to me then, and I am not quite sure that it has not been the greatest in the world to me ever since!"[44] One might suspect that this statement was politically motivated, as it was included in McCaskey's inaugural address in 1906, his first year as mayor of the city. However, it was more than political spin: Throughout his life, McCaskey spoke proudly of Lancaster and said he had never wanted to live anywhere else. And other than those first years on the farm, he did not.

After four years at Zook School, McCaskey moved on when he was 11 to Oak Hill Academy in Paradise, a village several miles from the farm. Its library and course offerings far exceeded what he had been exposed to at Zook. "At Oak Hill Academy what a world was opened in the books of Mr. Fetter's school library,"[45] McCaskey would write years later. For him, books were "the true Elysian fields."[46] In addition to a library, the school offered science and chemistry equipment and a collection of minerals and shells. Subjects were mathematics, English, Latin, Greek, German, and French, as well as instrumental music, drawing, and painting. Science would not be neglected; during the winter term, lectures on "Natural Science in general, will be delivered with experimental illustrations."[47] It also provided physical exercise: "[I]n the academy at [age] eleven," McCaskey remembered "wrestling, climbing, running, swimming, playing 'shinny' and corner ball."[48]

Purchased in 1847 by Edwin T. Fetter, its schoolmaster, the institution was sold only three years later.[49] McCaskey attended one or two sessions,[50] each five months long,[51] during Fetter's brief tenure. It was "an excellent school . . . [in] a beautiful residence at the eastern end of the village,"[52] where it encompassed nine acres.[53]

Oak Hill promised to cocoon the students from the world as it prepared them for their role later in life. Students would be "retired and apart from all public concerns; . . . and aloof from all corrupting influence from abroad." Fetter also advertised that he would pay special attention to "the personal appearance, health, and comfort of the pupils" and he would have as his main objective making them "practically useful and moral members of society." To that end, they could worship "each Lord's Day at either the Presbyterian, Episcopal, Methodist, or Mennonite churches" in Paradise.[54]

Today, Christ's Home, a facility for orphans, operates on the same site. It sits high above Route 30, aproned by a sweeping lawn with, yes, oak trees.

McCaskey would continue his education in Lancaster. The switch from the academy to the city schools occurred for several possible reasons. Neither Leacock Township nor other county districts had a high school, but the city of Lancaster did. Also, Oak Hill charged $50 for juniors and $60 for seniors for tuition, "boarding," and "washing."[55] Following Grandfather John's death in 1847, the family's prosperity declined. After McCaskey, there were six younger children to educate.

McCaskey arrived in the city of Lancaster in May 1849. He saw this move in terms of great good fortune. He had struck it rich, he wrote, richer than "the new Argonauts, 'the Forty-niners,'" who had sailed away for the Eldorado of California in that same year.[56] He attended a secondary school on Duke Street[57] before going to Boys' High in 1850. He remained a student in the city schools, except for one year, until February 1855, when he dropped out. Thus ended McCaskey's formal education.

So what about the college education Grandpa had promised him? McCaskey wrote his brother Will and sister-in-law Nellie in 1895 that "[t]he education I never got in the way he used to think of it, and perhaps it is far better *not*. At all events I am content."[58] Despite this assertion of contentment, however, McCaskey advocated higher education and wished that he had attended college: "A teacher should have scholarship," he said. Even though one could get that scholarship in other ways, a university education would be the best, he continued, adding, "the older I grow the more I appreciate the value of a thorough College or University course of study. Tens of thousands in money would weigh little with me now against an early four years' course under the good men of Franklin and Marshall College, and a post-graduate course in some great University. I did not and could not have it."[59]

He balanced that regret with gratitude, writing: "But I had the supreme good fortune to be started well, and my best teacher was my mother."[60] He certainly made the most of educating himself, defining *his* university: "My university has been the book, the newspaper, the play, the concert, the opera, the lecture, the sermon, the church, the world of nature, the world of art, the printing office, the dictionary, the cyclopedia, the poem, the restraining influence of the school, the blessed association of friends. Time and money have been of value only as they could be changed into what I wanted more."[61]

To attend plays, concerts, operas, lectures, art exhibits, and other cultural events, McCaskey rode the train to Philadelphia or New York, doing so for 50 years and following a demanding schedule: "He could leave Lancaster after school on Friday evening, take in some good play that night, attend to business on Saturday morning, see a matinee in the afternoon, another performance of high grade that night, get home after midnight, and be at church Sunday morning just as usual. All the great actors and actresses in their leading roles from all the world, and many of them many times year after year—he thinks no university life anywhere could match this in its high privilege."[62]

McCaskey's definition of his university reflects his irrepressible desire for knowledge. In a birthday speech at age 89, he mentioned that he had just been reading *The Outlook*,[63] which was among the ranking weekly news magazines of the early 20th century. He was a life-long learner and expected the same from his students and family. "He was always drawing people out to be educated," great-granddaughter Kay McCaskey Adelman recalled. "He seemed to turn people inside out . . . to see the potential, and it didn't matter if you didn't have any potential, he still stuck with you, you learned something."[64]

Grandchildren were quizzed at the dinner table about a word they used. McCaskey would have them pronounce it properly, spell it, give its meaning, and use it in a sentence.[65] Even the children's guests were not spared. A grandson brought a young woman, who later became his wife, to meet the family. McCaskey asked her, "What's the longest word in the dictionary?" She thought for a moment and then responded, "Forever." "Excellent, my girl!" he exclaimed.[66]

Great-grandson Edward McCaskey was put on the spot one day when he came home for lunch:

> "What did you learn in school today, young man?" Great-grandfather asked.
>
> "Nothing, sir," he replied.
>
> "Oh, nothing," Great-grandfather said. "We must never have that. Fetch the Longfellow."

And before he ate his lunch, Edward had memorized a verse from Henry Wadsworth Longfellow's poem "A Psalm of Life."[67]

Franklin & Marshall College awarded McCaskey honorary degrees that attest to his scholarship and accomplishments. In 1872 he received an honorary Master of Arts degree from the college[68] and in 1887 an honorary Doctor of Philosophy. [69]

The second State Superintendent of Public Education, John Pyle Wickersham, seemed to be speaking about McCaskey in an 1888 Lancaster High School graduation speech, at which McCaskey was present. "Remember the greatest scholars the world over are self-made," Wickersham said. "Schools and colleges are valuable aids, but no one ever accomplished much who did not in the main make himself. In the race of life success comes oftenest to the man who has learned to row his own boat."[70]

Perhaps McCaskey smiled to himself. After all, by then he had already done a great deal of rowing.

Chapter 3

When the Sands of the Hour-glass Ran Gold

"[Charley McLenegan and I] were cronies in the old days, and many a time sat side by side at the long red desks in 'Old Coley's' class-room when the sands of the hour-glass ran gold."[1]

Among McCaskey's young classmates at Zook School was a boy with whom he dreamt about going away to school some day: "One bright Sunday morning, William Leaman and I, little boys, lay on the grass under one of . . . [the] oaks [in the Old Leacock Presbyterian cemetery] and talked of going away to school."[2]

For McCaskey, that came soon enough, first to Oak Hill Academy. Ultimately, "away" led to Lancaster city in 1849. The twelve year old's arrival occurred simultaneously with the opening of Lancaster Boys' High School, the second public high school in the state offering a four-year course.[3] Here he received the rest of his formal education. Here he studied the same subjects he would teach.

The availability of a high school meshed with McCaskey's own educational needs exactly at the right moment. He wrote: "High schools had not yet become the fashion. There were not at that time a half-dozen free schools of this grade in the State."[4] The Lancaster school board permitted children from outlying districts to attend for $10 "if there be a vacancy and if on examination before the superintending committee they be found prepared."[5] McCaskey boarded with his uncle[6] Andrew White, Andrew's wife Eliza, and their four children in the southeast ward of Lancaster.[7] He rode the train to Gordonville on the weekends, perhaps, or took the stage-coach.

Lancaster included a high school from the beginning of its public education system, even though high schools had not been mandated by the Common School Law. The board resolved in 1838 that "a High School should be established as soon after the Common Schools are in operation, as may be practicable."[8] All grades, including the high school or "Upper Room-Higher Department" were initially housed together in the former Lancasterian building on the corner of Chestnut and Prince Streets.[9]

However, rapidly increasing enrollments necessitated expansion into other buildings and rented spaces. In 1846 the board formed a partnership with Franklin College, which provided for the education of 40-70 boys from the city.[10] This partnership was dissolved in the summer of 1849 when the board took action to "at once proceed to the establishment of a sufficient High School for the Instruction of such of the Male Youth of the City as may require the benefit of an Establishment of that grade."[11]

A "sufficient High School" was opened in the Presbyterian Session house on the corner of Cherry and Grant Streets in August 1849 but relocated the next year to the second floor of the Lancasterian building. Girls' High School was also moved to the first floor of that building from the Seminary Building at the corner of Prince and Orange Streets.[12] The girls entered from the Chestnut Street side, the boys from Prince Street.[13] The name "Lancaster High School" encompassed both schools.

Students from Kersey Coates' Duke Street Secondary School were the first to attend Boys' High in 1849. McCaskey was in Coates' class, but he was not promoted with them. However, he had only joined that class in May, and he didn't mind, for "it was his great good fortune to be left behind for what he thinks [was] one of the best years of his school life,"[14] for Howard Worcester Gilbert was his teacher, and McCaskey regarded him as one of his best ever. McCaskey entered high school in the fall of 1850.

Built in 1824 at Prince and Chestnut Streets for the Lancasterian School, this building became the first Lancaster High School in 1850, housing both boys and girls on separate floors. (Photo from One Hundred and Fifty Years of School History in Lancaster, PA.)

Among the high school regulations were the following: Teachers were to take roll "by the town clock." Morning exercises began with the principal or one of the "professors" reading a chapter from the Bible, without commenting on its meaning. Students not seated before 9 a.m. for the morning session or before 2 p.m. for the afternoon classes were marked tardy, and they would be required to stay after dismissal for twice the amount of time they had been late. Dismissals were at noon (for lunch) and 5 p.m. Acceptable excuses for missing a day of school included the necessity for the child to work at home; the student's or a family member's illness; "want of proper clothing"; absence from town with parental consent; and attendance at a religious function.[15]

Absenteeism was common. An 1849 board report admonished parents on this issue. Was there any better use of their children's time than "that of causing [it] to be sedulously and regularly devoted to their mental and moral culture?" Parents were also chastised for "the *small degree of interest* which very many [of them] seem[ed] to feel in the welfare and actual operations of the schools." The board encouraged "intelligent" parents to make frequent visits in "friendly and right spirit" to stimulate teachers and pupils and to provide good suggestions to the board, which would be happy to receive them.[16]

High school subjects included geography, grammar, arithmetic, composition and declamation, general history, algebra and advanced mathematics, book-keeping and surveying. The classical languages of Latin and Greek or the modern languages of German or French were offered.[17] Study halls were part of the schedule for both high schools and were supervised by the principal and teachers.[18] Advanced students from both schools attended lectures in the natural sciences (astronomy, geology, chemistry, natural philosophy, and physiology) each afternoon at 4 p.m. To assist students in their comprehension and retention of the subject matter, the lectures were not "to be formal written discourses, to which the pupils are to listen without any further means being taken to impress the subjects on their minds; but familiar oral explanations, illustrated by proper apparatus and experiments of which the pupils are to take notes, and on each of which they are to be carefully examined."[19]

All teachers were expected to pay "the strictest attention . . . to the handwriting and orthography of all the pupils, in their written exercises of every kind."[20] The emphasis placed on good handwriting and grammar is confirmed in Civil War letters written to McCaskey by younger brother Will, who had been among McCaskey's students at Boys' High. In April 1861, Will wrote from camp responding to a letter from McCaskey, who apparently had admonished the young soldier for writing errors. Will suggested that such matters paled compared to war: "I am thankful to you for kind remarks in regard to capitals and sentences but would ask of you to excuse all such things at present, as we must labor under many disadvantages and have very little time for such things, . . . but getting a place to consider capitals and sentences in writing is impossible."[21] Two years later, from Tennessee, Will became the critic, turning the tables on his brother. Will complimented McCaskey for seeking to improve *his* handwriting: "I am glad that you are taking instructions in penmanship, for I agree with Ellie [McCaskey's wife] 'that it is a necessary study . . .' and I only regret that I ain't there to do the same, but live on 'Hope!'"[22] The chiding proved worthwhile, as Will noted in a letter several months after that: "[There is] a decided improvement in your writing."[23]

McCaskey's view of himself while a student at Oak Hill was that he was quiet but observant: "I was a little fellow, quiet and almost unnoticed, I suppose, but all eyes and ears and mental touch."[24] In Lancaster he was "unconsciously learning to listen to voices, to look in to faces, and to gather definite impressions of people, less from what they said than from what they were."[25] In 1896 he drew from this reservoir of impressions as he addressed the Pennsylvania State Teachers' Association in Bloomsburg. He recalled with joy and judgment many of his teachers, prefacing his remarks with this: "As boy or man I have known them all, and I think known them well, in their soul habit as they lived."[26] He regarded his years as a student at Boys' High as golden and reflected on them with great warmth.

McCaskey began with three teachers whom he did not regard too highly. First was Kersey Coates, his Duke Street schoolteacher in 1849, who "was a very strong man with a taste for literature."[27] Coates left teaching in 1854 to move west to make his fortune, an unworthy aspiration, McCaskey maintained. Coates, he wrote, "read law with Thaddeus Stevens while teaching in the high school, went west to Kansas City, was a fearless defender of Freedom in those stormy days in Kansas, grew wealthy through his real estate and railroad investments, and died a millionaire. He was an efficient teacher, and to turn from the school-room to pile up gold like this is hardly a good thing for the average man to do. He usually pays too big a price for the money."[28] Despite McCaskey's sentiment, Coates is still remembered today as a leading figure in Kansas City's history for his anti-slavery efforts, his Civil War military service, his successful efforts to get a bridge built across the Missouri to the city, and other civic causes.[29]

Second was Samuel Becker, principal from 1849 to 1851, "a linguist, trained in the best schools in Europe, at home in six . . . languages and knew English as though it had been his mother-tongue."[30] Becker received a low grade from McCaskey because of his questionable character: "[Becker was] a general scholar of extraordinary attainments . . . but he was not a man of integrity or moral force. His habits were bad, and he made wreck of what might have been a brilliant career."[31] Becker was censured by the school board in 1851 for unspecified conduct but was allowed to be a candidate for a teaching position the next year if he promised to conform to school rules and "regulate his conduct in the school as well as out of the school in such a manner as to deserve the future approbation of the Board." Even though the board amended its censure the next day, saying that not all charges had been substantiated, Becker was not re-elected to his teaching position.[32]

The next teacher was Joseph Colburn, 1849-1853, who received the kindest treatment from both McCaskey and a local newspaper, which ranked him as "the best of the three" and called him "a delightful old man . . . [who] was the especial favorite of the boys."[33] Unlike Coates, Colburn died "poor in pelf [money] but rich, we believe, in treasure that lasts—cared for tenderly in the home of an aged sister."[34] McCaskey assessed him as "a guileless, gentle-hearted dreamer, always too near-sighted physically and not quick enough mentally to deal with the average Arab among school boys."[35]

Charley McLenegan sat next to McCaskey "at the long red desks in 'Old Coley's' class-room when the sands of the hour-glass ran gold," and the pair often misbehaved. Mr. Colburn, McCaskey wrote, was "a large man, with a big, soft hand—like his heart, it has often seemed to me—which he could lay with vigor and very suddenly to the near side of your head. We never thought it punishment, only fun. Soon he would forget everything, and be telling us of 'the nice times we'd have if we'd only be good boys.'" This admonition was heard but ignored, for "Charley's private opinion was that there was a world more fun just then in being 'bad boys,' and I think I fully agreed with him. But he liked us all the same, and we knew it, and we both had an abiding affection for 'Old Coley.'"[36]

Despite such fondness, McCaskey and others gave Colburn trouble, so much so that he was relieved of supervising the study hall.[37] McCaskey felt the sting of remorse when he was an adult and wanted to make up to

"Old Coley" for having given him a hard time. However, by the time he wrote his words of regret, both Charley and "Old Coley" were dead. "Perhaps Charley and I may find each other somewhere in the eternities. Then we will look up the old man, to learn that there was no day when he ever had a score against us, but is only glad beyond all telling to know that we have got to the same blessed country to which he has surely gone."[38]

The remainder of McCaskey's teachers received only accolades. Before turning the spotlight on them individually, he spoke about their goodness collectively, elevating them to glorious heights: "There have been other teachers also here under whom it has been good to live, with whom it has been a privilege to draw the vital breath of thought and feeling, to see the vision of beauty, to feel the throb of power, to triumph in heroic achievement, to know the glory of unselfish endeavor, to give ear to the gospel of wonder second only to the gospel of grace, to know the God of Truth."[39]

Howard Worcester Gilbert, his teacher in 1849-1850 at the Duke Street School, garnered high praise. In fact, McCaskey said that he was "perhaps the most influential in shaping [my] thought and life."[40] Gilbert nurtured McCaskey's love of books: "[Gilbert] introduced me . . . to a number of his favorite authors, and to some good things in literature which I could then in some good measure appreciate, and which have had for me an ever-growing charm."[41] Gilbert gave his protégé books. At that time, "Charlotte Brontë was . . . writing her stories. The first copy of 'Jane Eyre' that came to Lancaster [Gilbert] brought here, and one day he gave me this and 'Shirley,' by the same author, which he had bound for me in one volume."[42]

McCaskey, only 12 years old, counted himself as an abolitionist and attributed this to Gilbert's influence. He said that Gilbert was an "ardent lover of . . . human freedom. He wrote for the Anti-Slavery Standard [a weekly newspaper of the American Anti-Slavery Society], both in prose and verse, and often gave me the paper to read. He would not vote under a constitution that perpetuated human bondage."[43] (Several years later, Gilbert resigned to travel in Europe. When he returned, he was not re-hired because of his political views.[44])

Gilbert was also a role model for McCaskey as a teacher. More than half a century later, McCaskey wrote that he had been fortunate to attend a public school where they had the usual subjects: "reading, writing, spelling, arithmetic, algebra, geography, history." In addition, however, the "charm of literature, with its perpetual uplift and suggestiveness, and the wonder and beauty of nature from flowers to stars" pervaded the whole school.[45] Much the same could be said of the school over which he himself would preside for years.

The next beloved teacher was the Reverend John S. Crumbaugh, principal at the high school from 1851 to 1853. He was "a lover of learning, a fine scholar, a diligent student, a good teacher and a noble man. In person he was tall and well-formed, of great physical strength, but manner quiet and reserved; a man of presence, from whose reserve of power virtue seemed to pass to his pupils."[46] When Crumbaugh died at 27, McCaskey, by then a teacher at the school, had a "life-size and life-like portrait in crayon" made. It hung in the high school study hall even into the 20th century.[47]

"The most remarkable" of all to McCaskey was Elnathan Elisha Higbee. He taught at Boys' High for just a year, 1854-55, and later on became Pennsylvania's third superintendent of instruction: "[Higbee] never seemed to be trying to teach. . . . He was just living his ordinary life of interest in things at hand—and we lived with him!"[48] McCaskey wrote: "To us boys he was a sort of 'admirable Crichton,' able to do almost anything, from fencing, skating, sparring, and playing the flute, up to Latin, Greek, and Hebrew, and—what we had more respect for yet—all the mathematics!"[49] More than Higbee's scholarship, McCaskey praised his manner with the boys, saying Higbee was always ready to answer their questions and was constantly obliging. He was friendly and witty and did not exhibit "that dignified reserve which teachers sometimes affect."[50]

The last teacher McCaskey touted was William Van Lear Davis. English teacher and principal, Davis "was an accomplished and successful teacher, painstaking and faithful to his trust. It was good fortune to be under a man like him, and many a boy knew it well."[51] Years later, McCaskey found old roll-books covering more than 40 years in a desk drawer at the high school. "How vividly present do they make the past years!"[52] The books brought Davis into sharp focus. "I seem to hear Wm. Van Lear Davis call these names again with quiet deliberation. He stands in his pulpit-like desk on the high platform on the second floor of the old building at the corner of Prince and Chestnut, . . . I see him adjust his spectacles. I know the kind of pencil he is using. I see him pause a moment to adjust the lead, as its point is worn. He goes on with the roll-call."[53]

The memory expanded for McCaskey, as his mind moved back and forth between the 1850s and 1896 in the Bloomsburg speech. He ended his recollections of teachers and life at Boys' High poignantly: "All comes up as it were but yesterday. I am back among the old boys, in the old days. A child's voice in the street recalls me to the present! and I am walking among grass-grown graves where some even of the memorial stones are growing old. . . . As other rolls follow, that have been called day after day, changing from year to year, until the old are gone and all are new—class following class, hundreds following hundreds, through forty years of time—I seem to stand aside and see the procession go by, some faces in shadow, others in the light, but all moving steadily westward—westward—toward the sunset. In the moving column some go by slow and listless, others with the step of courage and confidence. There are kind eyes, smiles of cheer, pleasant faces, brave hearts of hope, honest and true. It is a goodly show!"[54]

The study hall for Boys' High at Prince and Chestnut Streets. (Photo courtesy of LancasterHistory.org.)

Chapter 4

Was Ever June Day More Beautiful?

"It was a bright day in June when I took a few hours from case [work as a printer] to see the members of the School Board and say that I would be an applicant for the old place. Was ever June day more beautiful? . . . I was to be a teacher."[1]

As much as McCaskey was enjoying life as a student at Boys' High, he returned to the Leacock Township farm in 1852. This was a year of crisis for his father. Tax records indicate that William had incurred debts up to $2,000, and he no longer owned the farm; he was listed as its "tenant farmer."[2] McCaskey returned to school the next year, but in February 1855, he left for good, just months shy of graduation to help his parents once again. William and Margaret McCaskey had moved with their six younger children from Gordonville to Lancaster that year, where they rented a home in the North West Ward. William had lost everything: his land, his money, his livelihood. He and Margaret would eventually move in with their daughter Catherine ("Kate") McCaskey Marshall and son-in-law James ("Jim"), with whom they resided for the rest of their lives. After the move into the city, William worked as a railroad conductor and left an estate valued at $300.[3]

William was considered one of the most popular conductors on the Pennsylvania Railroad, and at the time of his death in 1884, he was the oldest on the line. He committed suicide at age 68 on a Sunday morning in January. He had suffered for a number of years from chronic kidney and liver pain, which worsened and forced him to quit his job, leading to depression.[4]

Despite this sad end for William, the move to Lancaster proved to be a most propitious one for his offspring. The city schools provided free education for the remaining six children, and several of William's sons pursued successful careers in education, dentistry, and the military, while the daughters married and raised families.

McCaskey does not disclose the reason for leaving Boys' High before he graduated but rather dismisses it without elaboration as "an accident." In an address to the Alumni Association in 1906, his last year at the school, he said, "Many graduates are gathered here tonight from many classes. Alumni, I greet you! and would have been one of your number myself, but for an accident. The class of which I was a member graduated in July 1855, but in February of that year I was offered a place in the Lancaster Savings Institution."[5]

The William McCaskey family, 1876. Seated left to right: Joseph ("Joe"); daughter Margaret ("Cis"); father William; mother Margaret; John ("Jack"). Standing left to right: James ("Newt"); son William ("Will"); Cyrus ("Cye"); and Catherine ("Kate"). (Photo from private collection.)

And with that "accident," McCaskey's formal education ended.

McCaskey's earliest foray into the business world did not go well. The Lancaster Savings Institution, his first place of employment, failed, and he recognized in hindsight that this would be the template for his many other financial endeavors: "I did not then know the fatality that usually attends my financial ventures."[6] Of the circumstances surrounding that job, he wrote, "[A] few months after I went there, the bank broke! which ended my career in that line of business. The bank couldn't stand it. They didn't put me to jail for it, but they did the cashier, and I've sometimes been amused to think that perhaps they got the wrong man!"[7]

The "cashier" was the institution's treasurer, Charles Boughter, who had been in that position since 1842. In May of 1855, "some of the Trustees came to suspect a deficiency in the accounts of [Mr. Boughter]" and began an investigation. Mr. Boughter was dismissed, after having assured the trustees that the accounts were accurate and the institution solvent.[8] However, further investigation contradicted Mr. Boughter's protestations and by June 1855, he was in prison. His "lamentable defalcation" led to the bank's defaulting.[9]

At some point McCaskey sold geographical maps.[10] After the banking fiasco, he turned to the study of law under Newton Lightner, a school board member and a member of St. James' Episcopal Church, which was also the McCaskeys' church. Studying legal history was trumped by reading English literature: "I tried law, in the office of Newton Lightner, Esq., a most courteous gentleman, and long a member of the School Board. I got Blackstone's Commentaries into pretty good shape. [Lightner] advised that, by way of variety, I should read Pickwick, Oliver Twist, Martin Chuzzlewit, *et al.*, which I did, to find Dickens a good deal better than Blackstone."[11]

Neither lack of aptitude nor boredom, however, ended McCaskey's legal study. It was, again, the need for money: "But I had to make some money, as nearly all of us must, and left the law office for the school-room. County Superintendent Wickersham was then making his first examinations [of teaching candidates]. I got my first provisional certificate from him one evening in the early summer of 1855, in the dining-room of the old Lamb Hotel, on West King street, where a small class of applicants for such credentials were examined."[12] He would turn 18 that fall.

The requirements to be a teacher were based on two things, and McCaskey possessed both: integrity and scholarship. He was well known by his teachers and board members, many of whom attended St. James. As a student, he had been chosen to deliver Dr. Higbee's greetings to his peers,[13] and he was also among the student speakers at the first ever commencement exercises of the high school in Fulton Hall in 1854, delivering an address about "Mad Anthony."[14] Such honors attest to his leadership abilities. His interest in education was quite evident; while still a student, he attended the first three sessions of the newly-formed Lancaster County Teachers' Institute, the first in January 1853, when he was 15.[15]

He was elected "third assistant teacher of the Male High School" in August 1855.[16] The class he had left as a student in February graduated just a few weeks earlier. And so, McCaskey began his teaching career with provisional certificate in hand.

McCaskey's first stint in the classroom was brief. In August 1857, he resigned his position.[17] With no hint of regret but rather the casual abandon of a 20 year old, he quit, with plans that were quickly thwarted: "After spending two years in the high school, I thought I would go to California. I had resigned to do this, but the financial crash of 1857 came on, and the plans I had reckoned on miscarried."[18] The Panic of 1857 was a world-wide financial crisis. The United States was affected by a falling-off of demand from Europe for goods, a decline in the value of land in the West, and a drop in grain prices. Railroad companies shut down. Banks failed. McCaskey was forced to change course. He spent some months in several Pennsylvania cities, West Chester and Easton among others, before "drifting back to Lancaster"[19] that autumn.

McCaskey did not return to the city intending to teach again, but rather "with the purpose of learning the printer's trade."[20] He had been introduced to printing years before when he first came to Lancaster and lived with his uncle, who was friends with John W. Forney, editor of the *Lancaster Intelligencer*. McCaskey said, "The office was on Market street, near the house of the Union Fire Company. . . . My uncle was in the habit of calling on Mr. Forney at this office in the evening, and sometimes I went with him. I remember [Forney] distinctly. He was to me a very interesting man, pleased to greet his visitors, always busy at desk or case, coat off, his work never interrupting his talk, for he seemed able to do two things at once about as readily as one."[21]

McCaskey went seeking a job where none was being offered: "During the [1857] Christmas holidays, I went in to see Mr. John H. Pearsol, in the *Evening Express* office, on West King street, and told him what I wanted. He said every place was filled. I said to him, 'I want to learn to set type. I don't want any money until I am worth it.' 'Oh,' he replied, 'if that's it, I'll get up a case for you. Come in after New Year.' I did so, and one of the first pieces of copy I remember was a sermon by Bishop Bowman, in his strong, bold hand. It had nearly all the vowels omitted, only consonants used, but these were plain and clear. In six or eight weeks I hailed Mr. Pearsol for an advance in wages. 'How much do you want?' 'A dollar a week.' 'All right; go ahead.' Three or four months later I wanted another advance. 'How much?' 'I'm worth two dollars a week now.' He agreed to it, and at the time I left the office, after eight months of steady work, . . . I was receiving three dollars a week."[22]

Although the American writer Mark Twain claimed that he had, in 1862, been the first to devise such a ploy, a "great and infallible scheme for finding work for the unemployed," and it was "one of [his] great prides that [he] had invented it,"[23] he was wrong; McCaskey had already done so four years earlier. Even so, forty years later, McCaskey deferred to Twain and published the following anecdote entitled "One Way to Get a Position" in *The Pennsylvania School Journal*:

"A young man had asked Twain to help him get a job. The humorist replied: 'If you will obey my instructions strictly I will get you a position on a daily newspaper. You may select the paper yourself; also the city or the state.' The young man answered with a promise to do whatever was required and named the paper he wanted to work for.

"Twain sent him these instructions: 'Almost any man will give you a situation,' he wrote, 'if you are willing to work for nothing. The salary will follow presently. You will only have to wait a little and be patient. Therefore—

"'You are to apply at the office of your choice. You are to go without recommendations. You are not to mention my name, nor any one's but your own. You are to say that you want no pay. All you want is work—work of any sort. You are so tired of being idle that life is a burden to you. All you want is work, and plenty of it. You do not want a penny's worth of remuneration. You will get the place, whether the man be a generous or a selfish one.

"'When you have it, do not sit around and wait for others to find work for you. Keep watch and find it for yourself. When you cannot find it, invent it. This will make you needed friends among the members of the staff. When you see a thing that is worth reporting, go to the office and tell about it. Soon you will be allowed to put such things on paper yourself. Thus you will drift by natural and sure degrees into regular reporting, and you will find yourself on the city editor's staff, without any one's quite knowing how or when you got there.

"'Meantime, though you may have made yourself necessary, possibly even indispensable, you are never to mention wages. You can afford to wait, for that is a matter that will take care of itself. By and by there will be a vacancy on a rival paper. Some reporter of your acquaintance will speak of you, and you will be offered the place at current wages. You will report this good fortune to your city editor. He will offer you the same wages, and you will stay where you are. After that, when higher pay is offered you on another paper, you are not to take the place if your original employer is willing to keep you at a like price.'

"The young man wasn't looking for such instructions, but he kept his promise to Twain, and found a place on the newspaper he wanted. Within 30 days, he was on the regular staff of reporters. Then, he was offered a job on another paper with pay. He informed his editor of the better opportunity, who then offered him a comparable salary, so he stayed there. He got salary increases and became editor of a prominent newspaper in the South."[24]

McCaskey's apprenticeship in the print shop filled much of 1858. "I spent nearly a year in the old *Evening Express* office," McCaskey remembered, "getting some practical notions of the printing trade under my venerable friend, George W. Schroyer, . . . who in those days could make up a form, haul it down the rickety stairway and anchor it on press, ready for 'Doctor' Hitz, the pressman, in quicker time than any other man I have ever seen do similar work. He was a lightning foreman."[25]

McCaskey was soon being paid in gold dollars. He recalled that "[the gold dollars] were very small, but as they lay on [the paymaster's] desk, how big they looked! I've made a hundred thousand dollars and more since them. . . . And that work in the printing office was the most profitable in some respects that I have ever done."[26] McCaskey's printing knowledge would prove invaluable to him throughout his life in his work as a teacher, editor, and publisher.

That summer, however, the call to teach pulled McCaskey back to the classroom. Years later, he wrote of that moment: "It was a bright day in June when I took a few hours from case to see the members of the School Board and say that I would be an applicant for the old place. Was ever June day more beautiful? One of the first men I called on was Dr. Burrowes, who was then mayor, his office in the City Hall. He was pleased to know that I thought of going back, and so was I."[27] McCaskey later felt that this career path had been ordained: "I had at last learned my lesson, slowly, stubbornly, but at last. I was to be a teacher. Was it the irony of fate that drove me to this work? or did a kind Providence bar me in and direct my way? I prefer to think the latter; and I am very grateful that, with my small measure of ability and strength, I have been permitted thus to spend these forty years of life."[28]

The criteria for becoming a teacher were being ironed out in the 1840s and '50s, driven more by need than specificity. A provisional certificate had "no fixed standard of qualifications . . . [but rather] . . . [t]he grade of school, the supply of teachers, the wishes of directors and citizens of the district were consulted."[29] The first school board statement, in 1838, about requirements for selecting teaching candidates was short and general: "[t]he preferment of Instructors shall be predicated only on their literary and moral merits and practical skill."[30] In 1845 the requirements had become more specific and focused: "the art of discipline" was weighted as equal with applicants' ability to dispense knowledge, both considered more important than their expertise in subject areas: "The Board, in selecting teachers or employing instructors, will consider the art of discipline, the capacity to govern a school and preserve order by intellectual rather than physical means, and skill to impart knowledge, essential attainments to qualify applicants for election."[31]

In the 1850s, review by the county superintendent and permanent certification were added to the requirements.[32] To turn his provisional certificate from 1855 into a professional one, McCaskey needed to meet three requirements: "First, thorough qualifications in the branches named in the certificate; Second, a course of reading on the art of teaching, attendance for a satisfactory length of time at a normal school, or experience and success as a teacher; and Third, good moral character."[33] For the first and third requirements, McCaskey was undoubtedly qualified: he was well-versed in his subject matter, and his moral character was deemed good. For the second, whether he took a course on the art of teaching is unknown, but he did not attend a "Normal School" (a teacher training school). However, by 1857 he did have two years' teaching experience; that sufficed.

Pennsylvania Normal Schools (which have evolved into state universities that today number 14) were forming right along with the Common Schools. The first one was established in 1855 in Millersville, just a few miles from Lancaster. Teachers in the city were encouraged to attend county teacher institutes and read professional books, such as *Education: Intellectual, Moral and Physical* and *Science of Education and Art of Teaching*[34] and subscribe to *The Pennsylvania School Journal*, for it "bids fair to be eminently useful to the cause of education amongst us and all to whom that cause is committed."[35]

In 1858, McCaskey was elected to the same position he had resigned, third assistant to the principal.[36] By 1869 he would become the principal of Boys' High School, where he remained as teacher and principal until 1906. He was, first, a student and then teacher and principal in the same school and district for 52 years.[37]

McCaskey simply moved from a student desk to the desk up on the platform. Discipline techniques, subjects, the regulations to enforce, the duties to perform—all of these were familiar to him. The teachers were expected to promote a sense of general well-being in the schools and classrooms: They "shall endeavor to make their schools a place of agreeable resort to their pupils, promote neatness and order, cultivate habits of purity and truth, good manners and refined feelings, prevent profanity, and see that the pupils engage in no pursuits prejudicial to their health."[38] For students absent without an excuse, the teachers were expected to make a home visit.[39] Given that communicable diseases were prevalent in those years, such an assignment carried with it some danger.

Teachers evaluated students on their "performances in recitations and in conduct," and recorded their assessments in class rolls under the headings of "good, bad, and indifferent." They sent a summary to the parents once every 12 weeks. If a student did not attend school regularly, the teacher sent a sealed report to his parents, "delivered by a trustworthy student."[40]

The principal was expected to give instruction in all the subjects of the school, including Latin and Greek. He was in charge of the school and its professors and responsible for the condition and cleanliness of the school, grounds, and furniture. Supervisor of the study halls, he was to "maintain strict order and discipline, see that every pupil is studiously engaged in his studies; and shall afford such advice or assistance as each pupil may require in preparing for recitations before the proper Professor."[41]

McCaskey's teaching career had begun. He was an assistant to the principal, William Van Lear Davis, one of his favorite teachers whose recommendation had landed McCaskey his first teaching job in 1855. However, while McCaskey worked alongside him as his colleague, Davis was disgraced.

An incident was recorded in the board minutes of October 1859: Davis appeared at school on September 20, 1859, under the influence of liquor, "intoxicated to such a degree as to attract the notice of all present—his conduct and deportment was [sic] so influenced by his inebriate condition as to excite fear in some of the girls and elicit remarks from many of the scholars. His intoxication was particularly apparent at the time of calling the Roll and while reading the Bible in the opening exercises in the morning. Many of the children reported his unfit condition to their parents on their return home at noon and then in the evening. . . . So general was the condition of the Principal noticed by the pupils and freely spoken of by them at home, that his intoxication while in the schoolroom on the above occasion, has become notorious in this community."[42]

A motion to discharge Davis was tabled.[43] By the next August, a Mr. Reigart was elected principal of the Boys' High School, and Davis was no longer mentioned in the board minutes.

McCaskey's early years as a teacher, then, began with the beauty of a June day, but they were also sometimes clouded over by human failings. And the storms of the Civil War were gathering.

Chapter 5

Out of the Window Yonder

"Out of the window yonder, within a stone's throw of where we write, at a desk in the Lancaster High School building, stands the simple but massive tomb of Thaddeus Stevens."[1]

The national tensions of the 1850s rumbled through Lancaster. Near the beginning of that decade, a local tragedy foreshadowed the tsunami that was to wallop the country 10 years later. In those years, the adolescent McCaskey was going to school, helping his family, and working. A very young abolitionist,[2] he most certainly would have known about the Christiana Riot, a local incident in which a slave owner tried to retrieve his "property." Thaddeus Stevens and James Buchanan, ideological opposites on the slavery issue, were Lancaster residents and often subjects in the local newspapers. They were familiar figures to young McCaskey.

Pennsylvania was a "free" state where slavery was not practiced. In 1775, it was first among the original 13 colonies to organize a society "for the purpose of ameliorating the condition of the slaves."[3] The group became known as the Pennsylvania Abolition Society, and Benjamin Franklin, an early society president, implored the U.S. Congress in 1790 to end slavery. Ten years earlier in 1780, the Pennsylvania legislature had called for "the gradual abolition of slavery," and the Act of 1826 made "the free-born children of escaped slaves citizens of Pennsylvania and put them under its protection."[4] Abolitionists in Lancaster City and County worked for decades prior to the Civil War to move escaping slaves along on the Underground Railroad, risking their own lives and those of the people they were helping. The railroad had three different tracks through the county towards Philadelphia, Canada, or other havens of freedom. One came out of eastern Maryland and Delaware into southern Chester County and along the eastern border of Lancaster County. Another ran from farther west out of Maryland across the Susquehanna River and over the Pennsylvania border into southern York and Lancaster Counties. The third line came through York, Adams, and Franklin Counties, ending in Columbia, a river town in western Lancaster County.[5] On both sides of the Chester-Lancaster County border, Quakers living out their pacifist beliefs were among those helping the enslaved.

Lest one view such actions too rosily, not all of the state's citizens believed in freedom for everyone. Being a "free state" did not mean unanimous support for an end to slavery. Racism permeated 19th century Pennsylvania society, both rural and urban. While whites tolerated blacks, integration, acceptance, and equality were not part of the social fabric. An uneasy peace prevailed, and some Pennsylvanians were overt in their cruelty towards African Americans.[6] The American Colonization Society, begun in 1817, rejected freedom for the slaves, promoting instead their return to Africa, specifically to Liberia.

Along the state line between Pennsylvania and Maryland, kidnappers in the decades prior to the Civil War hunted down runaway slaves in York and Lancaster Counties and returned them to their owners in the South.[7] It mattered little to these marauders whether the blacks were escaped fugitives, and therefore "property," or "free" persons, those blacks who had been born and reared in Pennsylvania. For example, in 1850 a free Henry Williams was allegedly "seized without right or legal process and sold into perpetual slavery South."[8] In Bart Township, a man named John, known for his post-hole digging skills, was cuffed, gagged, and thrown into a covered wagon in the presence of his family, and then gone forever.[9] In a few instances, whites intervened in such despicable acts, such as citizens of Columbia raising $700 to buy former slave Robert Bennett's freedom before he was forcibly returned to Maryland and slavery.[10]

In 1850, the U.S. Congress passed the second Fugitive Slave Act, intended to strengthen the first one of 1793. Slave owners could reclaim runaway slaves, even in non-slave states and territories. Anyone aiding an escaping slave would be fined $1,000 and sentenced to six months in jail. Citizens were required to assist authorities who had arrest warrants for the apprehension of slaves. This, however, did not produce the desired effect of getting more compliance from white citizens. The act "had now become odious to the largely increased and rapidly increasing number of persons who were opposed to all forms of slavery, regardless of its constitutional protection or right at law."[11] Thus, it produced less compliance and more resistance and, in fact, civil disobedience. Such was clearly the case in the Christiana Riot.

In September 1852, reports of a riot near the hamlet of Christiana, one of the stops on the Underground Railroad in eastern Lancaster County, spread quickly throughout the area. A slave owner, Edward Gorsuch of Maryland, had come to Pennsylvania to claim six of his slaves, four of whom were reportedly in Lancaster County. Gorsuch, several relatives, other men, and a deputy marshal, armed with arrest warrants and guns, went to the farm of William Parker, a former slave. In the house that morning were Parker, his wife, and Gorsuch's fugitive slaves. Gorsuch and the marshal showed Parker the arrest warrants, but he resisted. Parker's wife and the other occupants fled to the second story, and while the two parties argued below, Mrs. Parker sounded an alarm of trumpet blasts out a garret window. Between 75-100 African Americans responded and came armed with firearms, rails, knives, corn-cutters, scythes, and axes.

Arriving on the scene, as well, were Castner Hanway, Elijah Lewis, and Joseph Scarlet, white neighbors who had heard the commotion. The deputy marshal showed Hanway and Lewis the warrants and told them it was their duty as citizens to aid him. They refused, Hanway saying he "wouldn't have a thing to do with it, that the [fugitives] had a right to defend themselves . . . [and he] didn't care for the Act of Congress or any other law."

Lewis, a Quaker, supported Hanway. Both men warned of bloodshed and then started to leave the scene.[12]

At this juncture in the narrative, accounts differ, and it is from the conflicting versions that the subsequent defense of Hanway and Lewis would dangle. The prosecution contended that, as he rode away on his horse, Hanway spoke to the African Americans, sparking gunfire. The defense contended that he had said nothing. Another variation suggests that the riot erupted when words led to blows and gunshots between Edward Gorsuch and one of the fugitives, who stood just outside the house: "The catalyst for violence, the lightning bolt that started the riotous blaze, was a confrontation between Gorsuch and . . . Samuel Thompson [one of the fleeing slaves]." Thompson told Gorsuch that he should go home to Maryland to which Gorsuch replied, "You had better give up and come home with me, . . ." Thompson responded first by striking him on the head and then shooting him. At that point, other African Americans attacked Gorsuch.[13]

Whatever the truth, as Hanway and Lewis were leaving the scene, chaos broke out, and in the ensuing skirmish, Edward Gorsuch was killed. Others from both sides were wounded. Parker and several African Americans escaped and eventually made their way to Canada, having found refuge in the home of Frederick Douglass along the route.[14]

This local incident was a microcosm of the devastating conflict to come. In a newspaper report 60 years later, the event was described as "the fatal affray that many critics contend marked the first bloodshed of the Civil War."[15] An historian has likened the event to the one that ignited the American Revolution: William Parker and the others who fought that morning at the little stone farmhouse "had engaged in a battle for freedom comparable in significance to the Minute Men's engagement of British troops at Lexington and Concord seventy-five years before. Like their predecessors in the War for Independence, Parker and the heroic black men and women who had fought at his side had won a signal victory in the war for the liberty of their race."[16]

Within days, 117 indictments for treason were handed down; of these, 38 led to charges brought before a grand jury and to the subsequent trial. The accused were held in the city prison. Early newspaper coverage of the incident was relegated to the second page of the four-page weekly *Lancaster Examiner and Herald*, the first page being reserved for fictional short stories and poetry. By the time the actual trial began in November 1851, reality had displaced fiction, and trial coverage filled the entire front page and spilled into the second.[17]

The successful defense was provided by a team of five lawyers, including Thaddeus Stevens.[18] All of the African Americans were clean-shaven and dressed similarly (by a committee of women from the Abolition Society) with red, white and blue scarves around their necks. Lucretia Mott, a famous Quaker abolitionist, sat with them at trial and knitted, seemingly unaware of what was transpiring until testimony went against the prisoners.[19]

John Read, one of Stevens' team, argued extensively on the law of treason, which "knocked the breath out of the prosecution, and Mr. Stevens was content with but a few words. The prisoners were acquitted, and from that day the fugitive slave law was a dead letter in Pennsylvania. The great merit of Mr. Stevens in this transaction was in the bold, firm stand he took at the beginning. His defiant attitude kept up the courage of those who would otherwise have desponded. His share in the trial was not very conspicuous, but there were good reasons for the course he pursued. The great object was obtained, and that was all he desired."[20]

Sixty years later, the incident and treason trials were commemorated with a ceremony and placement of an 11-foot, 3-ton gray Vermont granite obelisk in the town of Christiana, two miles from the riot house. With the wisdom and forethought so often exhibited by those given the challenge of memorializing events of epic proportions, this monument lauds the courage of William Parker, "Bold as a Lion, A Leader in the Fight for the Freedom of his People." It acknowledges the nobility of following one's conscience, noting that Castner Hanway "suffered for freedom." (Hanway, while in prison for 97 days, "never once complained. He wrote to his wife, '. . . I do not regret my course; I have simply done my duty.'"[21]) It also preserves the memory of Edward Gorsuch and his wounded son, noting that Gorsuch "died for law." The fourth side of the obelisk lists the 38 defendants who were indicted for treason but acquitted.

Thaddeus Stevens was a resident of Lancaster, having moved here from Gettysburg in 1842. He had been a teacher briefly before becoming a lawyer. He served in the Pennsylvania legislature in the 1830s and early 1840s and in the U.S. House of Representatives from 1848 to 1852 and again from 1859 until his death in 1868. As Speaker of the House, he was one of the most powerful men in Congress. McCaskey ranked him as "the second man in Washington,"[22] who "stood next in power and influence to Abraham Lincoln himself during the tremendous era of the Civil War."[23]

Despite Stevens' accomplishments, his local and national reputation waned in the 20th century, and he was even labeled "the greatest unknown person in American history."[24] However, his far-reaching contributions have recaptured deserved attention. For instance, Steven Spielberg's 2012 movie, *Lincoln*, places him in the forefront of the effort to pass the 13th Amendment abolishing slavery. In addition, a campaign for a U.S. commemorative stamp honoring Stevens was begun in 2013.

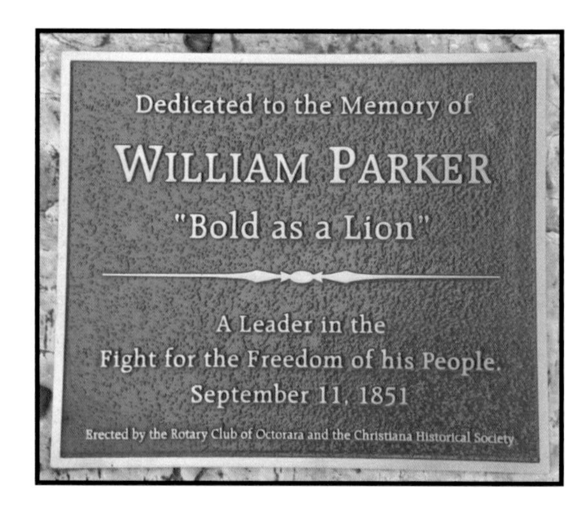

Marker next to obelisk in Christiana. (Photo courtesy of author.)

Obelisk in Christiana. (Photos courtesy of author.)

During the Civil War years, the newly married McCaskey and his wife, Ellen, lived in the same block of South Queen Street as Thaddeus Stevens, and they would have witnessed some of his comings and goings. McCaskey, most likely, reported in the *Lancaster Evening Express* on Stevens' return one Friday evening in 1864 from Washington, D.C., after an absence of seven months. Stevens had arrived by train quietly and unannounced, but the Union League Band began playing in front of his home at 9:30, which attracted neighbors and friends. The Congressman spoke to the crowd briefly about several issues, including his belief that liberty would win out over slavery, although he was unsure when that would occur, for the nation had perhaps not "yet been sufficiently chastised for [its] cruel oppression of a harmless and long suffering race; a portion of God's children." Stevens noted that the constitutional amendment abolishing slavery had been stalled in the House of Representatives. Then, tired from travel and the heat, he took his farewell, the reporter noting that he looked well and was in good health.[25]

McCaskey had also known Stevens as a teenager in the 1850s when Stevens was practicing law during his hiatus from Congress. "[I] knew [Thaddeus Stevens] both long and well," McCaskey said.[26] He recognized Stevens' significant achievements, writing " . . . [O]f all men who have lived in Lancaster, it may be that Thaddeus Stevens has, in the providence of God, done most for humanity—in the vast reach and ever-growing influence of his work, which was of State, National, and world-wide importance."[27] McCaskey placed a picture of Stevens on the first page of the *High School News* in 1906. The caption reads in part: "Thaddeus Stevens was the mightiest man I have ever known. He seemed granite or steel in the mobile form and garb of a man. So he always impressed me, as I have seen him in his office, on the platform, before the Court, or upon the street—though halt and lame—leaning upon his old hickory cane."[28]

Known as "The Great Commoner," Stevens was unwavering in his defense of and support for any oppressed individuals or groups, and much of his work as a lawyer was devoted to representing them in court. He worked in both the courtroom and Congress to free the slaves and grant them equal rights. He was instrumental in getting not only the 13th but also the 14th and 15th civil rights amendments shaped and passed.

Stevens lived his convictions. He helped his first housekeeper, an African American, and her husband attain their freedom, and he was active in defending and freeing many slaves. Evidence indicates that he and a subsequent housekeeper, Lydia Hamilton Smith, were involved in the Underground Railroad: beneath his office in Lancaster, a cistern, only recently discovered, had been used as a hiding place for fugitive slaves.[29] The home, at 45 South Queen Street in Lancaster, was added to the National Park Service's list of official Underground Railroad sites in 2011, and Stevens has been linked to seven sites in the county and nine in the state.[30]

Stevens' generosity was legendary. "One of his most remarkable endowments was that never-failing spirit of generous kindness, which made it his pleasure to do good to and confer benefits on all who came within his reach. . . . No man, woman or child ever approached Thaddeus Stevens, worthy or unworthy, and asked for help, who did not obtain it when he was possessed of the means."[31] The schoolboys of Lancaster in the 1850s, McCaskey related, "had no dread of him, for he was a very generous, kindly man. Again and again he was on our list when we were raising funds for some school purpose or other use. We always knew that we could count on Mr. Stevens—or 'Old Thad,' as everybody knew him—for five dollars when we wanted it."[32] In his most enduring act of charity, Stevens left the bulk of his estate to establish an industrial school in Lancaster for orphan boys, with no restrictions as to race. Today that school continues as Thaddeus Stevens College of Technology.

Stevens was also notoriously cantankerous and irascible. McCaskey, however, was not intimidated, and he offered this metaphor for the contrast between Stevens' outer countenance and inner magnanimity: "During the last eighteen years of his life, Thaddeus Stevens was to us one of the familiar

McCaskey's lithograph of Thaddeus Stevens. (Photo from High School News 1906).

and most striking figures in the city of Lancaster. . . . As we think of him, moving along slowly, with deformed foot and heavy cane, grim and unsmiling, save for the look of pleased interest or recognition that often spoke from his eyes, he reminds us of the gnarled oak with sweet juices at the heart of the old tree."[33]

McCaskey captured Stevens' wit and sarcasm as he described Old Thad's reaction to being dubbed the "Father of the Common School System." While Stevens' 1835 speech preventing the repeal of the 1834 Common School Law was recognized as absolutely crucial in saving the fledgling institution, he had been wrongly credited as the system's "father," and he himself knew it. About this, McCaskey wrote: "Not many men have had so keen a sense of the ridiculous. [Stevens'] wit flashed like light or scorched like flame; his humor was sometimes playful, sometimes severe. He never missed the ridiculous if anywhere present, and one of the things that used to afford him a grim sort of amusement was the would-be knowledge of such as declared him the Father of the Common School System of Pennsylvania.

'Why,' he would say, with the emphasis of humor, 'I never did anything but make a speech or two for the schools.'"[34]

Rather than Stevens, it was Dr. Thomas Burrowes and his remarkable leadership in structuring the inchoate Common School System while he was Secretary of the Commonwealth that warranted his being called "Father of the Common Schools," according to McCaskey.[35]

The opportunity to reflect on the life of Stevens presented itself to McCaskey daily for 30 years, for from his office window in the rear of the high school, he could see Stevens' resting place in the Shreiner Cemetery (now Shreiner-Concord): "Out of the window yonder, within a stone's throw of where we write, at a desk in the Lancaster High School building, stands the simple but massive tomb of Thaddeus Stevens. On one end of it is the single word 'Stevens,' on the other the dates '1792-1868;' on one side his name, place of birth, etc., on the other a word of explanation as to his burial place, that has been copied and printed thousands of times." McCaskey predicted that visitors would come by the thousands to the site out of curiosity or reverence.[36]

The "explanation" on the tomb was about Stevens' choice for his burial place. Although he had considered lots in two other Lancaster cemeteries, he rejected both upon discovering in their charters that "no person of color should be interred within their limits."[37] Shreiner's charter made no such restriction:

"I repose in this quiet and secluded spot,
not from any natural preference for solitude;
but finding other cemeteries limited as to race
by charter rules,
I have chosen this that I might illustrate in my death
the principle which I advocated
through a long life:
EQUALITY OF MAN BEFORE HIS CREATOR."

Decorating the grave with a flag, flowers and evergreens was a task McCaskey and his students undertook annually.[38]

The Pennsylvania Historical Marker at the Shreiner-Concord Cemetery. (Photo courtesy of Noah Brundin.)

Stevens' tomb. (Photo courtesy of Mary Alice Gerfin.)

James Buchanan was Stevens' political antithesis. As young lawyers, the two men had worked together on a case in York, but the collegiality faded quickly and they never spoke again. A year prior to their deaths, both in the same summer, Stevens was said to have attempted reconciliation, but Buchanan refused to take the extended hand.[39] The scenario might be fiction, but their antipathy was real. Buchanan's stance on slavery was clear. Convinced that the U.S. Constitution sanctioned the practice, Buchanan viewed it as "one of those moral evils from which it is impossible for us to escape."[40] Personally opposed to the "peculiar institution" of slavery, he nonetheless believed the Constitution protected the rights of slave holders and individual states.[41]

As a young man, Buchanan moved to Lancaster in 1810 and became a lawyer and politician. He served in the state legislature and then in the U.S. House of Representatives for 10 years and in the U.S. Senate for 11. He was also ambassador to Russia under Andrew Jackson, Secretary of State under James Polk, and Minister to Great Britain under Franklin Pierce.

Nominated as the Democratic Party presidential candidate in 1856, Buchanan conducted his campaign from the front porch of his home, Wheatland; it is a majestic mansion at the west end of town, preserved and open to the public today. Because of illness, Buchanan did not travel to campaign but invited supporters to come to Lancaster. The trains were full, and McCaskey's father, after his day's work on the railroad, must have had quite a few stories to share at home. Lancaster hotels were filled; restaurants were buzzing.[42]

James Buchanan, 15th President of the United States.

Buchanan became the 15th President of the United States. He spent much of his time in office trying to preserve the status quo and avoid the war that inevitably came. In December 1860, South Carolina was the first of the southern states to secede, followed by six others in the next two months, and the Confederate States of America was established in February 1861. Local papers reported on the disarray in Buchanan's cabinet and the rumors of war, and McCaskey wrote of the beleaguered President's last days in office: "A distinguished citizen of Lancaster, weary of the perplexing and difficult task of administering the government, was anxiously awaiting [Lincoln's] arrival at the White House."[43]

McCaskey stated that the citizens of Lancaster had known "President Buchanan well and had seen him often."[44] In 1848, when McCaskey was at Oak Hill Academy, he was classmates with "Jim" Buchanan, who was a nephew of the future president and a son of James' brother Edward Young Buchanan, rector of All Saints' Episcopal Church in Paradise. Buchanan was serving then as Secretary of State under Polk.[45] Jim served his uncle in the White House as his "personal secretary," a position now known as Chief of Staff, from 1858 to the end of Buchanan's presidency.

Among Buchanan's final executive acts was the proclamation of January 4, 1861, as a national day of "general Humiliation, Fasting and Prayer to the Great Ruler of Nations, in view of the alarming dangers which imperil the Union." Americans were asked to refrain from "worldly or secular employment" and instead devote the day to "such religious exercises as suggested by the Chief Magistrate of the Nation."[46] Lancaster gave "the appearance of a quiet Sabbath," with all the stores and shops closed (except the cotton mills) and all the churches open. At the First German Reformed Church, the Reverend J. W. Nevin began by noting that "our country is divided, her councils distracted, business deranged, the Union being in imminent danger of being rent into fragments, with the great calamity of civil war impending."[47]

James Buchanan died in June 1868, Thaddeus Stevens two months later. Stevens' grave continues to attract visitors, as McCaskey said it would. Buchanan's burial site is in the Woodward Hills Cemetery. Neglected for a time, it is now tended by a local Boy Scout troop.

James Buchanan's grave in Woodward Hills Cemetery. (Photo courtesy of author.)

Re-enactors as Fencibles at Buchanan's tomb, 2012. (Photo courtesy of author.)

Chapter 6

Goodbye to Mr. Reigart and Mr. McCaskey

"Thursday, September 11th: . . . Emanuel enlisted in the 93 regiment . . .
Friday, September 12th: . . . Emanuel and Sam Rathvon came to school to say goodbye to Mr. Reigart and Mr. McCaskey. . . ."[1]

McCaskey married Ellen Chase, a teacher from Bath, New York, in 1860. Celebrating their golden wedding anniversary, McCaskey told their children, "It was a warm day, August 8, 1860, fifty years ago, in Bath, New York, when your mother and I rode down to the church [St. Thomas Episcopal] where Rev. Mr. Howard waited in his clericals to solemnize a marriage. There were many people assembled, and most of them seemed afterwards to be at the depot as we waited for the noon train. You never saw me in white kids and a silk hat, but I had them that day. The hat I traded for another as soon as I got home . . ."[2]

Another of McCaskey's hats did not even make it back to Lancaster, a tale he shared with his students. One recalled: The newlyweds were on their honeymoon trip "by passage on a canal boat pulled by two mules and plying to Albany, New York. Young John on this occasion was wearing a plug hat [a rounded felt hat with a narrow brim]. His charming young bride was not impressed by said hat. So, striving to please her, he straightway tossed the offending headgear into the slow moving waters of the canal, never to be seen again."[3]

A third hat, many, many years later, was neither traded nor flung away. After Ellen's death in 1918, McCaskey honored her memory each morning as he came down to breakfast from his bedroom on the second floor, dressed for the day complete with a hat. He would pause on the landing where her portrait hung, bow while tipping his hat, and say, "Good morning, my dear."[4]

The hatless groom and his bride settled in Lancaster, where they lived just off Center Square on South Queen Street. He walked to his jobs: a block west on King and two blocks north on Prince each morning to school and, in the evenings, to the nearby *Lancaster Evening Express* newspaper office in their block. She tended to the home. The looming threat of war pervaded their domesticity with proclamations, the news of factions organizing, headlines blaring, rallies on the square, and loved ones volunteering.

The Civil War was threatening to destroy and permanently divide the nation. It was a war that would devastate the landscape from Gettysburg to Atlanta, from Texas to Virginia, a war that would yield 620,000 dead and stretch to the shores of the Susquehanna River, menacing the very city in which McCaskey and his family were living. It would pull in two of McCaskey's brothers, Will and Cye, and their sister Kate's sweetheart, James ("Jim") Marshall, as well as friends and neighbors, news of whose deaths or injuries might be posted in the newspaper or telegraph office windows any day.

President Buchanan's lame duck proclamation of the day in early January 1861 for "general Humiliation, Fasting and Prayer"[5] closed city businesses and filled churches,[6] but did not avert the inevitable. His failures filled the local papers. So did notices of Union meetings, Democratic meetings, meetings of the People's Party, and news of compromises still being sought, such as the Peace Conference in Washington in February.

In early March, when Buchanan vacated the White House, he was treated harshly in the *Lancaster Examiner and Herald*, which claimed that the ex-President would "meet with nothing but contempt" upon his return to Lancaster and branded him as a "vain, foolish and unprofitable public servant."[7] An *Express* article, most likely penned by McCaskey, was kinder.[8]

(McCaskey wrote the "Local Intelligence" column for the *Express*. However, only one can be credited to him with certainty.)

In April, as the Fort Sumter crisis boiled over, the headlines exploded into capital letters: "THE WAR" and "WAR! WAR!" The tension had been punctured. Tremors rattled Lancaster as news of the Southern aggression blared from the papers and over the telegraph lines, filling citizens' hearts with incredulity and rage: "[The attack] consumed the thoughts and movements of every man, woman, and child, . . . In Lancaster, disbelief soon turned to unbridled anger, then patriotism, as news filtered in and was confirmed. . . . All of those who had opposed the policies of Lincoln and the Union were not to be seen; it might not have been very healthy with passions running so high. . . . The streets were filled with people hustling about, trying to find what the latest news was. Telegraph and express offices as well as post offices posted dispatches for all to read as soon as they were received."[9]

Within days of the attack, Lancastrians responded. Judges, lawyers, commissioners, and others signed a resolution, crafted in part by Thaddeus Stevens, that renewed their oath of fidelity to the United States.[10] A day of affirmations of loyalty to the Union was held on April 17, this in response to President Lincoln's call to state militias to raise 75,000 men. So many arrived at the courthouse that morning, hours before the program was to begin, that the crowd spilled out into the streets. After a prayer of "great solemnity and most thrilling eloquence" came speeches and resolutions, punctuated by wildly enthusiastic cheers and applause, and the playing of the "Star Spangled Banner" and "Yankee Doodle Dandy" by the cornet band of a local militia, the Fencibles.[11]

The resolutions (in response to Southern states' secession, their attack on federal property and outrages against the flag) expressed Lancaster's eagerness to demonstrate its loyalty to the national government, its support for the President, and its approval of Pennsylvania's provision of resources to the cause. When Stevens was called upon to speak, he deferred and moved that the meeting be adjourned to Center Square for a flag raising. The flag was, after all, the flash point, as an earlier speaker had noted: It had been "stricken to the dust and we must not rest until we replace it, wherever it has been pulled down."[12]

And so, dignitaries and citizens walked to the square, mere yards from the McCaskeys' home, to witness the raising of a "liberty pole," a tradition from the Revolutionary War era.[13] The hickory flagstaff, 150 feet high and topped by a pine spar, was hoisted in place despite strong winds that day. Its successful erection must have come from the power of the people, the *Express* reported: "[I]t went up so steadily that a distant looker-on might imagine it was literally raised on the enthusiastic cheers of the patriotic crowds." As the pole "slowly and majestically rose to its place in the free air of heaven," men cheered, women waved their handkerchiefs, a cannon bellowed and the band played a patriotic song. The mayor ran the flag up as wild enthusiasm filled the air.[14]

All Lancaster now stood united. Now, "*[e]very man has taken his place in line*—treason has no sympathizers in old loyal Lancaster—we have but one heart and one purpose, and that is a heart of Patriotism and a purpose to stand by the flag of our country to the last."[15]

Two days later, with a myriad of flags rippling above the streets, the Lancaster Fencibles marched from their armory, past the Mayor's office, and up Queen Street to the railroad depot. Organized in 1855, this militia was one of the first volunteer units from Lancaster (along with the Jackson Rifles) to answer Lincoln's call for troops. More than 100 soldiers were surrounded by huge crowds of men, women, and children, cheering, crying, and waving handkerchiefs.[16] They were going to Harrisburg to be mustered into Company F as part

The Lancaster Fencibles, 1857. (Photo courtesy of LancasterHistory.org.)

of the First Pennsylvania Volunteer Infantry.[17] Their departure was the "most impressive and affecting scene ever witnessed in Lancaster," and the size of the crowd exceeded that of the one gathered for Lincoln's brief stop two months earlier.[18] The Fencibles were finally seated in the train, and it moved off.[19]

In the crowd were McCaskey and his family, for among the ebullient volunteers was McCaskey's brother Will. He was 17 years old.

Will had left high school in 1859 at age 15 and became, like his brother, a printer at the *Lancaster Examiner and Herald* office. Fascinated with the Fencibles militia, he joined it at the same time. He served as a Union soldier for the duration of the war and then made his career in the United States army. He and "Jack," the name McCaskey was called by his family, exchanged many letters during the conflict and throughout their lives.

When Will died in 1914, his wife Eleanor ("Nellie") sealed off two rooms of their California home; these were filled with many of the brothers' letters, documents, artifacts, uniforms, photos and other memorabilia from Will's military years. In 1983, a great-grandson, Henry ("Hank") Henley Chapman, was instructed to remove 12 trunks full of items from the rooms and burn the contents. Chapman determined not to carry out the directive but set about safeguarding the treasure,[20] a providential action. He edited a book, *The Letters of William S. McCaskey*, which includes Will's letters to McCaskey during and after the war. Without all these resources, most of the information about Will and McCaskey's relationship would not have been available, nor would a recent biography of Will, *Last Man Standing: William Spencer McCaskey,* have been possible.

The letters provide a fascinating, detailed account of a Union soldier's experiences while giving insights into his brother's civilian life in Lancaster. McCaskey was proud of Will's part in the war, and Will praised McCaskey for his newspaper articles about the conflict and his support of Lincoln. They remained best friends throughout their lives.

Three days after the Fencibles' departure, Will wrote to his siblings from camp: "We left you and host of friends with joy and sorrow intermingled, happy to be able to defend the glorious flag, and sorry to part with our endearing friends."[21] Nonetheless, the fledgling soldier was already enamored with the military life, writing: "There are many disadvantages and discouraging prospects in the life of a soldier, but as myself is concerned, I am delighted with it."[22] His resolve to honor the flag and punish those who did not was unflinching; he related an incident at camp in which the Stars and Stripes had been defiled: "[I would like to] have my desire gratified in shooting [the traitor], for I would have thought it an act of humanity to have done so, . . . [and I] do not seem to dread the shooting of a man who has in any way insulted or dishonored our flag."[23] Will's loyalties never faltered, and his dispassion never ameliorated.

While the Fencibles served in Maryland and Virginia, the citizens of Lancaster kept up their war efforts. More companies were formed; more volunteers boarded trains. Two Ohio regiments, consisting of 1,800 men, arrived and were quartered in the courthouse, Fulton Hall, and several churches, and they then encamped on the Lancaster Fairgrounds in "Camp Dennison"; hundreds of Lancastrians visited them.[24] The county commissioners appropriated $20,000 for families of volunteers. The Reverend Jacob Mombert, rector of St. James' Episcopal Church, organized the Patriot Daughters of Lancaster, which was the first society of women in the Union to minister to the soldiers throughout the war.[25] The women held concerts and charity bazaars to raise funds to ensure that each volunteer had a suitable outfit to wear. They gathered flannel shirts, haversacks, stockings, muslin "prepared in 8 and 12 yard bandages, one large box lint, rolls of linen, . . . and patches."[26]

After 90 days, Will and his fellow volunteers returned to Lancaster. McCaskey remembered their homecoming: "We saw them return with a like hearty popular ovation [as their departure]."[27] During August, Will and others, working in the new Fulton Hall, signed up recruits for Company B of the 79th Pennsylvania Infantry. In early September, he left Lancaster once again, joining the 79th to oppose "the rebellion against constituted authorities."[28] Jim Marshall also joined the 79th that September.

A photo of Will from that year shows him in a Fencibles' uniform of light-colored trousers, dark jacket, and kepi (a cap). He has pulled himself up straight and tall. His face is clean-shaven, and his wide-set eyes, overarched by dark, angular brows, hold their gaze at the camera, bespeaking both resolve and hesitancy about what is to come. While some of the look can be attributed to the need in the nascent field of photography for the subject to remain still for many seconds, in which case a straight face is easier to hold than a smiling one, the letters to his brother and family confirm that Will, young, middle-aged, or old, was indeed a man of resolve.

McCaskey struggled with his own sense of duty to the nation, as was clear in an October letter from Will: "I am very glad to hear that your military fever has subsided, it makes me feel much more at ease, for your lovely wife."[29] While Will's concern was for Ellen, McCaskey must have been worried about the schools, too. Teachers were volunteering or being drafted into the militia those first war years. Pennsylvania, given its border location between the Union and Confederacy, was among several Northern states with their own drafts prior to the 1863 federal draft. Of the 8,500 male teachers in the state in 1861, 1,800 left the classroom to join the army by the second half of 1862. To stanch that drain, Governor Curtin exempted male teachers from service in the militia in November.[30]

McCaskey, who had risen from third to second to first

Will in Fencibles' uniform, September 1861. (Photo from private collection.)

assistant of the principal at Boys' High between 1859 and 1862, watched as each position he vacated was eliminated due to budget constraints.[31] Torn as he was between his loyalty to both the country and the Common Schools, he must have felt a strong compulsion to remain in the classroom rather than volunteer for military service. Someone needed to stay in the schools, so stay he did.

McCaskey and Will were among the first generation of Pennsylvania children to be educated in the Common Schools. Enthusiastic praise and the high value of this new phenomenon, public education, resounded for many, many years. Leaders and educators believed that without public schools the Union would have been destroyed in the Civil War. Both McCaskey men concurred.[32] In a *Pennsylvania School Journal* editorial written 25 years after the war, the writer, clearly McCaskey, opined: "When the volcanic outburst of overt secession fell upon the unsuspecting North like an earthquake shock, it was the pervading influence of the Common Schools that rose to the occasion and made itself felt as an unconquerable force in the continental field of strife. The schoolmaster had been abroad long enough to enlighten the popular understanding, warm the patriot heart, and strengthen the popular will. . . . It is beyond dispute that the preservation of the Union was largely due to the Common School."[33]

In another *Journal* article seven years later, similar sentiments were expressed, this time making the schools *the* reason for the Union's preservation: "Had it not been for the Common Schools of the Northern States the Rebellion would have been successful." In fact, the article continued, "We are by no means convinced that the Common School System of our own State of Pennsylvania may not, in the providence of God, have been the pivotal agency upon which turned the mighty question of Union or Disunion. Had Pennsylvania been as illiterate in 1861-2-3 as in 1835-6-7, when the system of public education was adopted, her sons—more ignorant of the vast issues at stake and more easily misled by scheming demagogues—would not have been in the field to the number of hundreds and thousands in solid phalanx, as they were, doing battle for the integrity of the Union."[34]

Immanuel ("Manny") C. Pehrson was one of McCaskey's students during the war years. Manny kept a diary in 1862 and 1863 and wrote often about his teachers, Mr. McCaskey and Mr. Reigart. McCaskey, the ingenuous Manny noted, would occasionally stray from his lesson plans, due to his own loquaciousness: "Tuesday, November 4th: This morning Mr. McCaskey talked to us so long in history half-hour that he could not hear us our lessons." Manny commented frequently about "philosophy" [science] class and McCaskey's successes and failures in that subject. "Wednesday, November 19th: Mr. McCaskey wanted to try an experiment but it was raining and he could not get up electricity." December 10th, "Mr. McCaskey . . . shocked us and made Sam McCleery light the gas by touching it." December 17th, "Mr. McCaskey tried some more experiments. He shocked us two or three times. He lit some ether and alcohol by the machine." On Christmas Eve, "Mr. McCaskey explained about the works of a watch to us and I showed him my watch." In March, "Mr. McCaskey tried experiments with chlorine gas and succeeded very well." A week later, the results were not as good: "Mr. McCaskey . . . spilt some [phosphorus] on a globe and burnt it."[35]

An orphan, Manny lived on a farm near the Conestoga River with "Aunt Sally" (Mrs. Frederic J. Kramph) and her family, including her stepchildren Emanuel and Annie. The war wove itself seamlessly into Manny's account, starting with his very first entry: "May 6, 1862: Today I was 14 years old. Aunty gave me my diary and pen and pen holder. Annie gave me a picture and Emanuel a knife. Yesterday we heard news that Yorktown was taken last Saturday. Today Williamsburg was occupied by our forces. The loss is not yet known. I am in Mr. Erisman's first class, we study geography, reading, writing." Some days later, Manny recorded that Norfolk was taken and the Merrimac blown up. He and Emanuel "went into grandma's for tea. General Banks was rebuffed at Winchester." Manny picked strawberries and sold them, skipped school to see Van Amberg's menagerie that had come to town, hopped on the back of a wagon driven by a driverless mule and rode along for awhile, went to church, went to school, "went to a tent to hear some preaching." He found "a swallow's nest in the barn with seven eggs in it" and "[t]he president called 300,000 more troops." He and his friends put on a little theater, "Annie was dressed up like a gentleman, Emanuel like a lady, and Miss Benedict like a bride." In the same entry he wrote that "Mc-

Clellan was forced to retreat 17 miles and spike their siege guns but he took 2000 prisoners and a general," and his friend Dave Stamm came in a boat and they "went near to Rocky Springs." On July 4th, Manny and Emanuel went into town to the courthouse, heard readings of the Declaration of Independence and Jackson's Nullification speech . . . and "Mr. McCarter made a speech in Centre Square about the Union" and Manny had four packs of firecrackers. At a school picnic, he played cricket and "[s]ome of the boys stole a farmer's whiskey bottle and drunk all the whiskey," and Manny and a friend returned the bottle.[36]

The newspapers were urging boys and young men to get into good physical shape for military service, so Manny exercised ten minutes every day.[37] He and his friends observed much military activity around the city: "We saw about seven companies go past to camp [and his friend] Sam Potts enlisted in Captain Neff's company." Emanuel hankered to enlist, too.[38]

On September 2, 1862, "Aunty gave Emanuel her consent," and he joined the 93rd regiment on the 11th. On Friday, September 12, "Emanuel and Sam Rathvon came to school to say goodbye to Mr. Reigart and Mr. McCaskey."[39]

Chapter 7

Steel to the Hilt

"You give them steel to the hilt at home,
and I'll represent the household in the field."[1]

The patriotic fervor and indignation swirling about in Lancaster in the early months of the war sputtered into a cloud of gloom by 1862. Union disasters portended a drawn-out war and potential defeat. Residents gathered outside the newspaper and telegraph offices, no longer expecting news of a quick victory and an end to the rebellion. Now they came to scan casualty lists, their breath held in fear that the name of a family member, friend, or neighbor would be posted there.[2] The McCaskeys came there, too, as they joined others at these message boards of sorrow, not knowing then that, ultimately, their loved ones, Will, Cye, and Jim Marshall, would all come through almost unscathed.

McCaskey and his editor, J. M. Willis Geist, were among the first to have access to incoming telegrams. Geist wrote: "In the early stages of the existing rebellion, when our friend Mac and ourself used to spend night after night in the telegraph office, waiting for the war news . . . we had plenty of leisure to form opinions, and discuss the merits of matters and things in general connected with the war."[3]

As busy as McCaskey was as teacher by both day and night, journalist by night, family man, engaged citizen, and member of several professional and civic organizations, over the four years of the war he found time to do Will's bidding. Will sent money home with directions on how it was to be invested or used, including paying the rent and household expenses, such as coal and oil. Once, he directed McCaskey to give their mother money on the condition that "these $50's are intended to be used for her own private use,"[4] suggesting that their father William had not improved in his ability to handle a budget. Will fretted in several letters about sister Kate not being able to get her furs, and he directed that part of the $100 he was sending home be used to pay for them.[5]

McCaskey bought clothing for the soldier. Will needed boots, "a capital pair, just the fit and right weight, come mighty handy too, for my old ones were most pegged out on our last scouting trip,"[6] and more boots: "I wish you to call on my friend, Charlie Bickens, and buy me a pair of boots, made up exactly on the style, as the last ones, with the exception, of being lighter, not so heavy. I want him to get the finest material he can procure for the uppers, and do the job in tiptop style. Tell him, the others pleased me exceedingly well, could not have hit the mark better, just suit me."[7] He wanted pantaloons: "I wish you would step around to S. S. Rathvon's Clothing establishment, and order a pair of dark blue pantaloons for me. Tell him to make them exactly like Lieut. Blickenderfer's, they fit me exactly, I want the same material." He requested material for a collar: "I also wish you would get me a piece of black silk velvet for my coat collar, get enough, for I have a pretty big neck—15 1/2."[8] He called for hats: "That monstrous—just-the-thing-Planter hat came at last and just in time," and it was just what Will wanted.[9] McCaskey sent him gloves, not all of which were satisfactory: "The cloth pair were a good fit, but the others were monsters, could not make use of them."[10] Will received, as well, handkerchiefs, collars, and "good strong cotton socks."[11]

McCaskey also sent him books, including one on military law,[12] and Will ordered a "'Sword-belt' of the pattern of Captain Whiteside's, and a tiptop article at that. Send it along as soon as possible."[13] McCaskey sent shoulder straps and a tent. He arranged for a watch repair, about which Will had sent specific instructions: "You will have it taken apart and rigged completely, the hinges are loose, the center post is too high to allow a crystal being on, the cases are twisted, and the chain is too short, for it only runs 21 hours, and fast, going about an hour in every 24, last have it cleaned."[14] He sent him postage stamps,[15] and he renewed Will's subscription to the *Army and Navy Journal*.[16]

Pictures of family and friends were most essential. Will requested a "photograph album of card size, that will hold about 20 or 30 pictures" for he wanted to see "Ellen's, Kate's, Father's, Joe's, and all my friends' pictures I can get." He already had pictures of McCaskey, their father and mother, and one of a friend, Captain Drunkemiller.[17] He had lost youngest brother Newt's picture, jesting that "the Rebels captured Newt, or rather his photograph. I received it on the march, and put it in one of my boys' knapsacks, to carry for me, and the knapsack, picture and all, was captured. I suppose Newt never thought he would get into a secessor's hands."[18]

In the spring of 1865, Will requested maps for his company. "One thing, Jack, we have been sorely in need of in the last two campaigns, and that is maps. Now I wish you to send me, as soon as possible, the best maps that can be procured of the states of Virginia, North and South Carolina, Georgia and Tennessee. Remember, I want them on separate sheets, each state by itself and laid out in counties. The best thing in the market and of not too much cost, also Alabama and Mississippi."[19]

Letters from home provided the greatest joy for the soldiers. McCaskey wrote a grateful Will frequently: "Dear Jack, To you I would return my heartfelt thanks for your attention, and furnishing me with most all kinds of reading matter, also your punctual writing to me. This latter is a favor which I greatly appreciate, and I think no one can be more fully supplied with home news than your humble servant. I have never had much cause to be dissatisfied on this point, for you, Ellen and Kate, have kindly kept me posted on current matters. . . . Four letters from you are before me."[20] A note from home was the "the King of pleasures," and Will said that the soldiers wore pitiful expressions at mail call when they were told "'Nothing for you.'"[21]

Writing letters from camp was difficult. In an early epistle, Will said: "[W]riting, and on a white washed board door, such as are used on pig pens, is not an easy matter."[22] Weariness also stymied correspondence: "You must know that after 23 days campaigning, and most of the time without shelter of the least kind, without change of clothing, and slim rations, a man feels completely exhausted. Yes, we were entirely fatigued, and I pray you excuse me."[23]

The brothers sought each other's advice on many issues, receiving it usually with good grace. However, when it came to military matters, Will, six years McCaskey's junior and still an adolescent, rebuffed his older civilian brother. He was particularly strong in his rejection of McCaskey's advice on how he should behave on the front. In a letter from Tennessee in January 1863, Will, by then a two-year seasoned soldier, wrote: "[I]n my last [letter] I told you of my being on picket, and near the rebels, who drove me back on the next morning. You, in return, intimate rashness, needless exposure of myself and men & etc. Now, while I justly credit you with much 'book learning,' and extensive civic ideas, I must say you are very deficient in mili-

A letter from Will to "Jack." (Photo courtesy of Richard Abel.)

tary knowledge, whether it be strategic, or compulsory attack." Will went on to explain what he had done and said he expected praise rather than chastisement. He had taken on a dangerous assignment because his commander, Lt. Colonel David Miles, had confidence in him. He would obey orders and do his duty to his family and country even if he were killed; disobeying would have meant a dishonorable discharge and brought ridicule on him and disgrace upon his family: "Suppose I should have skiddeled [sic] in this hour of peril and said no, I should have been dismissed dishonorably, been the jest of all my companions in arms, and would never have the heart to look upon my family, who I hope would have courage and patriotism to spawn a son that would not act this cowardly and bring disgrace at their doors. I am sorry that you do not give me more credit for caution."[24]

While the two men occasionally disagreed, in the area of politics they never did. They were Republicans and supported Lincoln and the policies of the federal government. McCaskey joined the Union League, begun in 1862 to promote loyalty to the Union and Lincoln's policies, and Will congratulated him on his membership.[25] Among the Democrats, on the other hand, there were those who wanted peace at the expense of union. Also, "Copperheads," a radical faction of the Democrats, were sympathetic to the South and secretly worked for a Southern victory. The *Lancaster Examiner and Herald* labeled them "Northern traitors and agitators."[26] Will lambasted the Democratic League as "sympathizers, demagogues, poltroons, and friends of the Rebellion," and he accused them of keeping the war going.[27] The Lancaster Democrats' most notable member was George Sanderson, mayor of the city and also editor of the *Lancaster Intelligencer*. Sanderson, Will wrote, was "a traitor or rather a Union man conditionally."[28]

Sanderson was the target of many editorials in the *Express*, the paper McCaskey worked for. McCaskey wrote not only local news but editorials, as well. Because journalists' names were not included with their articles, only one opinion piece can be attributed to him with certainty. Will, however, knew which ones his brother had written, and in 1863, he praised McCaskey's work, mentioning that the soldiers in his company wondered who the journalist was:

"Your articles in the dailies are shot straight at the mark and I have heard numerous individuals around here wonder 'who that fellow is' that gets up those squibs."[29] ("Squibs" were satirical or sarcastic opinion pieces.)

In 1864 Will commended McCaskey again: "Your articles in the *Express* have been read with a kind of particular family pride, and have been handed around [extensively], . . . The 'Contrast' was a crowning effort, I never saw [or] read a better bit, and after my friends were informed who wrote it, they would say [you] were the master of your pen and should be a contributor editor or something of the kind, rather than a teacher, and my opinion. . . is the same."[30]

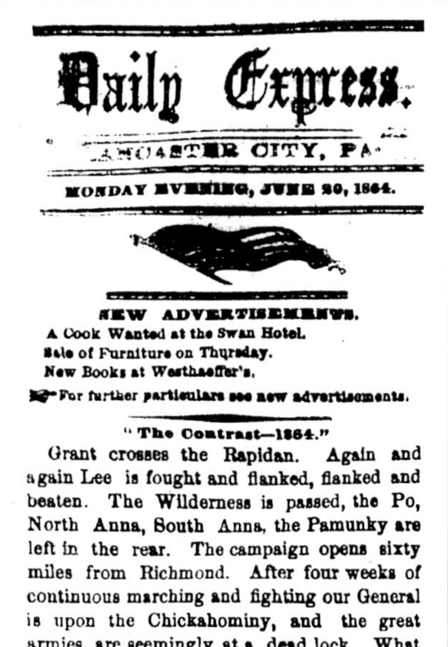

Daily Express.

[illegible]CASTER CITY, PA.

MONDAY EVENING, JUNE 20, 1864.

NEW ADVERTISEMENTS.
A Cook Wanted at the Swan Hotel.
Sale of Furniture on Thursday.
New Books at Westhaeffer's.
For further particulars see new advertisements.

"The Contrast—1864."

Grant crosses the Rapidan. Again and again Lee is fought and flanked, flanked and beaten. The Wilderness is passed, the Po, North Anna, South Anna, the Pamunky are left in the rear. The campaign opens sixty miles from Richmond. After four weeks of continuous marching and fighting our General is upon the Chickahominy, and the great armies are seemingly at a dead lock. What now? Siege works upon the line of the Chickahominy with this fatal season upon us? Is McClellan's failure to be repeated upon McClellan's chosen ground? Not so. The past history of the Lieutenant-General forbids the dreadful supposition. Gen. Grant is equal to the emergency. He has studied strategy to some purpose. The rebel works cannot be taken by storm. He does not "butt his head against them" a second time. Lee is hoodwinked by a skirmish line, and the entire army, crossing the Chickahominy and the James, suddenly threatens Richmond from the south.

Grant is at last *upon new ground!* It is a movement which the military historian will never tire of telling. One whose counterpart would have shed additional lustre upon the fame of the First Napoleon. Petersburg, the second town in Virginia, is surprised and taken. Hundreds of prisoners and many guns fall into our hands. The railroads are effectually cut, and General Lee seems caught in a trap at last. Richmond is threatened from a new and far more dangerous quarter.

Opening paragraphs of McCaskey's editorial "The Contrast" in the Express, *June 20, 1864.*

In "The Contrast," McCaskey wrote about the reaction in the U.S. House of Representatives to the news that General Grant had, in a flanking movement, captured new ground and was closing in on Richmond. He described the scene: "[T]he Union (loyal) members 'let themselves out' in the wildest applause, in which the galleries heartily join" but only four Democrats join in. Some 50 other Democrats, whom McCaskey labeled "copperheads," sit silently, grieving "at our success." They claim to be friends of the soldier, but their "hearts leap only at news of his defeat." A painting should be made of this moment, he claimed, for it would "immortalize the infamy of Copperheadism" and show "by contrast the beauty of loyalty and the excellence of true patriotism."[31]

Will believed McCaskey's newspaper work to be so significant that he wrote in 1863: "You give them steel to the hilt at home, and I'll represent the household in the field."[32] Will understood the power of language. The expression "steel to the hilt," connoting achievement beyond the maximum, carries with it, in this case, its literal meaning as well: warriors running the enemy through with the sword all the way up to its handle. That was Will's job, and yet he assigned the honor to his brother, assuaging McCaskey's conflicted feelings about not serving in the war as a soldier by inferring that McCaskey was, indeed, doing battle for the President and the Union.

Will's representation of the household in the field was laudatory. His devotion to duty, to the Union, to the flag never wavered. Unlike Henry Fleming, the protagonist in Stephen Crane's *Red Badge of Courage,* which is a fictional narrative of a young Yankee soldier's war experiences, Will never gave in to the urge to turn tail and flee from battle and bloodshed. As his company was lined up for its first engagement in April 1861, the 17 year old from Lancaster was ready to sacrifice himself: ". . . the boys were in a stew, but for myself, I tell you I felt composed, not flinching a muscle and prepared to render to my Country all that service that was in my power to do so."[33]

In an 1862 letter to McCaskey's wife, Ellen, Will saw death as a mercy when he responded to her sorrow about the regiment losing so many in a battle in Kentucky: "Sorrowful as people seem to be in and around the birthplace [Lancaster] of the shattered 79th, quite different is the appearance of solemnity in these quarters, for the boys have had so much hard usage, seen so many dead and mangled bodies, that pity does not seem to have any say. True as I tell you, we think the unfortunate are much better off dead as far as bodily sufferings are concerned, the mental sufferings, or end of our comrades we have no right to judge."[34]

During that battle, Will wrote, he experienced "that remarkable feeling . . . that seemed to have given way to a much more needed sense, that of calmness."[35] When his friend Fred Sener was shot alongside him, Will fought on to avenge him, "and bullets never went into hotter muskets with a more steady and determined hand. You could see the miserable looking varments [sic] trying to creep up on you, crack would go our muskets, down go the game."[36]

In *The Red Badge of Courage*, Henry Fleming would come to know the calm Will experienced. He would evolve from coward to hero when he came to understand, as Will always had, the great symbolism of "the colors," which were the company flags that provided the rallying point in the chaos of engagements. It was the company flag that empowered Henry: "Within himself, as he hurled himself forward, was born a love, a despairing fondness for this flag which was near him. It was a creation of beauty and invulnerability. . . . Because no harm could come to it he endowed it with power. He kept near, as if it could be a saver of lives, and an imploring cry went from his mind." When the color sergeant fell, Henry and his friend leapt to keep the colors upright.[37]

Will knew that love as well. Captain of Company B by 1865, he urged McCaskey to see the governor about getting flags for his unit immediately, for at some point they had been lost: "One great error in our composition, and one which cause[s] us many a sorrow, is our want of colors. We have not had a stand of colors since we left Marietta. There was a stand of colors at Chattanooga for us, but we never received them, and I tell you it is very galling to us, to be asked, 'where are your colors?'" Will did not explain their disappearance, other than to refute that they had been lost on the battlefield. If that had been the case, he declared, his body would have been lying there, too.[38]

Will understood the necessity for the war he was fighting in. He called it the war of "secessia," "the rebellion against constituted authorities," "this great contest between right and wrong," and "the mammoth Rebellion."[39] He was in favor of emancipation of the slaves but not equality.[40] He gave voice to the tragedy of the war and his outrage against it: "Who after this campaign shall have been over can be fortunate enough to have escaped the calamity of having lost a friend, an associate, or kinsman. Oh, cruel war, may deep dire damning punishment be inflicted upon the founders of this rebellion. Not one of them are fit to live on a soil like that of America. They should be swept from the land like plague."[41] As the war drew to an end, Will wrote his brother that two more of his men had died from their injuries suffered at Bentonville: "Two more men have been offered up, for what? The redemption and purging of the Nation."[42]

Will's four years of service in the Army had begun by taking him out to Pittsburgh, down along the West Virginia western border, into Kentucky, farther south into Tennessee and Georgia and then north through South and North Carolina and into Virginia and Maryland. He survived many battles, including Perryville, Stone River, Chickamauga, and Peach Tree Creek. McCaskey wrote about Will's good luck in a biographical sketch for a book about prominent Lancastrians: "[Will] seemed to bear a charmed life, for, though present in each of the twenty-eight battles[43] in which the regiment was engaged (never absent from the regiment at any time for any cause), and constantly on active duty, he was never wounded. Bullets cut his clothing, spent balls hit him, and he was knocked down by the impact of a cannon ball striking the timbers near his head, but he was never hurt."[44]

In 1864, Will sought an appointment to West Point and asked McCaskey to see Thaddeus Stevens about one. However, it was not forthcoming. Will wrote: "Well, my last hope for West Point has been shattered, cast from me, be it so, for it seems to me that destiny has marked out a different path for me, and whatever that may be, whether of long or short duration, I hope I may do my duty like a man. Accept my heartfelt thanks, Jack, for your kindness all along in this West Point matter. You have been untiring in your energies, I shall always remember you, but as you truly remarked to the Hon. Stevens, it is my last effort."[45]

In the waning months of the war, Will wrestled with what to do when it was over, but he was emphatically uninterested in pursuing a military career.[46] At war's end, he sought McCaskey's advice, and McCaskey directed him to Eastman's Business School in Poughkeepsie, New York, and paid his tuition and expenses. Will's letters home indicated a discontent, but he persevered. Then, in February 1866, a meeting in Lancaster between McCaskey and Thaddeus Stevens, Jr., Stevens' nephew, changed everything. Congressman Stevens had an army appointment to make and young Thad had recommended Will, with whom he had served in the Fencibles. McCaskey wrote Will, but even before he could get a response, young Thad returned to say that the appointment had to be made immediately. McCaskey accepted it on his brother's behalf, and Will was commissioned into the regular army February 23, 1866.[47] He served with distinction in the American West and in the Spanish-American War. His military career spanned 46 years.

Major General William Spencer McCaskey. (Photo from private collection.)

In a 1903 letter, McCaskey's son Donald wrote to Will, by then a colonel, about Will's career and hopes for a promotion: *"Dear Uncle Will,"* he began, *"Father recently sent me a sketch of you which he has prepared for a Lanc. Co. Biography, I believe it is. I've just finished reading it a few minutes ago, and was much surprised at what a fine record you have, Uncle Will. I never knew near so much about it before . . . I hope you will be appointed to a Brigadier before the time arrives next year when you have decided to retire from your present command. You are too good a man for the Army to lose from active service, in my youthful judgment."*[48]

Donald praised his uncle for having served so well, even if the honors were not always readily forthcoming for him or other McCaskey military men: *"Somehow there is in almost every McCaskey, inborn it must be, a quality that makes him do duty wherever he is and not to make much fuss about it. Somehow, also, the merited recognition seems to glide by them to land on the head of someone more fortunate, and often less efficient. This has been your case, Ed's and Walt's [McCaskey's military sons]. How it has been with Garrie and Doug [Will's sons, also career military men] I don't know. Whatever occurs to the recognition—the duty is always done and well done, as is instanced in your record time and time again."*[49]

Will received a promotion to brigadier general in 1904 and retired from the Army in 1907 as a major general.

Chapter 8

Times of Tribulation

"Well, we must not look at [the] dark side of the matter but hope for the best. These are times of tribulation, and our only remedy is submission."[1]

In 1863, the flames and blasts of the war closed in on Lancaster, and the newly-passed Conscription Act first waved its tentacles towards the four McCaskey brothers still at home—Jack, Joe, Cye, and Newt. McCaskey continued his reporting and teaching, although even that was in jeopardy. For all of Will's devotion to soldiering and his conviction about the necessity of this war, even he was growing weary.

The happiness borne of weddings and babies that year helped distract from the great uncertainties. In January, Jim Marshall had proposed to Kate, and Will wrote to McCaskey approvingly of Kate's acceptance and Marshall's integrity: "I must heartily congratulate her on choosing, and if she could only see how high Jim stands in the estimation of rank and file of the regiment, I think she would be amply paid for kind remembrance of him. Oh, I tell you he is a boy that you may be proud of as a bro-in-law, honest, brave, full of fun, but always sensible."[2] The couple married in May while the regiment was home on leave. Edward William, McCaskey and Ellen's first child, was born in August. Will called Ellen his brother's "lovely angel-half," and wished the couple "a long and happy [life], with many 'Juniors' to bring up in the paths of right, which I know you are both capable of doing."[3]

Joy in May was supplanted by fear in June. The war was creeping in on Lancaster and other places near the Pennsylvania-Maryland border as the Confederates pushed across the Mason-Dixon Line. In October 1862 the rebels under J.E.B. Stuart had already made a raid into Chambersburg, unnerving the populace. Now, in June, the news that the Army of Northern Virginia was nearby alarmed citizens living west of the Susquehanna so much that they packed up their families and valuables, drove their livestock ahead of them, and hastened eastward, crossing the river on the Columbia-Wrightsville Bridge into Lancaster County.

Governor Curtin called for the state to prepare for an invasion, and the federal government created the Department of the Susquehanna. Lancaster city and county men volunteered for homeland defense under Colonel Emlen Franklin. In mid-June, "To the Susquehanna" was the rallying cry, as Franklin designated rendezvous points along the river.[4] Daily drills were mandatory in Lancaster city,[5] and Cye, two years younger than Will, was among those manning battlements along the banks of the Susquehanna.[6] By month's end, rebel troops approached Chambersburg and Carlisle, and General Stuart and his men raided the area around Hanover and York. General Jubal Early destroyed Thaddeus Stevens' Caledonia ironworks[7] and occupied York. Confederate troops marched towards Wrightsville, a York County town on the river opposite the burg of Columbia on the Lancaster County side.

The militia defending the river town could not hold out long against the enemy's artillery fire and, retreating across the mile-long Columbia-Wrightsville Bridge, set it on fire the evening of June 28th. This act effectively destroyed the access the invaders had been seeking to reach Lancaster to "lay that town under contribution"[8] and then move beyond to Harrisburg and Philadelphia. The fire's flames leapt so high into the dark evening sky that they were visible in Lancaster.[9] The next day, news that the rebel troops were withdrawing brought great relief to the frightened populace.

Despite the great fear the invasion engendered, Will responded with little sympathy: "Well my boy," he wrote McCaskey, "they had you on considerable of a scare around Lancaster, about invasion, and all the imaginary evils inherent to an invading army. In one way, I wish the rebels would give all your Northern cities and counties a slight scouring, to let your memories be brightened slightly. The people of the North have not the remotest idea of war." He railed against those who opposed the war, Lincoln, and Congressional policies, and he chastised the ungrateful Northerners: "They . . . seem to forget they have persons of their own blood, trying to save them all the horrors of war, and endeavoring to thwart the rebels, whenever an opportunity offers, and in return what are their thanks, from many nothing more than a repudiation of our doctrines, dissensions from the great all absorbing, necessary policies of the times."[10]

After this defeat (which a local historian has called the real turning point of the war[11]), the Southerners moved west and rejoined the Army of Northern Virginia under General Lee to battle General Meade and the Army of the Potomac at Gettysburg for three days in July. Reports of the engagement there kept Lancastrians on edge, and the roar of the cannons on the last day could be heard as far east as Lancaster and far to the west.

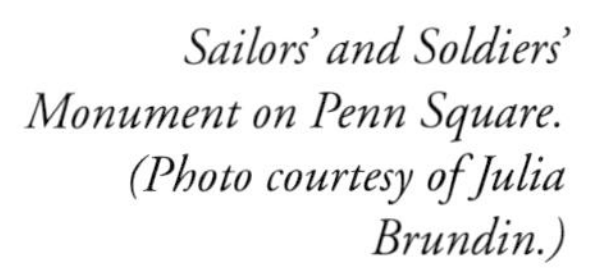

Sailors' and Soldiers' Monument on Penn Square. (Photo courtesy of Julia Brundin.)

In the days and weeks following the battle, Lancaster sent food and medical personnel and supplies to Gettysburg.[12] The Patriot Daughters of Lancaster traveled west, crossed the Susquehanna by ferry, and nursed 150 wounded soldiers for four weeks. When the men's conditions had stabilized, the women came home, only to receive news that their patients were starting to decline (apparently due to their nurses' absence) and so the women returned to Gettysburg.[13] (The Patriot Daughters were responsible, in 1874, for the erection in Lancaster's Center Square of the Sailors' and Soldiers' Monument, made of white granite with a base of 18 square feet and a height of 43 feet. Dedicated to those who fought in the war, its central figure, the "Genius of Liberty," is positioned with her back to the South.)

Sometime that July, McCaskey was among the first civilians to visit the battlefield. Will wrote to him: "So you've been to Gettysburg, to get a slight idea of the battle, and but a slight one you would get too, for all the din of battle had ceased, all the wounded cared for, all the dead buried. Together with your observations, imagine the rest, and it's not such a nice picture after all. Hope you enjoyed yourself, however, and made a few useful observations."[14]

The "Genius of Liberty" atop the monument. (Photo courtesy of author.)

Earlier that year, on March 3, 1863, Congress passed "An Act for Enrolling and Calling Out the National Forces and For Other Purposes," the first federal Conscription Act. The need for more troops had become great, as heavy casualties depleted the ranks, and volunteers were not as quick to step forward as they had been in those early, heady days of enthusiastic support from the citizenry, optimistic about a short war. Peace Democrats, Copperheads, and other anti-administration forces were fracturing the naïve belief that all of Lancaster's citizens were of "one heart and one purpose."[15] For those who could afford it, there were two ways to avoid serving: commutation (which meant that one could pay a $300 fee instead of serving) or hiring a substitute. Dodging the draft was legal and part of the law.

Will believed that the Conscription Act had come so late that many of those in service would leave with no one trained to replace them.[16] He was also concerned that his brothers would now be drafted. In May he wrote Jack from Murfreesboro, Tennessee: "I suppose you'll be a candidate for the Conscription Act, Ah; my boy, well you may be exempted! I would sooner you would be allowed to stay at home, with your wife, I don't mind being in the army myself, but I don't like to see my brothers in it, not for the want of patriotism, but because the bill [of conscription] will not be of benefit and neither you or Joe could stand the hardships of a campaign."[17] (Will was alluding to McCaskey's somewhat fragile health as a child,[18] and he considered Joe "too tender hearted to be a soldier."[19])

In June, Will told McCaskey not to worry: "I don't think you need fear being drafted yet, those six months state troops will delay that, some time, so rest easy at present."[20] Despite Will's assurances to the contrary, McCaskey probably did not rest easily, as "the wheel" was scheduled to come to the Ninth Congressional District, which included Lancaster, in July. The draft was set up as a lottery executed by a federal provost marshal. Names were written on individual ballots and placed into the wheel, which was an enclosed cylindrical tumbler about two feet wide suspended on a wooden frame with a handle to turn it and scramble the ballots. The tumbler had a small opening with a sliding cover, and into that opening went all the ballots. Turn, tumble, turn, scramble. Then, one by one, out came each ballot in the fingers of a blindfolded person, usually a federal marshal, until he had pulled the stipulated number for the quota.[21]

When the wheel was turned in Lancaster on July 16, inside it were the names of brothers John and Joseph McCaskey and those of 386 other eligible men in sub-district 28, Lancaster City N.W.W. (North West Ward). In the Orphans' Courtroom that Thursday morning, with just a few people present, the work began of putting all the ballots into the wheel and then pulling out 116 to meet the quota. This time a young girl was the angel of doom: "All the names on the slips are read out before they are put in the wheel; they are drawn out by a little girl about ten years of age, who is blindfolded, and as each name is read out one of the clerks at once fills up a notice to the man drafted, to report at the rendezvous in fifteen days."[22] "Joseph B. McCaskey" was called out; "John P. McCaskey" was not.[23]

Will wrote to McCaskey in August about the results: "You were a lucky boy, this draft, but Joe not quite as much so. Hope by this time he has been exempted. That was rather a neat little speculation you embarked in, but I reckon you are satisfied. Whenever a person engages in any contract, he runs a certain risk, as your pocket-book can testify."[24] The speculation Will referred to was a common fund in the care of businessman John F. Sehner into which McCaskey and 24 other men had each paid $50. Six of the 25 were drafted in the lottery that July morning, and on September 12 each received $250 from the fund to help pay for his commutation.[25]

In the wake of the lottery results, many from the city and county, among them Joe, applied for exemptions at the federal marshal's office: "Last week was a busy time at the Provost Marshal's office, in this city. The number applying for exemption was unexpectedly large, and the diseased and otherwise incapacitated for military service, together with those who 'forked over' the $300, render it pretty certain that, of the three thousand and upwards drafted in Lancaster County, not one thousand, if that many, will trouble Uncle Sam for a new suit of clothes and the privilege of carrying a musket to the tented field."[26] Will was aware, too, of the many exemptions from that first draft, writing on August 2: "I notice by the papers, that Lancaster County is nearly spun fit of material for soldiers, if a person may judge from the long list of exemptions, nearly two-thirds, perhaps more."[27]

Joe was exempted due to chronic rheumatism.[28]

The conscription wheel was to come to Lancaster again in 1864. A more resigned Will responded to Jack's news of another draft in a letter he wrote on Christmas Eve, 1863, from Chattanooga: "Yours of the 13th inst., at hand, still around I notice, with slight cause for exemption . . . Well, we must not look at [the] dark side of the matter but hope for the best. These are times of tribulation, and our only remedy is submission."[29]

Will revealed in the letter that brother Cye had offered to take Jack's place if his name was drawn: "I am glad to see that Cye is so kind, and hope if the worse [sic] comes you will accept his offer for it would be more suitable for him to go than you. If I were out of the harness, neither of you should go, but as of present, can't be [done]."[30] Cye was unmarried and 17; McCaskey, the oldest son and manager of his parents' affairs, was 26 with wife and child.

While the Conscription Act skulked in the background of McCaskey's life, his work as a teacher was becoming less certain because male student numbers were declining and the Boys' High was perceived as deficient. The district's earlier dire financial situation had improved markedly, due to "rigid economy,"[31] but cut faculty positions were not reinstated. Boys' High was in danger of being closed. No student graduated in 1863. That July, a resolution to close the Male High School was made to the school board, but it did not pass. Instead, a committee was set up to "investigate what defects or deficiencies (if any) exist in the present management of the High Schools."[32]

A publicly announced meeting invited "all whom it might concern to appear and lay before the Committee for investigation as to their truth or falsity, whatever complaints or charges they might have to make respecting either the teachers, the management, order or discipline of the schools."[33] Other than the committee members and the teachers (McCaskey among them), no one else came. The committee, after waiting an hour, asked to be discharged.[34]

The Male High School stayed open. However, pressures on McCaskey and the school continued. Along with his evening newspaper work, he had begun teaching at the Male Night School in 1862. He was a member of the Lancaster County Teachers' Institute, serving on its committees and lecturing at meetings.[35] All of this, and family life as well, must have led him to consider quitting the newspaper office in the summer of 1864. By then, the number of boys at Boys' High had shrunk significantly: Only 67 males were enrolled, "somewhat on consequence of disarrangement of labor, caused by the war."[36]

McCaskey sought Will's opinion. Even though Will had encouraged him to leave teaching for journalism several months earlier, advising McCaskey that journalism was a "more desirable position" which would give him the opportunity to "get around the world some and come to notoriety, especially in the political arena,"[37] he now deferred to McCaskey: "You were better acquainted with your own opinions than anyone else, I suppose, and any action you might take, such as leaving the *Express* office and returning to school, are perfectly satisfactory to me, for I think you are a better judge than myself, and I will not endeavor to disapprove of anything you might wish to adopt."[38] McCaskey remained at the high school. In 1869, he became its principal.[39]

In July 1864, Will urged McCaskey to speak with Thaddeus Stevens about helping brother-in-law Jim Marshall obtain a position "as Captain and Commissary of Subsistence, U.S. Vols." Such a request meant circumventing the usual channels, i.e., through the regiment's hierarchy, because neither Will nor Jim liked or trusted Colonel Henry Augustus Hambright, a fellow Lancastrian and commander of the 79th, who was (and is) regarded in Lancaster as a great hero of the Mexican and Civil Wars. Will wrote: "[Jim] will never gain any promotion in this Regiment because of consequences of his connection with Col. Hambright, I am certain."[40] McCaskey used the *Express* in August to publicly question why Jim "has not long since been promoted."[41] Six months later, Will was still persisting. He encouraged McCaskey not to let Stevens rest: "I hope you will keep [this] before Mr. Stevens, by perseverance it can be gained. Don't leave the old gentleman rest, until he has given you satisfaction."[42] Jim was eventually promoted to first lieutenant and quartermaster of the regiment.

Will had first written disparagingly about Hambright in a lengthy letter in the spring of 1863, complaining that Hambright "never did a particle for [him]" in the area of promotions, favoring others, instead, who were sycophants and could neither read nor stay sober.[43] Denouncing him as "a two faced deceitful pimp" who lacked honor, Will accused Hambright of befriending Copperheads. When Hambright was in Lancaster on furlough, Will warned McCaskey, "[I]f you come across him, he tells you something, you cannot depend on it, for he never keeps his promises, and his word is all a lie."[44]

Hambright and the McCaskey parents did meet, after which McCaskey urged Will to rescind his criticism. Will refused: "With regard to Col. Hambright, I withdraw nothing, and you can tell both Mother and Father that! When he spoke to them of my promotion, he meant nothing. He is simply a man of promises, never can fulfill all he has promised, and let me tell you privately that no home dictation, or any one else can change my opinion."[45]

Another source of irritation for Will was the reports for Company B which he, as its captain, had to submit to his superior for approval: "Hambright and I have had a couple squalls. The other day I forwarded a document to Dept. Head[quarters], which document contained several sentences in which the past participle was used and which sentences he was unable to analyze, consequently he would not endorse them, and sent them back with his correction. I knew I was right but to test the matter, referred it to several grammarians, all of whom agreed with me. I again sent the same document in with the remark that it was in proper shape. He got considerably annoyed and wanted to know if 'I set my opinion against his.' 'Certainly,' says I, 'when syntax is the issue.' 'What do you mean by syntax?' I asked him if he ever studied grammar. 'Damn grammar,' says he. 'It ain't right, and I won't forward it until corrected to my liking.' . . . [T]o forward the document, I drew it up differently, but not as he dictated, and rather than do as he wished me, I'll not send it at all.[46]

Thaddeus Stevens visited the 79th in Chattanooga in the fall of 1863, after which Will asked McCaskey to learn the truth about Hambright directly from Stevens: "I am glad that Thad came out here, and I wish you to go and see him, for he can enlighten you considerably, about the feelings and sentiments of the 79th."[47]

More egregious than Hambright's failure to promote Jim and Will, his misguided politics, and his rejection of grammar, Will thought the colonel a coward and a phony. He vilified him frequently, sometimes at great length and in great detail. Will and Jim were not alone in their disdain for Hambright. Col. Hobert of the 21st Wisconsin was another who was no admirer of Hambright's: "He's such an enemy of Hambright, held him in such contempt that it will make a capital case."[48] Jim, in September 1864, described Hambright's feigning illness to stay behind the lines in a battle in Georgia, saying, "He is a dead cock in the pit here. This campaign has completely used him up, in the estimation of men and officers. His conduct has been very bad."[49] Jim complained about Hambright in a December 1864 letter to McCaskey, writing that Hambright was seeking a sick leave of absence and "[i]t would be a benefit if he would go home and stay there."[50]

Will reported that at the 1863 battle of Chickamauga, another officer, Colonel David Miles, had led the men courageously, even after their line broke. Will wrote: "You could see poor Col. Miles here yet, rallying the men." The officers of the 79th "all but one (Col. Hambright), [had] done their duty bravely. . . Hambright was in the rear and came up like a skiddelling after we reformed our line."[51]

Miles, highly regarded by Will and Jim, was captured at Chickamauga and held in the South until the next summer, when he returned to Lancaster before returning to the regiment. McCaskey interviewed him and published the details of his capture and imprisonment in the *Express* in August 1864. McCaskey praised Miles' courage and hinted at the cowardice of others: "We are aware, however, that it is such exhibitions of unflinching courage that make men idolize an officer, while on the other hand they are quite likely to despise the officer who seizes any opportunity—a trifling injury, it may be—to be absent himself from his command in the hour of battle. The former, soldiers will follow confidently to death—the latter cannot but fail to gain either their confidence or regard."[52]

To this praise of Miles and the thinly veiled criticism of Hambright, Will responded: "Your defense and praise of Col. Miles is not unappreciated, you may be sure. He will never forget you, your condemnation of Col. Hambright is just as is considered so by most of the fighting men of this command. Keep the ball a moving. His charm as ceased, his authority doubted, and his thunder amounts to bubbles of wind."[53]

Despite Will's vitriol, Hambright, who had served heroically in the Mexican War, commanded the Pennsylvania 79th as its colonel from the beginning to the end of the war. He suffered from health problems in 1864 and 1865 that often kept him out of command.[54] Nonetheless, in June 1865, Hambright received a commission as Brevet Brigadier General of Volunteers from President Johnson "for meritorious services in the field."[55] In 1907 McCaskey, as mayor of Lancaster addressing a reunion of the 79th, found words to praise its commander: "You had in Colonel Hambright a tireless drillmaster, who held prompt obedience and strict discipline the first of military virtues. Drill was a passion with him—he had a will of iron in this direction—"[56]

The sword of Damocles continued to hang over the McCaskey men. In January 1865 Will encouraged McCaskey to hire a substitute if he was drafted in the next lottery, for Lincoln had called for 300,000 more men. (Commutation had been repealed in July 1864.) While Will was eager for new recruits, he hoped his brother would not be among them: "With regard to that draft, Jack, I am glad of it, but would not like to see it come too near home, if you are drafted, you must make some arrangements for a substitute, and he will see you through. Stand her like a man, my boy!"[57]

Ultimately, McCaskey never served in the army. The quotas for the Lancaster city wards in the two 1864 drafts, June and September, were filled prior to the drawings, and so the drafts were unnecessary.[58] Volunteers had stepped forward, or those eligible had found substitutes. Brother Cye, too young to be eligible, must have been among those volunteering, or he substituted for McCaskey or someone else. He entered the army sometime in early 1865. He served in Company B under Will, who wrote McCaskey that he was a good soldier: "All is well. Cye is an admirable soldier and pleases me much, performs his duty, and acts the private soldier under a brother with much good grace. Don't fear that we will not get along with him."[59]

Will was a wise older brother. As the regiment marched north in Virginia that spring, Cye kept asking local people how much farther to the next point, and "was nearly always disappointed in their answers," Will wrote. "He has not been in the Army long enough yet to stop his inquiries. I thought the best plan to have him discover the uselessness of such acts himself will do him some good, I think."[60] In June, Cye fell ill, and Will furloughed him to Lancaster for 20 days.

Another draft menaced in 1865. In March, both Will and McCaskey, war-weary, worried that their youngest brother, Newt, 16, might also be pulled into the war. Will wrote: "You speak a little despondently, Jack, of the prospects of an early settlement of this affair when you alluded to the probability of Newt's buckling on the straps, at some future day to give us a lift, that I never wish to see, if the rebellion should ever last. One of us was enough to fight the battle though, and two are plenty, no more needed from that family, that draft Jack, don't suit me much, I tell you. It is well enough to have such things, but when they touch home they are not so nice."[61]

Newt did not serve.

Will, Jim, and Cye mustered out of the army July 12, 1865, in Washington, D.C. Cye, already putting the war behind him, wrote in a brief letter to McCaskey that same day: "Do not forget to attend to the two bouquets for Miss Bricker."

In the post script, he reminded him again.[62]

Chapter 9

The First Great End of Education Is Character

"The first great end of education is character. In this we all agree. The entire life of the school should have this end always in view. Thought determines life, and the best things that can be put into the mind of the growing boy or girl are good 'thoughts that breathe and words that burn.'"[1]

In a graduation speech for the Boys' High Class of 1906, speaker Howard Hersh reflected humorously and poignantly on his and classmates' high school years. Hersh noted his cohorts' accomplishments in subjects, sports, and mischief, and he provided hyphenated nicknames for his cronies, such as "Elmer Ain't-I-a-Sorehead Curry," "Kensel I-ain't-going-to-school Evans," "Charles Sad-and-Lonely Miley," "Edgar What-a-bashful-boy-am-I Worrest," "George Can-I-do-my-Greek-to-day Vatter," "Marriott Be-home-from-school-early Seachrist," "Morris What-do-you-think-of-my-hair Cohen," "William How-about-the Matinee Goodhart," and "Paulus Weary-Willie-please-don't-bother-me Weaver."[2]

The "peripatetic philosopher" of the class was "James Jolly-boy-balky-boy Stehman," who was the classmate best at memory work, even if he skipped school sometimes, according to Hersh: "[Jim] was always absent when there was a base-ball game scheduled. He was a chum of [Edgar Out-of-School-Always] Butz and [Harry Be-at-the-Baseball] Springer." "Good fellows enough," Hersh said, "but they had no use for books. In one thing Jim did excel, and that was our weekly memory work in prose and poetry. The doses were big and regular, but he took his medicine like a little man. I believe he liked it." Hersh continued by affirming the great benefit of such an exercise: "Well, if he got nothing else out of the school, [the memory work] should be to him of great value through all his life." Hersh asked: "What boy has not had good from our memory work in prose and poetry under the direction of our principal, Dr. McCaskey?"[3]

Hersh had benefited from the "big and regular" doses of memory work himself; his speech was interlaced with quotes from seven poems. Also, he, along with "Willis and-he-does-the-brainwork Schindle," "Frank Am-I-growing-any Diffenbaugh," and all the others had memorized the Gettysburg Address;[4] some had been on the field trip to the battlefield the year before.

After joking and encouraging each class member, Hersh concluded in a more serious tone: "A word more, and I am done. The hour strikes, the curtain falls, and we go our several ways to Life or Death. God grant it may be towards life and a life eternal of ever-growing wisdom, power, holiness, justice, mercy, and truth." He cited the final poem, reminding his peers that they all knew it: "In the words of Bryant, in his noble Thanatopsis, familiar to you each and all:"

So live, that, when thy summons comes to join
The innumerable caravan, that moves
To the pale realms of shade, where each shall take
His chamber in the silent halls of death,
Thou go not, like the quarry-slave at night,
Scourged to his dungeon; but, sustained and soothed
By an unfaltering trust, approach thy grave,
Like one who wraps the drapery of his couch
About him, and lies down to pleasant dreams.[5]

McCaskey and Boys' High Class of 1906. (Photo from High School News 1906.*)*

In "Life in a High School," a speech before the Pennsylvania State Teachers' Association in July 1896, McCaskey began by claiming that he really knew "nothing whatever" about the high school teacher, despite having taught 40 years. He said he had taught "one thing and another" to high school boys, had enjoyed it and had gotten much good from it himself. He hoped that the boys had benefited, too, but he did not regard himself as an expert. However, he would attempt to speak about life in a high school to be helpful, perhaps, to someone in the assemblage.[6]

Then, leaving self-effacement behind, McCaskey got to his point: "The first great end of education is character. In this we all agree. The entire life of the school should have this end always in view. Thought determines life, and the best things that can be put into the mind of the growing boy or girl are good 'thoughts that breathe and words that burn.'"[7]

How was this goal of character building to be accomplished? Through memory work, using only the best poetry and prose. The pupils' intellect, morality, and spirituality would all be improved by memory work: "The habit of thinking good things, strong things, beautiful things, in the very words of the masters . . . gradually weaves their precious substance into the very warp and woof of individual character, and so insures, in varying degree, intellectual, moral and spiritual development."[8] Borrowing from George MacDonald, a 19th-century Scottish novelist and minister, McCaskey asserted that pupils should not "be deaf and blind to celestial visitants, but courteously 'at home' to each worthy thought that comes knocking at the door of their souls."[9]

McCaskey said that such character development would bring forth angels, whom pupils and teachers should trust to lead them "day by day, towards their own Delectable Mountains," an allusion to the rest havens for pilgrims in John Bunyan's *The Pilgrim's Progress*. McCaskey even suggested that memorization work would direct students to immortality: "Let us then teach the supreme things, generous and noble, reverent and true. Let us determine character on high lines, and so make life 'worth living,' because it looks on towards a blessed immortality."[10]

In 1888, McCaskey, speaking at an Arbor Day ceremony, asked the students, "Why do you come to school at all?" The goal, he told them, was to "get good out of it—mainly in disposition and character" to which physical, intellectual, and manual achievements are secondary. He based the primary purpose of education on the Presbyterian catechism: "Man's chief end is to glorify God, and to enjoy him forever!" This, McCaskey emphasized, should be the outcome of education. "God is the essence of all that is truly good, of every kind, and in every degree. To desire the truth, and to love the good in nature, in science, in art, in literature, in morals, in spiritual things, is to love that which is of God; it is to 'glorify him' with an increasing love forever."[11]

Incorporating religion into education had been the practice in Pennsylvania from its beginning. William Penn set literacy as a major goal in education so that colonists could read the Scriptures. In the 1700s and early 1800s, with education in the hands of the churches, Christian teachings infused the curriculum. When the Lancasterian system was instituted in the 1820s, morality in general and Christianity in particular were emphasized. Wooden boards, "plain pine boards, twelve by twenty inches, hung upon the walls" with lessons painted on them, in particular "scriptural reading lesson[s]."[12]

"Characteristics to be Cultivated" were set forth on the walls of the Lancasterian school: "Good Scholars Will Be Amiable, Affectionate, Attentive, Benevolent, Conscientious, Consistent, Disinterested, Frank, Filial, Forgiving, Grateful, Generous, Humane, Honorable, Humble, Ingenuous, Modest, Mannerly, Obedient, Punctual, Patient, Self-Denying, Sincere, Studious." Directly across from these were "Characteristics not to be Cultivated—Unamiable, Malicious, Heedless, Covetous, Unscrupulous, Capricious, Selfish, Intriguing, Disobedient, Revengeful, Unthankful, Parsimonious, Arrogant, Unskilful [sic], Slothful, Impudent, Disrespectful, Obstinate, Dilatory, Fretful, Intemperate, Thoughtless."[13]

Additionally, students copied into small leather-bound books "sentiments and regulations" such as the following: "He who tells a lie is not sensible how great a task he undertakes, for he must be forced to invent twenty more to maintain that one." "God gives all things to industry." "If you would know the value of money, go and try to borrow some; for he who goes a-borrowing goes a-sorrowing." "Whoever speaks of another's failings with pleasure, shall hear of his own with bitterness of heart."[14]

When common schools replaced the Lancasterian system, moral instruction continued, and "cards were ordered to be suspended on the walls of the different rooms, on which were inscribed in large letters the Lord's Prayer, the Apostles' Creed and the Ten Commandments."[15] A controversy developed on the local school board in 1848 when the Reverend Samuel Bowman sought to mandate this instruction, requiring students to memorize and recite the texts on the posters once a week. Dr. Thomas Burrowes offered a lengthy substitute, which echoed William Penn's sentiment that persons were to be free to worship as they saw fit. However, Pennsylvania also protected Christianity, Burrowes argued, citing as crimes acts of blasphemy, profanity, and violation of the Sabbath because such crimes had a "malignant influence on society." He also called for the Bible to be used as a textbook, for the Old and New Testaments included "the authentic history of the origin of our race, of the condition of the whole race, for many centuries." Also, in the Bible was to be found the basis of the modern legal structure: "[It contained] also the best exposition of that system of Christian morality upon which our legal code of morals is founded." However, passages from the Scriptures were not to be extracted and taught separately "as an act of religion."[16]

A motion before the school board to postpone indefinitely the entire matter passed 13 to 11.[17] The practice of promoting morality and Christianity on the classroom walls and reading from the Bible carried throughout the 19th century and well into the 20th.

Beginning in 1892, articles about memory work began appearing in *The Pennsylvania School Journal*. Included were McCaskey's views on the value of such work, methods for teaching it, recommendations of texts, and titles of what he and his students had done in a year's work. In 1894-95, they learned over 60 selections, the next year over 40, and the following year they had learned 32 by March. Some selections were repeated "year after year that they may become familiar as 'household words.'"[18]

McCaskey, learning passages himself that he had assigned to his students, pressed his family members into the discipline. In an 1892 letter to Will's daughter Margie, he wrote: "Lizzie and Elsie, Dick and Bertha, and I have been taking hold of a new line of work—a psalm and a poem each week to commit to memory. It is a good thing to do. Go at it. . . . The psalms we have been learning are the 90th and the 19th. Also the verses of 'Home Sweet Home' and 'Crossing the Bar' the past two weeks. Next week Tennyson's prologue to 'In Memoriam' and [the] 23rd Psalm."[19]

McCaskey's love of memory work did not germinate in a vacuum. Memorization had been part of educational strategies for centuries. William Penn, who wrote *No Cross, No Crown* while imprisoned in the Tower of London for eight months in 1668, relied on his memory for quotes and commentary from 68 authors.[20] In his *State-Book of Pennsylvania*, Thomas H. Burrowes recommended that younger students memorize about 40 pages' worth of material and advanced classes 90 pages' worth.[21]

At Boys' High, memory work was implemented as follows: McCaskey assigned two selections each week for the boys' foray into this "finest of the wheat" of all high school activities. "The first [was] from the Bible or sacred song, and the second from the world of literature, prose or verse."[22] The teacher was to learn these, as well, because he "must love what he would have them love" and he might benefit even more than the students from such work.[23] He first used *Butler's Literary Selections, 10 Times 10 Series* and then the *Lincoln Literary Collection*, both which he edited. Each of the four books in the Butler series, published between 1877 and 1881, contained 100 selections. Students would question one another, "Are we going to Butler today?"[24] His *Lincoln Literary Collection,* compiled by McCaskey because he had not been able to find a satisfactory memory work text book,[25] was published in 1897 and included over 600 selections and methods for teaching memory work. The question students then asked was "Are we going to Lincoln today?"[26]

Tuesdays from 9 to 11 a.m. were designated for writing the pieces "from memory in books distributed for that purpose, with due attention to the arrangement of matter, punctuation, use of capitals, spelling, etc."[27] "Such book[s]," McCaskey said, "will be highly prized in after years."[28] He allowed nothing to interfere with the Tuesday sessions, which he and the students "regard[ed] [as] the most important of the week."[29] To ensure retention, McCaskey reviewed the selections often, and he assigned three or four that had been previously learned for "declamation day," (Fridays), when the students were to be ready to recite any of them from heart.[30] Sometimes the boys recited a piece in unison,[31] and group "recitations in concert" were performed at school programs, like Arbor Day.

Ad in the February 1878 Journal *for McCaskey's 10 X 10 Series.*

The written work was to be done as if it were to be set in type, Dr. McCaskey explained: "Get it as the author left it, the exact words he used, and each word in its place. See the capital letters, the spelling and meaning of unusual words, and the punctuation marks, so that you could write it as 'copy' for the printer. This requires care, close observation, thought, and encourages the habit of close attention."[32] A tool for memorizing that McCaskey recommended was the "four and tally" count. Students would draw a vertical line, hold the pencil on it, repeat the sentence or line, then make the next line, and so on, crossing out four lines with a diagonal one to equal five, so they could keep track of how many times they repeated it. Sometimes, this was done aloud with the entire class and in unison. "This means close strain on the attention, but it means definite result as well."[33]

An approach specifically for poetry was to assign a number to a keyword or phrase in the first line of each stanza. The teacher would then signal any one of the numbers with his fingers or other means and the students were to recite that stanza quickly. McCaskey compared such numbering to the white pebbles a fairytale character dropped along the way in order to find his or her way home again.[34]

McCaskey contended that this work was valuable for students of all learning abilities: "After months and years of this kind of work, even the

When the first Lancaster High School became overcrowded, Boys' High was housed in this building from 1869 to 1876. Used for an overflow of boys into the 20th century, it was called "The Annex." It is located at 116 N. Mulberry Street, opposite the Shreiner-Concord Cemetery and the location of the second Lancaster High School. McCaskey would cross Mulberry Street to conduct classes with those students. (Photo courtesy of author.)

Opened in 1876, this was the new Lancaster High School at the corner of Mulberry and Orange Streets. Girls' High occupied the first floor; Boys' High the second, and there was a gymnasium on the third. It was replaced by a new building for the boys in 1918. The school was a block from McCaskey's home. (Photo from "Souvenir of Dedication Exercises of the Boys' High School September 26, 1918.")

View of the new high school from the back. (Photo courtesy of LancasterHistory.org.)

slowest pupils get good out of it from increased power of the memory, and much more good from the side of thought and the literary charm of that with which they are brought so closely into contact."[35] McCaskey conceded that a few students might have difficulty memorizing things, and for them, he said, "some allowance must be made."[36]

Such drilling may sound tedious and boring, but memorizing the piece was only the beginning, a necessary prerequisite to more meaningful, higher level activities. McCaskey clarified: "Of course, there should be talk about the thought and language of the selection, something of its author, something of etymology, grammar, punctuation, scanning, etc. Thus the ear is accustomed to good forms of expression, the eye is taught to see, the mind to think, the memory to recall."[37] The texts were to be "thought about, talked about, committed to memory, pondered in the 'study of the imagination,' until the inner meaning of things is felt, their deeper significance seen, and not merely their outer semblance."[38]

Probing beyond the "outer semblance" provoked the analytical thinking that is evident in "Honest Doubt," a newspaper article written by a Boys' High graduate, Addison Groff. Groff discussed the poem "Abou Ben Adhem," which led him to appreciate someone who was different in many ways, most particularly in religion. Published in a Lenten column in the 1930s, the article, "Honest Doubt," began by crediting McCaskey's influence: "Maybe it's time for me to wash Mr. Ben Adhem out of my hair. But it will not be easy. For the aged, revered, and venerable 'Jack' McCaskey put that swarthy man there with an adhesive far tougher than 'Aunt Jemima's Plaster.'"[39]

Groff recalled McCaskey's visits to the boys' classroom in the annex on Fridays. There Abou Ben Adhem, an 8th-century Arab Muslim saint, came alive and would remain in Groff's mind and heart for life. Why, Groff wondered, did he "and the whole generation of yesterday" fall in love with this Adhem, given that he was not of Groff's "race, creed, color, or national origin." Also, Ben Adhem didn't "love and serve the Lord," as Groff said he himself was supposed to.[40]

The poem begins simply: Abou Ben Adhem awoke one night and saw an angel in his room, writing "the names of those who love the Lord" in a book of gold. Adhem asked if his name was one of them. The angel replied it was not, whereupon Adhem requested that it be added in as "one that loves his fellowmen."

At that point, Groff interrupted the poem to ask his Lancaster readers: "Now what would you write about this man, who, for all we know, accepts none of our creeds, never visits Church, Synagogue, or Meeting House?" The answer was in the poem: The next night the Angel came again and showed Adhem ". . . the names of those whom the love of God had blessed, And, Lo! Ben Adhem's name led all the rest!'"

In conclusion, Groff stated, "That just couldn't be right," but immediately reversed himself: ". . . it is right, and right in the middle of Lent. I confess I will not forget Abou Ben Adhem, nor those who led me to his feet."[41]

"Do the boys get great good out of memory work?" McCaskey asked rhetorically in an 1896 speech. "Many do," he answered, "to whom it will be increasing good through all their lives," and he noted that such work would be especially helpful to college-bound students.[42] One of his college-bound boys had fallen ill, and McCaskey visited him at his home, remembering, *"When I called to see him a day or two before he died, his voice had sunk to a whisper and he was quietly awaiting the end, glad to think it so near. As I sat on the side of his bed and talked with him of familiar things, I recalled his having learned the ninetieth Psalm, and said, 'You know the grand old verse, "Lord, thou hast been our dwelling place in all generations." With a glad smile, 'Oh, yes!' he whispered, for he could no longer speak above his breath, and went on with the verses that follow, adding eagerly, in a whisper, when he had ended, 'O, how good many of those sweet and noble things that we learned in the High School have been to me when I have been kept in the house all these long months! What pleasure it has been to think them over and over again!' He was dying but these things out of his school life he recalled with rare gratification even then. Not mathematics or science or Latin or Greek—and he was foremost in all of these studies—only this! Is it good to do such work? I think so."*[43]

As McCaskey's young student exemplified, one benefit of memorization was company and consolation in moments of loneliness, sickness, and in dying. McCaskey told an audience: "Commit to memory, choosing the best things . . . Know many of these things in the dark. Know them when you are apart from books, or sick, or tired, or lonely. Then go away in thought with the poet, the hymn writer, or the seer, with the wise and the good of the past or of our own time, and in the study of the imagination commune with them in blessed companionship.[44]

McCaskey in 1880, age 43. (Photo from a private collection.)

Memory work was not only to be carried on in the common schools from the primary through the high school, McCaskey believed, but also in the Normal Schools, Sunday Schools and the YMCA.[45] He even found opportunities to instruct the public. Arbor Day programs often included a memory work session. During the 1897 program, "Mr. McCaskey occupied a few minutes in having the school and the audience commit to memory [a] pretty little fancy in verse" consisting of 12 lines.[46] At that same program, the boys gave "Recitations in Concert," five selections totaling 118 lines. On another Arbor Day, the girls learned by rote Mary Howitt's "The Spring," consisting of seven stanzas of five lines each.[47] The first verse of the poem follows: "The Spring—she is a blessed thing!/ She is the mother of the flowers,/ She is the mate of birds and bees,/ The partner of their revelries,/ Our star of hope through wintry hours."[48] Memorizing poetry, McCaskey suggested, might provide better entertainment for young people than a popular card game called progressive euchre.[49]

In July 1897, McCaskey's son Donald accompanied him to a convention of the American Institute of Instruction in Canada. Donald recalled the event in a letter to his son, Townsend: "Your grandfather was a teacher, too, of committing beautiful poems to memory. At Montreal—at a big teachers' convention there—I saw him get out on the platform and TEACH THOSE 1,000 or more teachers in his audience—HOW TO BE BOSS OF YOUR MEMORY. The old gentleman worked from scratch—without a single note."[50]

Memory work was the vehicle to build character, "the first great end of education," because it was a way of putting good thoughts into students. "In the deeps of the human heart are good and evil. Let us put in all the good we can, and put it deep, as deep as we can," McCaskey urged.[51]

Chapter 10

The High-Souled Teacher

"For the greatest good that comes to the average pupil out of any ordinary, every-day school worthy of the name, comes not from the books he is using or the drill he is getting, but from the life he or she is living with the high-souled teacher, the man or woman of noble aims, who is not a mere day-laborer in the school-room, but an artist in love forever with strength and beauty, and goodness."[1]

William Riddle wrote in his book *One Hundred and Fifty Years of School History in Lancaster, Pennsylvania*, published in 1905, that he and McCaskey "labored together in that trying field of child development, the 'boys' night school on the hill'" in 1865 and 1866. Riddle endorsed the opportunity that night school provided for those children, an opportunity sometimes unavailable due to school budget shortages. This was regrettable, for according to Riddle: "[R]ich, indeed, was the prospect among the boys whose only opportunity of seeking an education was under the light of the 'gas jets.'"[2]

A boy named Zeke was among the night school students. Riddle described him as *"a tall, thin, shambling, rawboned figure of a young fellow well up in his teens. His face was long and lean, its most prominent features being its great nose, diverted by nature slightly to one side and flanked by a tremendous pair of cheekbones. A grinning smile, showing a set of pearly-white teeth; long bony arms, with long bony hands; a long lank lean body, a loose pair of pedal extremities, with a pair of rawhide boots, extending well up in the direction of his 'intellectuals'; a cheery voice bubbling up from the vast depths below."*[3]

Then, Riddle chronicled an incident involving Zeke and McCaskey:

Principal McCaskey was in charge of the study hall one October night, Halloween to be precise, and "all went along in the usual manner until the hour for dismissal came; the pens and copy books were being gathered up; the principal . . . stood ready with bell in hand to tap for the first column to move, when lo! a shower of white soup beans went soaring over the heads of teachers and pupils, landing against the window panes like a shower of hail in midsummer. A moment later the principal exclaimed in a determined tone, 'Will the young man who threw the beans please come forward?' No response. Again and again the summon was repeated, but the culprit, whoever he was, sat with the others the very picture of stolid indifference. 'Boys,' added the master in charge, 'take your own time; this school will here remain until the bean-thrower steps forward.' Another half hour passed, as innocence sat depicted on the countenances of the hundred or more half-sleepy lads. At last, as the hands of the old clock told the hour when all night school boys should have been sleeping the sleep of the 'innocent,' came, from a remote corner, a squeaking voice, 'Zeke threw the beans!' A moment later, a hundred eyes were centered on the now disconsolate informer, as Ezekiel stood before the school with trousers jammed into the upper portion of a pair of long-legged rawhides, the very picture of injured innocence.

"'Young man, did you throw the beans?' to which came the prompt rejoinder, 'No, sir, I did not!' Under ordinary circumstances, this prompt reply might have served its purpose; but there was a certain something in the young man's expression, if not in his peculiar accent, combined with a knowing twinkle of the eye, that betrayed a guilty conscience. 'Take a seat and empty your pockets,' came in even a sterner voice, when out came a barlow knife, a few horse-shoe nails, a half-dozen broken slate pencils, an apple core or two, that had found lodgment therein, when the danger of detection became most imminent; the beans, however, were nowhere in evidence among the conglomerated mixture of odds and ends. Up to this trying moment, the young prevaricator had weathered the

storm, and stood ready to return to his seat to determine upon the proper course of treatment to be administered to the young scapegrace who had violated one of the unwritten laws which was held sacred by the average night school boy, never to 'peach' on a school comrade, when, to his chagrin, again, came, now, in a half-sleepy drawling tone, 'He's got 'em in-his b-o-o-t-s!' 'Off with your rawhides!' came the order of command, [and] the guilty offender of the majesty of law sat wriggling and twisting, now jerking at this then at the other of the rawhides with little hope of success. There being no boot-jack within hailing distance, it became necessary, as the only way out of the dilemma, to summon the informer in relieving the young man of his personal property which, having previously become water-soaked, stuck to the feet of the owner . . . . For five long minutes the peacher jerked and twisted, first at one, then at the other, while Zeke sat twisting and screwing his toes into an india-rubber ball, imbued with the idea no doubt that self-preservation was the first law of a night-school boy's nature. At last, after many fruitless efforts, off came the long-legged rawhides, and with them, a full pint of pearly, white soup beans. By this time the school was in an uproar of merriment. Ten minutes later, the boys were dismissed, with the admonition to Zeke, 'Gather up the beans, my boy; take them home and store them away for the early spring planting.' As the young man, years after, became a truck-gardener, it is only reasonable to assume that this supply of white soup beans furnished him with his first stock in trade. Zeke, it may be said, was ever after a favorite in the school."[4]

McCaskey's admonition to Zeke shows him to have been strict but fair, a teacher who expected honesty from his students and appealed to their integrity. He understood the impetuosity of youth and the need for the adults in charge to pay heed to adolescents' developmental stages. He encouraged them to do well and to learn from their errors: Plant the seeds, Zeke!

Corporal punishment was not forbidden in the classrooms of the 19th century, but *The Pennsylvania School Journal* (hereinafter referred to as the *Journal*) published articles against it. An 1852 piece made clear that corporal punishment, specifically flogging, would not induce a rapscallion to change his ways: "Flogging school-boys may make them *smart* but then it is in the wrong place. If a boy has intellect he will get along without the cane. If, on the contrary, he is dull and stupid, pelting him over the head will make him not so ambitious to overcome Algebra as to overcome the school-master."[5]

The Lancaster school board, while acknowledging that corporal punishment was necessary in extreme cases, encouraged teachers to use it rarely, and no "teacher shall punish any pupil while under the influence of anger."[6] Teachers not using physical discipline were to report such to the board; those who did were to provide a detailed account. Preferred was the teacher who appealed to the students' intellect to keep order.[7]

McCaskey was among the latter, although he was not above having miscreants use it on one another, as student Harold F. Diffenderffer documented: *"As [Dr. McCaskey] sat at his broad, flat-topped desk, busy on some school matter during the study period, he might hear in the distance some sound of disturbance. Then in a loud booming voice he would say, 'What boy did that?' If none answered, he asked, 'All those who were not involved in the noise raise your hands.' This was apt to put the guilty ones on the spot. When the culprits were disclosed he would command them to appear in front of his desk and hand one of them a good substantial ruler. Then he would say, 'Now use it.' Thus he [one of the offenders] brought it down upon a fellow culprit's hand, and he in turn, applied the ruler to the other chap. The results were very good. I can well recall he had some trouble with a pair of identical twins and at the length of the long school room he could not clearly distinguish them, so he would first ask, 'Is it Bertram or Walter?' Then followed the usual penalty. Sometimes these boys were not entirely fair to each other and the wrong boy took the rap."*[8]

While refraining from corporal punishment for his students, McCaskey did not spurn it for his own progeny. McCaskey and Ellen opened their home at 304 West King Street to siblings, aunts, uncles, children, and grandchildren as they had need of a home, particularly during the Great Depression. The influx of people brought with it the occasional conflicts. In his old age, McCaskey appears to have lost his patience with those creating a disturbance. When two adult grandsons got into a fight, he did not appeal to their intellect. Brothers Richard and Edward "fought up the steps and down the steps. J.P. [the descendants' name for McCaskey] called the police and they came. The police asked which brother started the fight and which one they should take in. J. P. responded, 'They were fighting with each other. Take them both.'"[9]

Townsend ("Townie") McCaskey, grandson of McCaskey and son of Donald, lived at 304 West King as a boy. He was full of mischief and spunk, which were rewarded sometimes with a spanking: "I still remember some of the tannings I used to get from J.P. for coming in after curfew in [Lancaster] (Curfew 9:30 p.m.; I was aged 14)."[10] However, the old man was much more tolerant when Townie and his friends engaged in battles in the backyard at 304. It was the Cabbage Hill Gang vs. the Well Known Defenders of Hill 304 West King; participants were between 10 and 14 years of age.

Townie recalled: *"The battlefield never changed. It was always the back yard of 304. If those pear trees and cherry trees could talk. . . . [T]he Cabbage Hill Gang, numbering a half dozen, attacked with great stealth . . . from the corner of the Folmer and Clogg Umbrella Factory [across from the McCaskey home]. . . . As the battle joined, the air was full of rocks, all sizes, big, small, medium and intermediate. As the ebb and flow of military might progressed, historians have likened it to Napoleon's victory at Ratisbon and sometimes to the 2nd Waterloo. Sometime a sortie, a flanking movement . . . was mounted by the defenders, a quick movement around the old abandoned outhouse and Aunt Bella's tomato garden, by this time accumulating its share of spent rocks. . . . At this point, the thump of rocks had reached crescendo as they rained from the out-house and could be heard as far away as Charlotte and Vine. . . . When the battle had reached its zenith, it was said that the upper floors of the . . . [f]actory were filled with spectators who, neglecting their machines, stopped making umbrellas long enough to observe the carnage.*

"At this crucial point in the heavily engaged battle, with both Aggressor and Defender filling the air with many kinds of rocks, suddenly, out of nowhere appeared in the middle of No Man's Land a figure that brought this desperate conflict to an end at once. . . . Aunt Kate [McCaskey's daughter-in-law] . . . who, becoming aware of the carnage outside, the shouts, the noise of battle, the tinkling of the glass windows in the kitchen and outer kitchen, would appear in righteous Irish rage in the middle of the field of conquest. . . . [T]his appearance was enough

. . . to cause an immediate cessation of hostilities, immediate quiet at once. Peace had descended. Aggressor, the Cabbage Hillers, had withdrawn . . . Defenders made great efforts to absent themselves from the scene but no good—it was clean up time!! . . .

"After these engagements, always victory for our side, myself, T. [Townsend] Hoopes, the General, suffered major Courts Martial from several high sources. (J.P., however, would regard these interludes with a quiet chuckle and nothing happened. Not so Aunt Kate, however, her punishment was most severe and consisted of stern glarings of well-deserved Irish rage for an hour or two . . . and I am sure caused many a chuckle later, in private with Uncle Ed. . . . And I am sure they are chuckling even now, way up there)."[11]

Later on, former enemies joined forces to wreak havoc on local fruit trees: *"Sometimes, after the battle, a few of both sides, enmities forgotten, would conduct night time raids on various targets of opportunity. Sometimes it was Mrs. Madigan's prize peaches, as long as they held up. Sometimes it even became necessary to skirmish far afield and raid the splendid ox-heart cherry tree of those rich people at the corner of Charlotte and Vine. They didn't have a dog either."*[12]

Townie was also a member of the Grant Street Gang, which engaged in other daring escapades, testing his Aunt Kate's Irish temperament yet again and inviting more chuckles from J.P.: The gang played *"Fox and Hounds running across factory roofs for a block or two and running the elevators up and down in the vacant tobacco warehouses on Sundays as well as putting cars in gear and running them up and down the street a few feet while the owner was making a living somewhere."*[13]

McCaskey himself had grown up under strict parents, and his father did not spare the rod.[14] Of him, McCaskey said that he was a "man of iron will, resolute and fearless."[15] A story from McCaskey's childhood hints at William McCaskey's sternness. The McCaskey children were required to sit straight and silent during services at Old Leacock Presbyterian, unlike the wiggly Woods children seated in front of them. McCaskey noted: "[Mr. Woods'] pew was next in front of ours. He was a man of giant frame, sat at the head of the pew, Mrs. Woods at the other end, and their playful boys between them. The little fellows had rather more freedom of movement than was permitted to us, and I often wished I was in their pew."[16]

That McCaskey expected students like Zeke, Bertram, and Walter to admit wrongdoing and that they complied is corroborated in letters from alumni: The boys "get into mischief often, but it is fine to see their hands go up upon inquiry as to the guilty ones. It matters not what the punishment may be, the boys are ready to stand up and be counted."[17] In a discussion about moral training at a State Teachers' Association meeting in York in July 1880, McCaskey said such admissions occurred in schools where a sense of morality permeated the institution.[18] He did not hesitate to ask students who swore to raise their hands, and he believed most would respond "because the public sentiment of the school scorned a lie. Some boys will swear, and lie too; but a good moral tone will break up the practice pretty thoroughly."[19]

McCaskey also asked students to raise their hands if they were willing to give up swearing. Some would and "by their promise . . . swearing was in a good degree banished from the school."[20] He and other participants drew upon the Bible for support, and he said, "There is nothing humorous about this matter; it is removed from the sphere of fun by the Third Commandment, which may be driven home with an emphasis that most boys will feel."[21]

McCaskey concurred with a colleague who said that asking students to confess taught them a sense of personal responsibility, which was preparation for life. That sense, McCaskey said, was the most important point in the whole matter. In his 25 years by then as a teacher he had put such questions to students and received acceptable answers. He did not punish those who admitted using profanity; rather, "[r]eformation must come from the inside, not the outside, and if you can put good impulses *into* the pupil, you have done him a good service."[22]

McCaskey believed that students, having memorized good thoughts, would have a storehouse from which to order up only good things to send forth over their lips. He cited two who had not had such guidance: *"At a play, in Philadelphia, I sat near two young men, college students, who in the freedom of the place talked, I suppose, as they would have done in their own room. Their talk was only blackguardism, profanity, and slang. The sweetest name, the purest thing, to them were nothing but interjections and by-words. If, during their school-boy days, and the helpful hours spent in the Sunday-school, thoughts sweet and strong and good . . . had been imbedded in the deeps of their being, could they be so coarse, degraded, and brutal in thought and language now?"*[23]

He gave another example: *"Some time ago in a popular restaurant, frequented daily by hundreds of ladies and gentlemen, two well-dressed young men sat down on the opposite side of the table at which I happened to be taking supper. There were but three of us at the table. The young [waitresses] were passing from place to place giving attention to the guests, and could readily hear their indecent conversation. After a few moments I told them that their blackguardism must stop. One of them said they were not directing their remarks to me. There was some emphasis to the brief conversation. Everybody around began to give it attention, and they were quiet enough for the rest of their meal. They got away as soon as they could—cowards as well as blackguards."*[24]

McCaskey felt such behavior was widespread: "And this shameless degradation, this moral rottenness, is not at all uncommon. There are thousands of just such young men to be found in our colleges, and tens and hundreds of thousands outside their halls. Can we, by encouraging better memory work, and much more of it, in our day schools and in our Sunday-schools, reduce this crop of dragon's teeth?"[25]

Memory work was, of course, one way to put good impulses into the students. Another was to keep maxims before them, just as the Lancasterian and first common schools had done and which McCaskey continued with his own *Lancaster School Mottoes*, the first of his publishing enterprises.[26] An influence on the minds of the pupils "which cannot be otherwise than good," these were published by the Inquirer Printing House, a local busi-

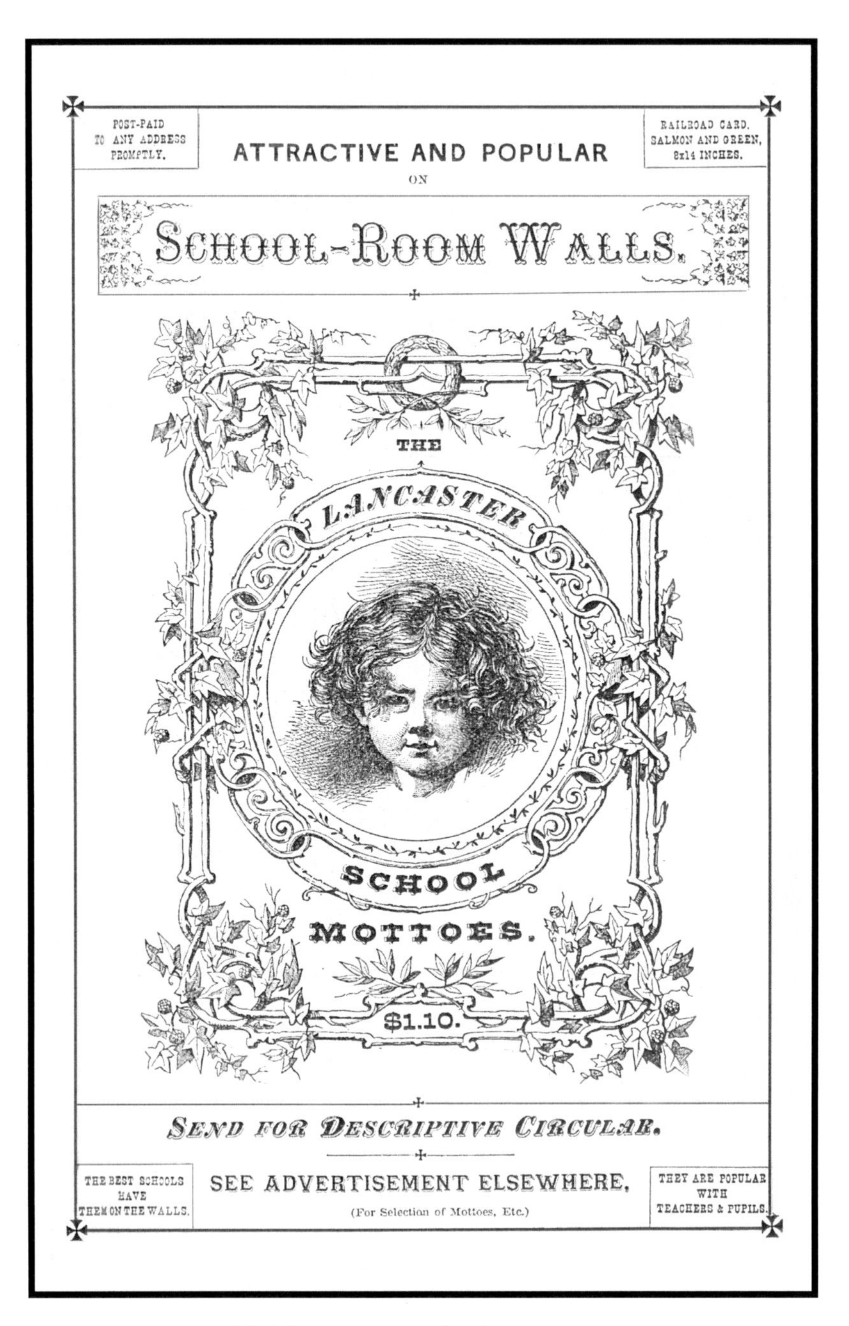

Ad for The Lancaster School Mottoes, *1875.*
(Photo courtesy of B. David Wagner.)

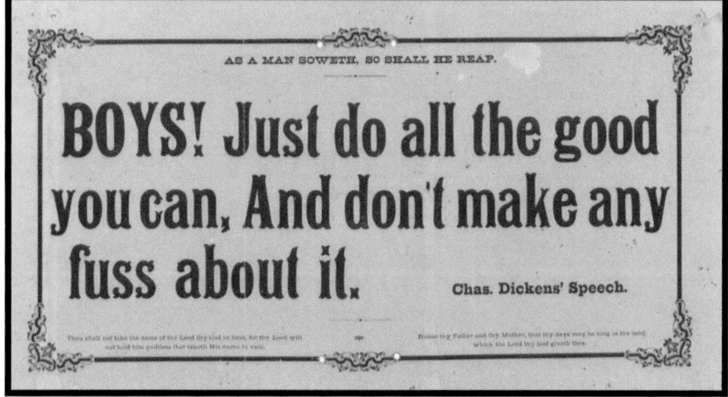

Some of the Lancaster School Mottoes. *Original set at Winterthur Library.*

ness in which he was an investor, and advertised in the *Journal*. The mottoes came as a set of 12 printed in "black type, bold and attractive" on both sides of an 8" x 14" green or salmon "extra-calendered 6-ply 'Railroad' (not China) board."[27] Some proclaimed good life habits: "Lost Time is never found again." "A silent worker is better than a noisy talker!" "Lost! Ten Golden Minutes! Each studded with Sixty Diamond Seconds!" "Thoroughness First, Then Progress." "Do One Thing At A Time And That Well." "Let no one consider the day as ended, until the duties it brings have been discharged." "Always Be 'On Time.' No Idlers Here." Two promoted the public schools: "The School Tax Is The Best Tax." and "God Bless Our School." Another card displayed the Lord's Prayer.

Other mottoes dealt with good behavior and faith: "No Bad Thoughts, Be Self-Reliant." "Do Right. Have Faith in God." "Speak the Truth, No Lie Survives." "Boys! Just do all the good you can, And don't make any fuss about it." "Be Polite. Strive to Please." "With Malice towards None, With Charity for All, Boys, Don't Be Mean!" "Never Forget That God is Ruling." "Our Life Is What We Make It." "Golden Rule. Do Unto Others As You Would Have Others Do Unto You." "Be Kind to One Another." One reminded the boys that they were being watched: "Thou God seest me."

One, in bold black letters, addressed swearing, lying, and other bad habits: "Chewing, Smoking, Lying, DRINKING, SWEARING! BOYS, THEY COST TOO MUCH!" As a young man, McCaskey had smoked but realized that "[t]obacco was killing him. . ." and so gave it up and "always urged the boys to let it alone."[28] He refrained from playing cards, too, for when he was young, "[h]e soon found cards a waste of valuable time."[29] He admitted to having sworn once.[30] He drank very little, if at all.[31] Grandson Townsend recalled that while Grandfather might abstain, other family members did not: "I remember J.P. was dead set against booze so the rest of the clan had an oasis back in the dining room or kitchen somewhere."[32]

Pictures adorning the classroom walls were another way to fill stu-

Top: "Old Mark Telling Fairy Tales," 1899. (Photos courtesy of the author.) All photos on pages 117 and 118 are from the Lincoln Art Series.

TRAIN UP A CHILD
IN THE WAY HE SHOULD GO, AND WHEN HE IS OLD
HE WILL NOT DEPART FROM IT.—Solomon.

"THE BETTER LAND."

dents' minds with good things, and McCaskey spread that gospel through the *Journal*, both in articles on the topic and advertisements for his *Lincoln Art Series*. The study hall at Boys' High was attractively decorated, with some prints from the series and portraits of U.S. presidents, prominent educators, and Stevens filling two walls.[33] Not only schools but also St. James and the Y.M.C.A. and Y.W.C.A. displayed many of McCaskey's lithographs. His picture of Thaddeus Stevens is displayed even today in the Caledonia State Park Visitors' Center.

Good pictures are silent teachers, McCaskey asserted.[34] He often cited John Ruskin, an English writer and artist, who said, "In the emptiest room the mind wanders most, for it gets restless like a bird for want of a perch, and casts about for any possible means of getting out and away. Bare walls are not a proper part of the means of education."[35]

Memory work, posters, and pictures were important, but it is "the teacher makes the school," McCaskey stated.[36] "For the greatest good that comes to the average pupil out of any ordinary, every-day school worthy of the name, comes not from the books he is using or the drill he is getting, but from the life he or she is living with the high-souled teacher, the man or woman of noble aims."[37] The teacher's walking the walk was the most important factor in education. McCaskey said: "[H]e must himself be what he would have his pupils become. He must love what he would have them love . . . The worthy person must always be a person good to live with."[38]

McCaskey's "morning talks" were legendary. Manny Pehrson heard them in the 1860s, and Howard Hersh did, too, in the first decade of the 20th century: "We got many an idea in study hall and class room, and especially from the earnest 'morning talks' to which we have listened for so long."[39] They were, Addison Groff recalled, "so highly praised that there was talk of playing them as recordings at the World's Fair in St. Louis [in 1904]."[40] The topics were wide-ranging, sometimes about the many places McCaskey traveled,[41]—he was particularly fond of Buffalo and Niagara Falls—or plays he had seen, other times about his faith or living virtuously. "Oftenest," a graduate recalled, "he talk[ed] of men and women, noble men and noble women, both living and dead, in the companionship of whose spirits he always [found] infinite delight."[42]

Student Diffenderffer recalled how McCaskey would swerve from the subject at hand to whatever topic he desired: "Often without warning he was apt to set aside the morning class for all and step in front of the boys and pour out his very soul in an impromptu lecture on some current or burning subject that brought all the boys to attention to hear this remarkable teaching. Their eyes were opened as never before to the great issues of life and of the Hereafter. Thus did the boys get so much more out of education which can never be found in the routine of a text book."[43]

Dr. McCaskey's teaching and talks also included "the high Gospel of Wonder," something all teachers needed to instill in their students, he believed, for wonder provokes interest and leads to knowledge. He justified the talks, even though they encroached on the time needed for the curriculum because "[t]here is so much effort to feed the intellect . . . that the spiritual man, the heart side of our complex nature, is often lost sight of."[44]

"[A]bove all, the teacher must be a clean man" McCaskey told an audience of teachers in 1896.[45] His remedy for getting rid of teachers who were "[r]otten-mouthed because rotten-hearted" was amusing but impractical: They should be dumped in the river above the Niagara Falls and sent over for "a bath and cleansing;" however, he doubted that even "all the waters of Niagara" would wash them clean.[46] McCaskey said that he warned his students about anyone whose "moral and spiritual condition" was so bad that "the angels must hold their breath, as well as their noses, when they come within range of these morally diseased but too often well-dressed people."[47]

McCaskey held Ulysses S. Grant up as an example of someone who abstained from profanity or inappropriate language. He cited Grant's friend, George W. Childs, publisher of the *Philadelphia Public Ledger,* who said of the 18th President: "I never heard him express or make an indelicate allusion in any form or manner. There is nothing I ever heard him say that could not be repeated in the presence of women."[48] These remarks about Grant's decorum came at the end of McCaskey's comments about "unclean" teachers. McCaskey suggested that such purity of language and manner was as much to Grant's credit as was his tomb at Riverside Park on the Hudson.[49] (Given Grant's reputation for drinking, he may seem to be a poor example. Perhaps one vice was enough.)

At a testimonial dinner in 1926, approximately 300 Boys' High alumni gathered in the Brunswick Hotel to celebrate McCaskey's 89th birthday. Dr. Henry H. Appel, president of Franklin & Marshall and an 1885 graduate, presented McCaskey with a basket of roses and said: "We love you now as we have always loved you. You were a great teacher because you had a great personality. Your courage for right and your condemnation of wrong live with us. Above many of the great works exalted in this city is your work in the building of these men. We bring this tribute to you as the Master Builder."[50]

McCaskey's grave marker is a simple, flat stone, inscribed with the words by which he wanted most to be remembered: "Builder of Men."

McCaskey's gravestone in the family plot at Greenwood Cemetery. (Photo courtesy of author.)

Chapter 11

Teach the Children to Love the Trees

"Let us teach the children to love the trees. One respects what he loves, and protects what he respects."[1]

In 1854 Julius Sterling Morton moved from green, wooded Michigan to the barren plains of Nebraska. Yearning for the trees and forests of his childhood, Morton advocated in his paper, the *Nebraska City News,* for their restoration and preservation in his new state. He began actively planting trees on his property, today preserved as Arbor Lodge State Historical Park, and he encouraged skeptical neighbors to do likewise. They laughed at him, "saying that fruit trees could not live upon the cold and bleak prairies."[2] Morton, who would hold several political offices, became Secretary of Agriculture for President Grover Cleveland (1893 to 1897). Most well-known for initiating Arbor Day, Morton called the effort "the battle against the treeless prairies."[3] The first Nebraska Arbor Day took place April 10, 1872; more than a million trees were planted that day. The concept soon spread to other states and countries around the world. Of the significant difference between this and other holidays, Morton clarified, "Other holidays repose upon the past; Arbor Day proposes for the future."[4]

In the same era, naturalist John Muir, founder of the Sierra Club, was in the West, climbing up 100-foot pine trees to ride in storm winds,[5] crossing glaciers,[6] accidentally somersaulting into bushes perilously close to a steep drop-off,[7] hiking uncharted courses to mountain summits and, once, even being swept down a mountain on the back of an avalanche.[8] A key figure in preservationists' fight to set aside thousands of acres as national parks, Muir shared his stories and awe of the great outdoors and the magnificent lands of the West in articles that appeared in *Century* magazine, *Harper's Weekly*, and other periodicals. McCaskey read about Muir's adventures and his campaign to preserve the wilderness.[9]

In 1876 McCaskey attended the Centennial Exhibition in Philadelphia and reported on it in the summer and fall issues of the *Journal.* Among the attractions was a sequoia display from California. A gargantuan tree, 24 feet in diameter, had been cut down and a 16-foot section was transported and then reassembled. Eastern viewers, who were not familiar with these trees, reacted in disbelief and dubbed the exhibit the "California hoax." Whatever McCaskey's take on the sequoia, he and the country were being exposed to much new information about nature and the environment. Concerns about deforestation and preservation of the great and wondrous lands were common topics, bubbling up like the Yellowstone hot springs in the newspapers and magazines of the time.

It is, therefore, not surprising that McCaskey would be impressed and inspired by the efforts of Morton, Muir and others. He grew up in the country, came under the influence of a teacher who loved botany, and went on to advocate for getting children into the woods and nature through his efforts in advancing Arbor Day, field trips, bird preservation, and his vigorous study of the stars.

McCaskey credited his childhood years on the farm and at Zook School with awaking in him his life-long awareness and love of nature. He wrote that he was born in "one of the oldest log houses in Lancaster county, with no cellar, built over a perennial spring in what may have been primeval forest."[10] Past remnants of that forest, McCaskey walked the half mile to Zook School. The entire area surrounding the McCaskey birthplace today is virtually devoid of woods. Farm fields, boasting some of the best non-

Sequoias in Sequoia National Park, CA. (Photo courtesy of the author.)

Marker for the stump of the tree cut down for the Philadelphia Centennial Exhibition of 1876, Sequoia National Park, California. (Photo courtesy of the author.)

irrigated agricultural land in the country, come right up to the road edges, with no allowance for trees or wildlife habitat.

About Zook School, McCaskey wrote, "The old country school was at a cross-roads, but out of the windows was the cool woods, with dropping nuts and acorns, where we played 'town ball,' where the birds sang, where I can see the flash of the flicker's wing and hear the woodpecker tapping yet."[11] He expressed the value of being out-of-doors for children, saying: "It is a blessed thing to have been a child in touch with Mother Nature, with time to see her sky, and breathe her air, and live such a life as can be lived nowhere away from the woods and the farm."[12]

McCaskey's sojourn at Oak Hill Academy in 1848 provided more exposure to nature, this time in an ordered, manicured way. The school building sat high, providing a grand view, and the grounds were landscaped with walks and plantings, including orchards: "The building has an imposing appearance, and standing on elevated ground, commands a broad prospect of a country justly styled the Paradise of 'Garden Spot of Lancaster county.' . . . About 9 ACRES of first quality land are attached to the property, agreeably laid out in walks and planted with ornaments and fruit trees, besides an excellent Apple and young Peach Orchard."[13]

The love of nature would burgeon in young McCaskey in Lancaster under teacher Howard Worcester Gilbert's tutelage. Along with Gilbert's impact on the young farm boy in other areas, he influenced him in the realm of botany: "On the Duke street hill, . . . I was introduced by Mr. H. W. Gilbert to the delights of the plant world from the side of botany."[14] Gilbert, McCaskey wrote, "was living his own life and enjoying it, and we were his privileged wards and companions in his walks to the hills and woods and streams, in our study of botany and other things. He took us with him and we often went alone—for the fever was in our blood and he had put it there. That was a teacher! . . . The flowers of sixty years ago have the dew of the early morning on them yet, the trees stand glorious yet, because of him!"[15] McCaskey recalled school excursions with Gilbert to "the high bluff at Rockford (Indian Hill),"[16] where they "gathered the columbine and the 'shooting star' from its clefts and crevices."[17]

Gilbert's field trips with his charges, McCaskey made clear, were the reason he, as principal, insisted that the man whom he regarded as one of his very best teachers be brought to the high school 26 years later: "The memory of those botanical excursions and the enjoyment we had in finding and analyzing plants and flowers along the Conestoga and elsewhere, led many years afterwards to the coming of Mr. Gilbert to the high school mainly that he might give to other boys, and to us all, what he had given to me."[18] Gilbert was elected in December 1876 as second assistant to the principal, a position last filled by McCaskey in 1862. The board meeting was heated, for the appointment was controversial, given that it was a rush job and that Gilbert was to teach only four hours a day but receive a full-time salary.[19]

Botanical excursions, a la Gilbert, became part of McCaskey's lesson plans. Teacher and students explored Chiques Rock,[20] a precipice overlooking a broad, sweeping curve in the Susquehanna River just north of the town of Columbia and reached on foot through woods on trails bordered by wild flowers. An October 1884 newspaper notice announced one such outing: "The boys of the high school expect to make their customary fall trip to Chiques tomorrow. Should the day be fair, they will have a good time."[21] The pursuit of flowers and plants led the teens and teacher along the Conestoga River, too. Student Diffenderffer recalled McCaskey guiding him and his peers, "a band of youths from the school into the woodlands and along the Conestoga River on botanical excursions. Wild flowers would be obtained and with botany book in hand, the blooms and plants would be analyzed on the spot."[22] "The usual trip was from Engleside, foot of South Prince Street, eastward along the river to Reigart's Landing, [directly behind the Greenwood Cemetery], foot of Strawberry Street at the remains of an old stone bridge."[23]

These excursions included crossing the river, which eventually led to a tragedy. "High School life was not always blithesome and joyous," Diffenderffer wrote. "Sometimes sad events must occur."[24] At 4:30 p.m. on May 17, 1888, McCaskey and his students were returning to the city. McCaskey's 10-year-old son Donald was along, as he often accompanied his father on such trips.[25] About 100 yards below Reigart's Landing, the party crossed the river in small groups on a rope-operated raft, for the bridge had collapsed and never been repaired. Such traversing was common practice for people and even their horses and wagons.[26]

Donald and several of the boys crossed first, safely. Then Professor McCaskey and five students stepped onto the raft. "As it was an ordinary means of crossing, we did not think much of danger," McCaskey said in the account he gave to the *Intelligencer*. "The boys were told to stand so as to have the weight pretty well balanced. We had gone but a little distance into the stream, however, when one end of the float began to sink. Before it could be righted, it slid away from us, leaving us in water beyond our depth." Two of the boys managed to get to shore.

"We had the rope but it was so slack as to let us down too deep into the water, making it very difficult to keep upright, because, being on the wrong side of the rope for the current, our feet were being constantly carried towards the surface and our heads going under the water. It was important, however, that the boys should keep to the rope, as none of them could swim."[27]

McCaskey explained that the boys were quite alarmed, and the cold water added to the shock. He struggled to help the two boys nearest him, holding on to them and the rope. William Smith, however, had slipped underneath. "As he came up," McCaskey said, "I called to him to catch the rope, but he seemed unable to do this, and I did not dare to [let] go in order to reach him lest one or other of the boys already at the rope should lose his hold and sink."[28] Two boys on shore threw off their clothes and plunged into the river to rescue Smith but could not. McCaskey and the other students were pulled on to land, where McCaskey lay "more dead than alive" on the bank, Donald recalled.[29] Donald assisted in removing his father's boots, which came off with great difficulty: "I still remember the 'squeezy suction' sound when we began to pull off the knee boots of my Father," he wrote.[30]

Smith's body was recovered at 5:30 p.m., about 20 feet beyond where he had gone under. "Clasped in his arms" was the botany book he had taken with him that day.[31]

After this, McCaskey stopped leading the annual excursions.[32] (Also, an avid swimmer, he gave up the sport after the tragedy, great-grandson Jim McCaskey believed.)[33] He turned the job over to his assistant, and the young men continued to "[analyze] the flowers sitting under the woodland trees," but no longer did they cross any rivers.[34] Student Howard Hersh recalled the trips he went on: "We have been tramping hill and vale and meadow after plants, which has done every one of us good."[35] McCaskey, when very old, recalled: "For a generation the boys scoured the neighboring country with their botanizing cans and brought in a wealth of specimens for class and for individual analysis. They named from practical analysis and knew at sight very many of our native plants and trees."[36]

McCaskey pursued botany and science outside of school, as well. He was a member of the local Forestry Association[37] and also the local Linnaean Society, begun in 1862 "for the study and development of natural science."[38] The association, with 75 active members who were interested in developing a natural history of the county,[39] met the last Saturday of each month at 2 p.m. in the society's museum housed in the Y.M.C.A. on South Queen Street. A charter member, McCaskey was its corresponding secretary and served on the committees for herpetology, ichtheology and mineralogy.[40] The Tucquan Scientific and Piscatorial Association evolved from within the organization and made day (and, later on, four-day long camping) excursions out into rural areas during the summers. McCaskey remained a member of both clubs for many years.

Trudging about in fields and streams led McCaskey to find a native fish that had not yet been identified. This discovery was detailed in a county history: "J.P. McCaskey, September 9, 1863, brought me [Jacob Stauffer, founder of the Lancaster Linnaean group] a specimen taken at Shenk's Ferry—nine inches long, of a yellowish or pale olive color, having a silvery reflective and metallic blue on the sides, lateral line straight, dorsal, spine serrated, nape of the neck depressed, anal fin wide and long, light colored, with prominent veins or blood vessels ramified over the fins. This I named *Ichthaelurus McCaskei.*"[41]

Fish, flowers, trees, all attracted McCaskey's attention. Thirty-five years after *Ichthaelurus McCaskei* was named for him, a vibrant yellow plant blooming in abundance along the railroad tracks caught his eye as he rode the train through the small town of Gap on a Saturday jaunt to Philadelphia, this one on May 28, 1898. Aware that the Scotch broom bush, with its deep taproot and lateral root network, had been planted there to prevent erosion from the banks sloping upwards on both sides of the tracks, he was nonetheless struck by its early blossoming: "We have known the plant to be there for some years, but thought of it as being in flower later in the season, and its glory of golden bloom on Saturday morning, as we passed, was a delightful surprise."[42] So captivated was McCaskey that he returned from Philadelphia earlier than usual in order to disembark at Gap to view the Scotch broom up close. He wrote, "The late afternoon was very pleasant, and the walk down the railroad, with a half dozen birds of different kinds in song, and the rich profusion of bloom upon the slope, was an experience not soon to be forgotten."[43]

This scene, McCaskey said, would be a memory for a lifetime; it brought to mind William Wordsworth's poem "Daffodils." (This is its first verse: "I wandered lonely as a cloud/ That floats on high o'er vales and hills,/ When all at once I saw a crowd,/ A host, of golden daffodils;/ Beside the lake, beneath the trees,/ Fluttering and dancing in the breeze.") At the end of his recollection, McCaskey provided the poem "The Broom-Flower" by Mary Howitt, which begins: "O the broom, the yellow broom!/ The ancient poet sung it,/ And dear it is on summer days/ To lie at rest among it." [44]

Driven by his own proclivities, then, and influenced by the Mortons, Muirs, and Gilberts of his world, McCaskey organized the first Arbor Day in a Pennsylvania school. The holiday, while observed in several states after Morton's 1872 launch, was not within the purview of the schools until 1883 when Dr. Birdsey Grant Northrup, a noted educator, suggested at an American Forestry Association meeting that schools become the locus for Arbor Day observations.[45] McCaskey led the way in Pennsylvania; Lancaster High School celebrated Arbor Day in October 1884.

On numerous occasions, starting in 1885, McCaskey credited the following for instituting Arbor Day in Pennsylvania: first, the *Journal* for its early coverage and continuous promotion of the day; next, Superintendent Higbee, whom McCaskey *repeatedly* praised as the man responsible for the first state-wide Arbor Day in the schools, then Pennsylvania governor Robert Pattison, and last, the legislature.[46] He did not include his own name. However, in 1904, twenty years after Pennsylvania's very first celebration of Arbor Day at his school, McCaskey inserted himself into the history of the holiday, making clear this time that *he* had been the initiator of the movement, using the *Journal* to accomplish it: "The *Journal*, . . . under the direction of its publisher [McCaskey], who was also principal of [Lancaster High School], *began the great movement* [author's emphasis] in a series of articles showing the results of Arbor Day work elsewhere, and urging the appointment of such a day in Pennsylvania." He then credited the politicians and Higbee. However, McCaskey continued with characteristic deference, saying that more important than any individual person was what the day had accomplished: "The important matter is not who are responsible for thus rousing the attention of the State in this direction, but that the people of the State could thus be promptly roused to effective action."[47]

The *Journal* was a powerful tool in the hands of a zealous man. Softening up teachers and administrators, the volume for 1884-1885 carried 23 articles and almost 20 editorials related to trees and Arbor Day. One editorial proposed that students plant "one or more growing trees" as a requirement for graduation.[48] A series on how to plant trees ran from October to April.[49] "Authors' Grove" listed trees that were planted to honor great American writers. The governor's proclamations, superintendents' circulars, suggestions for program formats, and detailed reports about the celebrations in Lancaster were printed. Justifying the large number of articles on the topic in the May installment, McCaskey called each reader to action: "The space given to Arbor Day proceedings in the present issue is commensurate with the importance of the subject at this time. The reader, after having gone through these interesting reports, should not be at ease until he or she has planted a tree in honor of the Arbor Day season and with generous thought for the future—and, by suggestion and example, induced others to the same good deed of largess."[50]

If all of this were not enough to drive the message of Arbor Day into the hearts and minds of the state's teachers and educators, McCaskey had other arrows in his quiver, as well. He printed songs, with the music and lyrics, such as "Swinging 'Neath the Old Apple-Tree"[51] and "Woodman, Spare That Tree"[52] at the ends of issues. He inserted a slogan for the first time in the *Journal*, this in May 1885. It read: "Ye may be aye stickin' in a tree, Jock; it will grow when ye're sleepin'."[53] He inculcated the saying in his students, one of whom editorialized about it in the 1902 *High School News*: ". . . [O]ur esteemed principal, Prof. J. P. McCaskey, has been striving to get the boys of the High School to see the wisdom in this saying and have them apply it." The boys, the writer continued, planted 175 trees that spring.[54]

McCaskey shot off another arrow, as he featured Johnny Appleseed in the *Journal* several times. Appleseed's real name was John Chapman, an eccentric character who roamed barefoot about Pennsylvania, Ohio, Indiana, Illinois, and West Virginia in the late 18th and first half of the 19th centuries, carrying along apple seeds, planting them in enclosures, and then returning a year or so later to sell the seedlings. McCaskey held Johnny Appleseed up to his students as an example, albeit a somewhat odd one: "He was a kindly man . . . but like many another benefactor of his race he was regarded a little daft, to give so many years of his lonely life to the dream of apple orchards rioting in springtime bloom and laden with autumn fruitage."[55]

Beyond providing practical information about trees, the *Journal's* greatest accomplishment was in convincing the state legislature and governor to designate a day for the entire state, for "planting trees, shrubbery and flowering plants."[56] The January 1953 issue of the *Journal* inaccurately names McCaskey as the "founder of Arbor Day;"[57] that was J. Sterling Morton's achievement. However, McCaskey was the one who pulled it over the Commonwealth's borders and into the schools and communities of the state. April 16, 1885, was the first official Arbor Day in Pennsylvania.

The *Journal* was influential throughout the state and beyond, even across the Atlantic. In Belgium, where forests were likewise being depleted, an article entitled "Belgium Demands Arbor Day" by Roger de Goey was published in the *Revue de Belgique.* De Goey proposed a Belgian Arbor Day similar to the American one. Based on information he had garnered from the *Journal*, he cited the speed with which the holiday had been introduced in Pennsylvania's schools, and he highlighted the Lancaster program specifically.[58] De Goey spoke of the schools' efficacy in initiating and spreading such work: "The example of America confirms our faith in the effects of education. . . . The [teachers] are teaching the children in the schools to love trees, to think about them, to plant them. . . Let us teach the children to love the trees. One respects what he loves, and protects what he respects. Let us institute Arbor Day, like the Americans."[59]

A major goal of the holiday was landscaping barren schoolyards, and everyone associated with the schools was called upon to pitch in.[60] Such work would provide pleasant areas for play and memories for the alumni, as well.[61] The school environs affected "the warp and woof, the essential texture" of children's character as much as what happened in the classroom, and "[t]extbooks are not all of education."[62] Additionally, "[c]hildren dearly love to have something to do. . . . especially if it comes in the shape of a holiday frolic, where work can be turned into play, and play be utilized into productive and enduring work."[63]

Productive it was. Over 50,000 trees were planted in the Commonwealth that first Arbor Day. A second Arbor Day was set for October because, in April, some of the schools had already ended their school year (the current mandate for a 180-day school year was not then in place), and in some of the northern counties the ground was still frozen.[64] Biannual Arbor Days continued to be observed into the twentieth century. By 1906, McCaskey's last year at the high school, some 9,000 trees had been planted in the city of Lancaster.[65]

The impetus for tree planting in Pennsylvania was strong, as the "sylvans" of William Penn's colony, an area of almost 20 million acres, were being decimated at a rapid pace. By the mid-1800s, the lumber industry in the state was thriving, due to growing demand, and improvements in logging equipment as well as rail transport hastened the destruction exponentially. Farming also contributed to the felling of trees. Clear cutting was carried out in many places, and by the 1920s, most of the trees were gone. A few stands of old-growth trees remain in the state, one in Cook Forest State Park, where today's visitors can hike past 300-year-old trees in an area called the Forest Cathedral, drop their heads back, and stare up in wonder. Simon P. Eby, a speaker at an Arbor Day celebration in 1885, wished that he and his audience could be out "under the branches of some of the giants that lift their tops far up into the blue sky, so high that it strains the neck and makes the head dizzy to look up at them."[66]

Interest in Arbor Day waned in the United States in the twentieth century but was rejuvenated by the first Earth Day in 1970, almost 100 years after Morton had established the holiday that "proposes for the future." Many states and countries continue to recognize and celebrate Arbor Day; Pennsylvania's is the last Friday of April.

Along with the trees, birds were being decimated. Slaughtered by the thousands, whole birds, or parts of them (heads, feet, wings, feathers), and even their nests were pressed into the service of haute couture. The local press made note of the hat craze, "where oddities are not at all odd this season, but common enough, as a pair of bird's feet extending from patched up breasts, or four or five dyed chicken feathers standing erect from similar foundations."[67] To protest the carnage, the superintendent of the Oil City, Pennsylvania, schools, Dr. Charles A. Babcock established Bird Day in 1894. Bird Day was promoted in the *Journal* and was celebrated in Pennsylvania concurrently with Arbor Day for a number of years.

McCaskey himself remained a birdwatcher from his early days at Zook School, where he had met the flicker and the woodpecker, and he observed birds in moments of leisure: "In a large Tecoma vine on the end of our house, and in a heavy growth of the Virginia Creeper on the eastern wall of our High School, the English sparrows have many nests, and their familiar chirping is always in the air. Now and then—but it seems at long intervals—a robin, or a song-sparrow, or a catbird breaks into song and makes everybody glad. We have for the past two or three days been making closer acquaintance through a good field-glass with a catbird that has a nest nearby." The song of the catbird, and therefore nature, McCaskey inferred, could have a civilizing effect on young ruffians: "[E]verybody listens, even the boy of half-savage instincts whose first thought is a stone. The boys always need missionary work in this direction."[68]

Another spring found McCaskey again observing the birds. This time he made a connection to the stars. As he listened to robins and song-sparrows "chirping and chattering outside the open windows, near their nests in the vine upon the wall," he said he hadn't heard either bird since the previous fall, an unexpected realization. He compared it to seeing certain constellations reappear in the autumn sky: "[A]nd it was as when in the Fall one comes, with a quick pulse of glad recognition, upon the Pleiades and Orion, which he has not seen for many months, leading up the starry hosts to blaze in the winter sky until the spring returns again."[69]

The Pleiades and Orion constellations McCaskey had learned to identify as a student. As a teacher, he taught astronomy: "We used to look to the heavens . . . We used no text-book . . ., but had the blackboard, and our lines of direction and distance. The boys had their blank books—and the brilliant sky of night was overhead."[70] Edward William McCaskey, McCaskey and Ellen's first child, had been one of his students and recalled: "[W]e located the constellations and more conspicuous stars readily by lines of direction and distance and angles and triangles. It was an easy and simple way of teaching the stars, and we all learned about 25 constellations and nearly all the more prominent fixed stars. We learned the difference between the planets and the stars, how near the former are to the sun and the awful distance of the latter. We knew nearly 100 of them, many of which we have never forgotten. We located three or five or more each week and made our list familiar. This was slight knowledge of Astronomy, but it was what the old Chaldeans learned, and it has been with me ever since."[71]

McCaskey taught the teachers, too. At a Lancaster County Teachers' Institute in 1878, he made astronomy presentations and urged the teachers to learn about the stars for themselves and their students. Teach the students, he told them, about the stars' enormous magnitudes and almost infinite distances from Earth and one another. "[The student's] interest is thus aroused to know more of so grand a science. He will begin for himself to look up to them, to note them singly, and soon to trace out in the sky the various diagrams from the star list that may be assigned to him."[72]

In the 1870s, McCaskey arranged for lectures on astronomy at Fulton Hall and organized the Star Club of Lancaster,[73] with more than 100 members. It met 10 times during the fall and winter months in the Lancaster Y.M.C.A. At the May 1880 session, McCaskey gave the members more stars—the list for the year totaled 125—to seek out in the night skies. He specified the viewing times (from 9 p.m. to midnight) and locations of constellations, such as Cepheus, Cassiopeia, the Dragon, the Eagle, Hercules, Ophiuchus, and Sagittarius.[74] And, to remind members of the vastness and perpetual coursing of the solar system, McCaskey pointed out that since the club's last meeting three months earlier, "the earth has swept through one-fourth of its mighty orbit about the sun, and, all unconscious of motion, we have traversed a distance in space of nearly one hundred and fifty millions of miles."[75]

McCaskey looked skyward throughout his life. In 1908 he sat in a Denver-bound train, gazing up: "Venus hangs clear and bright above the sky line of a grand mountain peak. These mighty mountains! And the splendor of the old familiar stars in this pure air and cloudless sky! I sit in the rear of the observation car for hours of the night—the wide universe, Milky Way and all that can be seen of the rest of it, in full view from this mountain height of vision. The most magnificent sight the eye of man ever looks upon is the clear sky of a winter night—or such a sky of stars as this."[76]

McCaskey taught astronomy and love of nature at home. Great-grandson James McCaskey, who lived at 304 West King Street as a child, remembered the walls of the bathroom being decorated with star charts.[77]

James' oldest brother Edward wrote about birds and blossoms at 304: "Along the side of the front half of the house grew a beautiful ivy vine which was the home of countless birds. Here was the outstanding feature of the entire place. The house itself was of red brick, and [when] the ivy bloomed, it made the picture perfect. At the foot of the ivy grew lilies of the valley, and to their right was the brick walk that so unevenly divided the yard."[78]

Why, asked McCaskey, study the stars or plants? He and his colleagues, he said, were neither scientists nor specialists. It was because, in science as in the humanities, God is to be found: "But as we have learned to enjoy music and poetry, painting and sculpture, literature, eloquence and the dramatic art, so we are learning more and more to enjoy the perfect work of God in nature."[79] He seemed perplexed that anyone would not look up: "It is surprising that any human being should go through life without being at times struck by the beauty of the sky above him, and led to acquire some knowledge of its most brilliant and remarkable stars."[80]

Whether he was planting trees on Arbor Day, listening to the birds, looking up at the night skies, or down into the waters, McCaskey echoed what Henry David Thoreau concluded while peering through the ice on Walden Pond: "Heaven is under our feet as well as over our heads."[81]

Chapter 12

A Miracle of Bloom

"Over the fence last spring we looked down from our school-room windows into the yard of the parsonage upon a peach tree which was a miracle of bloom."[1]

Arbor Day was official. Well, what kinds of trees and bushes should be planted? Where would funding come from? What would the day's activities entail? The *Journal* provided answers. Plant selection? Choose stock conducive to growing in the readers' areas. Suggested were deciduous trees, evergreens, fruit trees, bushes and shrubs: "hickory, walnut, sweet-gum, dog-wood, buttonwood, ash, bass-wood or linden, birch, beech, locust, willows, tulip-tree, pines, larches, firs, and others too numerous to mention. For shrubbery and vines, mock-orange, spireas, the burning bush, deutzia, lilacs, wigelia, hardy roses, honeysuckles, Virginia creeper, wistaria, the tecoma, and others."[2] In 1895 the only plants arriving at Lancaster High School were rose bushes, these as a memorial to Dr. Higbee.[3] In April 1886 two hundred fruit trees, "many choice varieties of apple, cherry, pear, apricot, peach, gage, and quince," and grape vines and honeysuckles were delivered.[4] Soon after the very first Arbor Day, peaches and other fruits from the young trees began appearing on Dr. McCaskey's desk, foreshadowing a bountiful crop of gratitude to come in the years ahead.

To guarantee that all students had a tree to plant, the *Journal* offered some funding tips. At one school, the principal purchased "choice varieties of peach trees at thirteen cents each" and then sought a 25 cent contribution for each tree from those who could afford to do so.[5] At Lancaster High School, teachers and students raised funds together.[6]

The day began with students receiving their plants and instructions. Then, off they, accompanied by the teachers, would go. It was important that *they* do the work, the *Journal* asserted, and that they plant *good* trees, for it took the same amount of time to plant a good tree as a worthless one. Such "practical and profitable training" enhanced the students' intellectual and moral training and guaranteed constant benefit to the community.[7] "It is a great thing for boys and girls to have their thoughts directed to such work as this, and their own hands actually employed in doing it. So many people talk . . . One tree-planter—be he man or boy, or even a good, wide-awake girl—is worth tons of people who merely talk about it."[8]

On the first official Pennsylvania Arbor Day, a Norway maple, white spruce, hemlock spruce, white pine, two sugar maples, two horse chest-

McCaskey and the Class of 1897 on the steps of vine-covered Lancaster High School. (Photo courtesy of LancasterHistory.org.)

nuts, two Japanese gingkoes, and three sweet-gums were planted at the high school. Shrubs and several vines were to be added later in the growing season.[9] In 1886 McCaskey predicted that "[I]n a few years—thanks to Arbor Day—our substantial school building will be embowered in greenery. Its walls we hope to see covered with climbing vines, so that it shall stand an object of attraction to all."[10] Eleven years later, the school's façade was flush with the triadic leaves of the Virginia creeper.

Beyond the schoolyard, students were encouraged to plant trees at their homes. They were, in fact, to plant a tree for every family member.[11] Should their property fill up, they were advised to extend their exuberance into their neighbors' yards: "Plant over the fence, in the yard of someone else. What matters whether you enjoy the shade or gather the fruit? Another may and will."[12] McCaskey wanted *everyone* to plant trees: "What good citizen, but should esteem it a privilege, find it a pleasure, and regard it a duty?"[13]

Lancaster benefited, as well, for it had no parks within its perimeters. While William Penn's layout of Philadelphia included parks, James Hamilton's design for the city, drawn up in 1734, did not. Hamilton had "thought, properly, of church and school and market and jail," McCaskey wrote, to help attract settlers, but "he had not looked to the distant future, and so . . . he did not think of reserving a few acres for a park or pleasure ground for the people of his little town."[14] Hamilton received a posthumous scolding from McCaskey, who accused him of thinking only of money: "[Hamilton] wasted no sentiment on parks, for that would have been to throw away real estate with cash value. The spirit of [the founders] . . . seems ever since to have dominated these two cities. It is a grand thing in any formative era to have a wise and noble leader—for his impress upon after-times! If the spirit of William Penn had impressed James Hamilton, Lancaster would be a somewhat different city from what we know it to-day."[15]

To counter Hamilton's failing, McCaskey targeted locations around the city for greenery, such as the Reformed Theological Seminary (today the Lancaster Theological Seminary). In October 1898 more than 20 trees were planted near College Avenue; they included "[s]ix oaks, six tulip poplars, two sweet gums, two Paulownias, one Lombardy poplar, one copper beech, one horse chestnut, and one Norway maple."[16] McCaskey trusted that some of the trees he had chosen "might be growing long after we are all 'away.'"[17] Indeed, a few, two red oaks, still stand today.[18]

This particular Arbor Day was named for the Marquis de La Fayette and the trees were christened "La Fayette's Row." McCaskey paid glowing tribute to the idolized Frenchman in a speech that afternoon and spoke of his 1824-25 return visit to the United States. A few in the audience had actually seen La Fayette when he came to Lancaster, McCaskey noted. His own aunt Margaret McCaskey White, who lived with him and his family, was one of the eyewitnesses. "An old lady," McCaskey said, "who sits by me daily at the table, and who in less than a month will be ninety years of age" spoke of the Marquis "with keen interest."[19] McCaskey had paid for the trees and expenses himself because he wanted

Oaks at the Lancaster Theological Seminary. (Photo courtesy of the author.)

all funds raised for the day to go instead to a proposed monument at La Fayette's grave in Paris.[20]

Treeless city streets were selected, as well, for as McCaskey explained: "Were the number of trees growing upon our streets increased four-fold, Lancaster would be more beautiful, more healthful, and its homes more comfortable during the season of midsummer. The value of real estate would also be increased, for the city would become more attractive as a place of residence." He noted one such barren stretch, on King Street from Manor Street to Lime.[21] When Superintendent Higbee offered to provide trees as consolation for his absence from an Arbor Day celebration, McCaskey chose that site: "I have had planted along West King and Mulberry Streets—of course, my own part of the town!—and on the property adjoining the High School building, some twenty-seven maples and American ash trees."[22]

Trees were planted where Long's Park is today; some—two large beeches and several white oaks—continue growing into the sky.[23] In 1933 a newspaper article about McCaskey's 95th birthday mentioned his continuing visits there: "Today he likes to ride through the park in an automobile and look at the trees he and his boys planted, some of them more than half a century ago."[24]

Trees were planted in honor of poets, politicians, historical figures, educators, and others of prominence. Elizabeth Barrett Browning, Thaddeus Stevens, Governor Pattison, Sir Walter Scott, William Penn and, of course, McCaskey, were among the many so designated. George Washington was recognized with the "Washington Centennial" horse chestnuts, clustered at the corner of Prince and Orange Streets.[25] On the occasion of such plantings, while a representative from each class declared, "The class of _________ names this tree in honor of ________," Principal McCaskey would move from tree to tree, shoveling dirt on the roots.[26]

With the planting accomplished, students, teachers, board members, citizens, religious leaders and local dignitaries would converge on the high school at 2 p.m. for a program which often lasted 2½ hours or longer. The building was decorated by the boys, who had been given free rein. One year, flags stretched from the ground floor to the top of the school tower, and a large streamer fluttered over Orange Street.[27] McCaskey exhorted` the boys to include the girls in the work: "Don't forget, either, that the girls are as pretty as the trees, and gallantly arrange to give them the best opportunity to embellish the occasion, and add to its attractions by their presence, and . . . contribute in their own way."[28] The study hall, crowded beyond capacity, was decorated with ferns and flowers.[29] Portraits of educators were draped with vines and surrounded by flowers and bouquets.[30]

1890s photo of McCaskey. (Photo from a private collection.)

Small programs listed the musical performances, readings, "recitations in concert," speeches, Scripture readings and prayer. As many as 17 musical numbers were interspersed throughout the program. The high school chorus, with 250-300 singers, performed songs about trees, nature, patriotism, and God; it was accompanied by the orchestra, which played three or four selections.[31] Students read several selections, including the Governor's Proclamation of the day and the Superintendent's "circular," and poetry and prose passages that centered on nature, e.g., "The National Flower," "Hidden Uses of Plants," "Apple Trees in Love," and "Legend of the Trailing Arbutus." Every program ended with the Doxology. The public was sometimes invited afterwards to attend physical education exhibitions by the boys and girls on the third floor of the high school, which had been converted into a gymnasium at McCaskey's prompting.[32]

The centerpiece of the afternoon's program was a speech by a prominent citizen, a forestry expert or state commissioner of forestry, the current state or county superintendent and occasionally even the governor; McCaskey generally had more than a few words to say. These addresses included a review of the destruction of Pennsylvania's forests and a denunciation of "American extravagance."[33] Some listed the benefits of trees and forests: shade; fresh, cool air; sources of lumber and fuel; modification of climate; prevention of soil erosion and evaporation; more even distribution of rainfall; absorption of carbon dioxide; regulation of water flow into streams and rivers, prevention of flooding, and protection against cold winter winds that freeze crops and cause snowdrifts.[34]

The children, presenters maintained, would receive the greatest salutary effects from Arbor Day, learning the laws and cycles of nature and the effect of trees on climate. The well-kept classrooms and landscaped school yards would serve as models for their own homes and families.[35] Expressed in a lengthy prayer at the first Arbor Day program was the hope that, learning from their own planting and tending, the children would reach out to others in love and not be self-centered.[36]

McCaskey, state superintendents Higbee, Wickersham, Schaeffer, all of them believed children should spend time outside. Higbee, on the state's inaugural Arbor Day, expressed the importance of children experiencing nature first-hand: "[W]e would, with special emphasis, call the children to a wholesome converse with *nature* herself; would withdraw them from the restraints of books and recitation tasks and woo them to her shady haunts, her valleys and hills."[37]

Speeches with titles such as "Moral and Religious Uses of Trees," "Tree Planting Considered with Reference to Its Moral Aspects," and "God's Trees" linked trees and their propagation to the spiritual and moral realms. State Superintendent Nathan C. Schaeffer proclaimed this in an 1898 circular: "The pupil who begins to see the beauty of the landscape, to understand the laws of vegetation and to grasp the thoughts which are everywhere enshrined in nature, is learning to think God's thoughts and to enjoy the things of a higher life."[38]

And so, Lancaster became dotted abundantly with trees and shrubs, bushes and vines. Securely rooted in the hearts of students were the values and benefits of such work. McCaskey regretted that he had not begun such efforts before 1884 but found solace in the idea that "[t]he work goes forward, but it is never done, which is perhaps one of its best features."[39] On his twice-a-day, block-long walk from his home at 304 West King Street up the hill along Mulberry to the high school on Orange, he could see trees where there had been none.[40] Visible from his office were trees and plants in the cemetery behind the school and in neighboring yards regaling him with their beauty, evidence of recurring rewards.

Several stories about fruit from trees students had planted must also have assuaged McCaskey's regret, although one is bittersweet. On the high school's first Arbor Day, some of the boys planted "choice varieties of peach trees." Two years later, produce from those trees arrived at the school, including some from a student who had fallen ill and died. Before his death, he had expressed his wish that the first fruit his tree bore "be sent to [the teachers]. His wish was regarded, and two beautiful peaches of exquisite flavor were brought a few weeks since from the hand of his mother." McCaskey ended this narrative, as he usually did when talking about someone's death, with the hope that he and the boy would meet again in the after-life: "It may be that one of these happy days we shall have the pleasure of acknowledging to himself [the student] the thoughtfulness that prompted the gift."[41]

A happier story told of a student named Neff. One spring day in 1887, McCaskey was looking "down from our school-room windows into the yard of the parsonage [next door] upon a peach tree which was a miracle of bloom." He recalled no particular interest in the tree, but was struck by its beauty.[42] That fall, he received a letter from a Boys' High graduate who had gone to Switzerland to become a missionary and who "spoke with kindly interest of the High School to which he belonged on our first Arbor Days."

A day or so later, McCaskey and another teacher were called to the same window from which he had observed the peach tree in the spring: "Miss Martin called Mr. Gable and myself to the window 'to see something fine.' Laden with ripening fruit, well set and shapely, it was the most beautiful tree we have seen during the present season. [Miss Martin] said, 'It is Neff's first Arbor-Day tree!' We were all somewhat in doubt as to this, the tree seemed so large and the fruit so fine, until the sexton of the church, who was there when the tree was planted, said, 'Yes, it is Neff's tree; he got it at the High School—and better peaches don't grow in all this country.'" McCaskey promised to write to Neff: "Our young friend will hear of this with pleasure beyond the Atlantic, among the mountains of Switzerland."[43]

Peaches and other fruits continued to arrive at the high school over the years. In his address to the students of Lancaster High School on the eighth Arbor Day, Mr. Gable spoke of such offerings: "If, during the last two months, you had seen and sampled as I have, the large and luscious fruit left by pupils and ex-pupils on the desk of our principal, you would certainly know that in this case 'Bread cast upon the waters has returned after not many days.'"[44]

Such affirmation of the good resulting from Arbor Day came to McCaskey even when he was very old. In his 93rd year, he wrote to Will's widow Nellie in California about pears he had received from her son Hiram, who had lived with his Uncle John and Aunt Ellen in Lancaster while attending Boys' High and was among the first students to participate in Arbor Day: "Hiram sent us a box of his wonderful pears. We never see such pears in this part of the country, although we have here many of the best things in the world, right here in Lancaster County. I hope to write him and Mary for their fine treat. They ripened in perfect shape and we were all delighted with them."[45]

Another Boys' High graduate provided more peaches: "For a year," McCaskey wrote in the same letter: "I have been getting up about 9 a.m. and taking breakfast in bed at that time. The best thing I know of is your monster yellow peaches from the Pacific coast, which seem to me the finest thing in the world. No matter what takes the second place they come first and I have them every morning. The president of the Erie Railroad, an old High School boy, has been sending them to me part of the time—three or four dozen cans."[46]

McCaskey helped plant trees in his own yard, removing tie and suit jacket to heft the shovel and dig up the earth.[47] He had done his part to inspire his students—among them his children and nieces and nephews—and his community and state to plant trees. He would have been sad to learn of the fate of the big flowering chestnut trees, pink and white, that lined his property along Mulberry and King Streets.

Following his death in 1935, McCaskey's property was sold to a man who put in one of the first gas stations in the city. The house was razed and the trees cut down. A great-granddaughter recalled, "They just dynamited everything, you know, exploded everything. So, we couldn't go near it. My mother would walk down the alley to market. She wouldn't pass the house. It was too heartbreaking."[48]

The memory of those chestnut trees might have inspired a great-grandson to smuggle trees into the United States on his return from England years after McCaskey's death. He had hidden two chestnut seedlings, one pink and one white, by strapping them onto his legs under his long pants,[49] a shenanigan of which even McCaskey would not have approved, although he was known to have a sense of humor and appreciated the pranks that his students often played on one another and even on him.[50]

Oil painting of 304 West King Street by Anna Stauffer McCaskey. (Photo courtesy of the author.)

That same great-grandson wrote about going to see the West King Street property after McCaskey's death: *"The first thing that I missed was the horse-chestnut trees. Only their stumps showed above the pavements. They had formed a right angle along the front and on up the hill beside the house. As my eye wandered along the line of stumps, I unconsciously counted fifteen; then I saw them in their glory! How they blossomed out in the tender green of spring one time on my birthday. I remembered that Saturday had been warm and cloudy, and on Saturday night a misty, filmy spider-web-like rain had spun itself over the town. In the morning it was clear and very warm. When we went to church, it was apparent that the buds on the trees were about to burst. When we came home, the leaves were all over the trees. It was quite a birthday surprise! And in the fall, all the school-boys would come to gather the horse-chestnuts. The old man had been very proud of those trees, but they were gone now."*[51]

Chapter 13

The Charm of Old Enoch Lytle's Fiddle

"... but the charm of old Enoch Lytle's fiddle in the big kitchen by the light of the evening fire—for whose music I had waited in glad expectancy all the long day—"[1]

By the last decade of the 19th century and into the 20th, McCaskey was at the zenith of his productivity. He sat at the helm of Boys' High. His work as editor and publisher of the *Journal* and secretary of the Pennsylvania State Teachers' Education Association continued. These were peak years for memory work and Arbor Day promotions. His songbooks were being marketed throughout the country. The *Lancaster School Mottoes* and the *Lincoln Art Series*, both printed in Lancaster, were being shipped across the state. He was a member of a number of civic organizations, and he was still serving on the vestry of St. James, having been elected to that body in 1867. 304 West King was full of activity. There, he and his wife Ellen, his secretary (Elizabeth McVey), his five children, a foster child, several nephews, and other relatives lived.

Given all of this, it is not surprising that by the turn into the 20th century, McCaskey expressed some weariness. In a lengthy 1901 letter to Nellie, he complained: "I haven't been at [brother] Joe's in a long time nor at [sister] Kate's, see them now and then and hear from them, but do not get away from the daily work routine to make any visits. Get to church once on Sunday, to the printing office often, school regularly, and other places where I must go, but not elsewhere. It's not quite right, I know, but habit—and is it the slower movement of old age? I haven't been so well at times for the past year or two and that may have something to do with it. Can't work so late at night—must sleep more. Dr. Crumbaugh and Donald [a medical student by then] have me in hand and prescribe diet (good things to eat) and treatment and I am doing very well. If I could take a week off every month, I would be in prime condition. As it is I am a trifle 'down', but you'd hardly think so, if you saw me. I look well enough."[2]

Physical weariness did not slow McCaskey down, however. In addition to all his commitments and responsibilities, he researched his family heritage in that same arc of years, an undertaking without which the family history and the genesis of McCaskey's love of music would be lost.

In an 1895 letter, McCaskey responded to brother Will's inquiry about their ancestors with a question: "So you have caught the genealogical fever?"[3] He applauded Will's interest: "Good thing to know something of one's forbears, and the more the better if they were worth knowing, as I think most of our own have been."[4] That letter and an earlier one from 1892 are filled with family history. In 1910, at his and Ellen's golden wedding anniversary celebration, McCaskey spoke to the family about his genealogical pursuits: "For some years I have, at intervals, been looking up our lines of descent, getting the personal history of our grandparents through a half-dozen generations, collecting their wills—some of which, 100, 150 and nearly 200 years old, I mean to read to you today—learning the countries from which they came, what languages they spoke, and, so far as may be, their personal disposition and characteristics. It has been a most interesting study."[5] In 1916, McCaskey sent Will's daughter Eleanor research he had undertaken to document her lineage, for she was applying for membership in the Daughters of the American Revolution. Uncle John was able to supply what she needed: Ancestors Thomas Edwards and Gabriel Davis were soldiers in the revolution.[6]

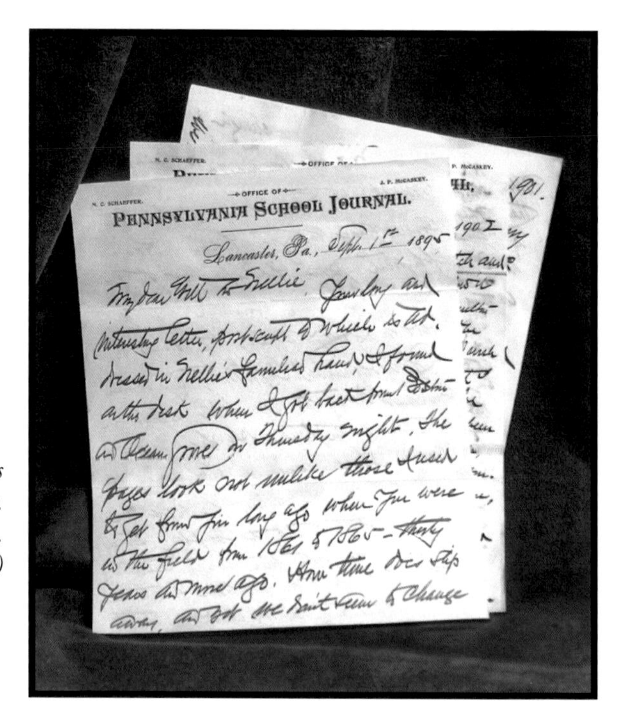

—OFFICE OF—
PENNSYLVANIA SCHOOL JOURNAL.

Lancaster, Pa., Sept. 1st 1895

First pages of letters written by McCaskey. (Photo courtesy of B. David Wagner.)

McCaskey solidified much of the family genealogy in his work for two publications, *Portrait and Biographical Record of Lancaster County, Pennsylvania* and *Biographical Annals of Lancaster County*. These books contain sketches of noteworthy citizens written by either the subjects themselves or someone close to them.[7] McCaskey composed the ones for ancestors from both sides of the family tree, two siblings, his own, two of his children, and a brother-in-law. He also wrote the sketches of Thaddeus Stevens, Thomas Burrowes, E. E. Higbee, and two teachers at the high school. For some, he provided portraits, and he paid for the inclusion of the sketches and pictures in both works.[8]

Due to his diligence, the McCaskey ancestry can be traced, often with great specificity and tender insights. He found this research very rewarding: "It stirs the blood at times to know one's grandfathers and grandmothers, remote and near, and is cause for profound gratitude, not shallow pride nor weak vain-glorying."[9]

When he was 85, McCaskey wrote an autumn letter to 76-year-old sister-in-law Nellie and listed those among his family with birthdays in September and October, including hers October 3rd and his on the 9th. Calling it "a season of birthdays," he grew introspective: "So we go, year by year, until we vanish and are forgotten like our ancestors. Whither do we go—and what to do? But how glad I am that I had the good fortune to be born into a world as good as this—even if we have in it 'Turks and infidels'—tigers, fleas and mosquitos [sic.]."[10]

He was wrong about being forgotten, for McCaskey himself lives on in the halls and on the walls of Lancaster City Hall, St. James' Episcopal Church, and John Piersol McCaskey High School. His genealogy efforts ensured that his forebearers would not be forgotten, either. From his hand have come tales of tragedy and heartbreak, determination and hope, renunciation of the old and embrace of the new. They tell of Atlantic Ocean crossings, one tainted by the death of an infant and another that brought family and immediate friends and "whatever promised to make life more comfortable in the new world. This included [c]hina and glassware, linens, bedding, household utensils, and much good furniture, solid mahogany and walnut upholstered in leather . . . [and] the Douglas clock, a large eight-day grandfather's clock, with fine works and very heavy brass weights, thought to be of French manufacture, brought from Scotland nearly two hundred years before . . . [I]t has ticked away the lives of a half-dozen generations on this side of the sea, and is doing its work [in 1903] for the seventh."[11] A 1592 Queen Elizabeth Bible made the crossing, too.[12]

In the American Revolution, two ancestors fought for independence from England, while a third, a British grenadier, fought for the crown. He returned to County Monaghan in Ireland, took his young son upon his knee, and told him stories of the war and America.[13] When grown, that child, McCaskey's grandfather, came to America and took up farming in Gordonville. Stories are preserved of those arriving throughout the 1700s, forced to migrate because of their religious beliefs or lack of food or employment. Here they prospered. They were farmers and millers, judges and justices of the peace, and one a member of the Pennsylvania Assembly. An early arrival from Wales bequeathed to "each of his three sons a farm of four hundred acres with buildings and livestock."[14] Another's progeny owned between 12,000-15,000 acres in the county.[15] Most settled in Pennsylvania; a few pushed on to Ohio.

A house built in 1735 and razed circa 1900 was home to three strands of the McCaskey line. McCaskey visited there frequently and wrote about the homestead, its spring water, the ancestors, and a dog: "There was an unfailing spring of excellent water within a short distance, shaded by a noble tree. We have frequently been at the old place, in and out of whose doorway passed many of the earliest settlers and of every generation since their day. We remember well 'Aunt Peggy,' 'Uncle Whitehill,' good old Dinah, the faithful ancient; the big kitchen, the old-time garden, and the house-dog that 'knew the names of all the cattle and horses on the farm,'—for they all had names—and was so great a favorite with everybody."[16]

McCaskey reported, too, about the grandmother who loved another better but married the grenadier's son (grandfather John) because her parents wanted her to, for he was a man of substance.[17] Though lively and attractive, "fond of riding and dancing and life generally, proud and handsome, too," she was not the equal of her husband in intelligence,[18] McCaskey opined. Among other ancestors, a husband and wife died within four days of each other; he was 40, she 38. A husband, after his wife's death, married his housekeeper. Another was left with nine children to raise when his spouse died at age 44. A widow married her husband's closest friend, the man who had been appointed guardian of her children. Mothers and babies died in childbirth. Men drowned. A teenager was kicked in the head by a horse and killed.

They had come from Wales, Switzerland, Ireland, and Scotland. Those from Scotland abdicated their royalty of a millennium's duration when they emigrated, but a few titles, lord and daughter of a lord, crossed the Atlantic and are still preserved on several of the oldest tombstones in the church cemetery where many of the earliest arrivals are buried. In McCaskey's account of this family, the Douglases, his opening salvo is a rousing tribute to the Old World ancestors, and it is full of swagger and erudition: "'The broad breast of a Douglas has been Scotland's best bulwark,' said the king. Archibald the Grim [a late medieval Scottish magnate who was the third Earl of Douglas], the 'Good Sir James,' and others of the name, are historic figures. For many centuries the [sic] Douglas was a man of iron will, dauntless courage, and a mighty force in Scotland."[19] However, all the titles—earl, lord, lady, would matter no more, as the Douglases relinquished such claims in their new land. McCaskey, scion of those swashbuckling Scots and the others, expressed his gratitude for his ancestors, not for their titles but for their courage, their character, and their faith.

Maternal ancestors made their "more or less reputation"[20] on lands straddling the Lancaster/Chester County border, with their church, St. John's Episcopal Church of Compass, as the center of activity. St. John's was founded in 1729, and the earliest arrivals populated, in turn, its congregation and then its cemetery. At the entrance to the church grounds, two stone gateposts, sentinels of the church's earliest days and still standing in 1929, witnessed soldiers trudging along to fight in the French and Indian War and, later, the American Revolution.[21] The current structure sits solidly and proudly on a knoll above the King's Highway, now Route 340, and is the building McCaskey would have known. Built in 1838 of gray fieldstone, the building's façade has large, clear glass windows with 32 panes framed in white. Double doors, flanked by tall columns, are capped by a leaded glass transom.

St. John's Episcopal Church, Compass, Pennsylvania. (Photo courtesy of the author.)

Interred in the oldest part of the graveyard directly behind the church are 16 Davises, 7 Douglases, 3 Piersols, and 18 Wilsons, according to church records transcribed more than 100 years ago. Among the cemetery's residents are "fourteen grandparents . . . and more than a hundred uncles, aunts and cousins" of McCaskey's.[22] In a weary line, their tombstones struggle to stand tall, some leaning off the perpendicular, others with one shoulder angled down, heaved about by winter freezes and thaws. Inscriptions on the old grave markers are being etched away and blurred by acid rain and weather. The stones, all with curved tops, are gray with spectral white splotches drizzling down, while lime green and black algae speckle the pocked surfaces. Several are chipped and battered, rounded corner flourishes missing. In this quiet place, some of the oldest headstones in Pennsylvania are to be found. In 1906 McCaskey hired George W. Killian to take photographs of this ancient country church and cemetery,[23] and the next year he took a 20-year-old granddaughter to Compass to have a picture taken "including herself and a stone at the grave of one of her ancestors, eight generations removed."[24]

It was to this church and this area that horse-drawn carriages and then automobiles filled with the William McCaskey family traveled first from Gordonville and later Lancaster to relatives' homes, among them the stone house with its smart farm dog. Visits included attendance at the church for worship, baptisms, weddings, and funerals. McCaskey's final return to the church probably took place in 1929. Driven there by son Donald, he had been invited to attend the church's 200th anniversary. His presence was certainly warranted. After all, he was a descendant of so many of its original members, including three of the Douglas brothers who were among the founders in 1729.[25] He was also remembered as "one of the most ardent visitors" to the church, although his last visit had been 21 years earlier.[26]

Twenty-one years since his last visit, and yet he was still regarded as an *ardent* visitor, a devoted, passionate, fervent one. And that he was, a man passionate about family and ancestry. In 1929, he could have described himself in words he had used for his ancestors: the "faithful ancient." He was 92.

*Two of McCaskey's ancestors' gravestones in St. John's cemetery.
(Photos courtesy of the author.)*

From the pages of McCaskey's research, violins whisper. The violins, he asserted, had unlocked his mother's innate musicality, her beautiful voice: "Whence came to my mother the untold blessing which she found in music? And whence has come to me, through her, such increasing enjoyment as words can never tell? She, no doubt, inherited her sensibility to such influences. This, however, would have remained comparatively dormant but for the violins in the home of her girlhood that filled her soul with melody; the old-time singing school, where again the violin was always present; and the church service that gave words and airs never to be forgotten."[27]

Perhaps it was down through the Wilsons, "a very staunch and vigorous people,"[28] that fiddle playing came: "We remember well how delight fully an old granduncle, John D. Wilson, used to touch the strings of his violin for his own pleasure or for the dance at home in the evening after the day's work on the farm was done. He was stalwart, had a mighty hand, and a voice that could be heard for a mile when he went out to call the hounds, or gave orders to someone at a distance."[29] In the cacophony and frenzy of the 21st century, one might yearn for the simplicity of a fiddle's sweet strains floating out across evening fields of early autumn dotted with grazing cattle or blanketed in golden grain, or for the joy of dancing away the weariness of the day's labors.

When McCaskey appealed for instrumental instruction in the city schools, he invoked Uncle John and another relative. In an 1888 Arbor Day speech, he told a large audience that none of the great violinists he had heard during the previous 25 years in Philadelphia and New York could compare to the music he had heard as a child on the farm: "[B]ut the charm of old Enoch Lytle's fiddle in the big kitchen by the light of the evening fire—for whose music I had waited in glad expectancy all the long day—or, later on and better still, the music that Uncle Johnny Wilson used to bring from the strings with his wizard touch—that charm is never broken."[30]

The Wilsons provided the violins, but McCaskey praised another branch of the maternal family tree for its vocal talent. John Piersol often came to visit, and McCaskey recalled him trotting up the farm lane on horseback, exciting the children's anticipation of sweets and sonorous tones: "[He was] one of the brightest, quickest, most versatile and attractive of men. Often on bright Sunday mornings did we little folks look to see John come riding up the lane, for on Sunday he frequently came over from New Holland, a distance of perhaps seven miles, to visit our mother, a favorite cousin. He always had a pound or so of candies in his coat pocket 'for the children.' In those days we thought his laugh and his voice simply delightful. It remains with us, like the memory of music that we love; indeed, we have never heard a man's voice whose tones in ordinary conversation were more musical, or whose cheery laugh was more infectious. He was a genuine Piersol, wiry, strong, fine, quick, fearless and generous."[31]

McCaskey's mother's voice filled the air of his childhood: "By the cradle, at her work about the house, at the milking time about the barn, in the meadow and at the spring, in the service of the church, what voice so sweet as hers, clear and strong and melodious in every tone, in ballads, songs, lullabies, and lilted tunes that had no words, but most of all in hymns with their high suggestion? 'Marget, sing something' . . . was my father's frequent request. And everybody else seemed to ask it, too; . . . I used to fancy that she had caught into her voice the tones of the violins in the home of her childhood."[32] McCaskey himself was known for his fine tenor voice.[33]

Just as McCaskey extolled Enoch Lytle and Johnny Wilson as better than the best violinists in the world, so, too, he asserted the same about his mother's voice, although he conceded a bias: "It was a clear, sweet soprano of rare quality and unusual power, that no one ever seemed to tire of hearing. She sang as the bird sings; it seemed as natural as to breathe; and toil grew lighter for herself and others. I never knew any one besides to sing so much or so well as my mother. 'So well,' do I say? I know it is the fond prejudice of childhood."[34]

In his old age, McCaskey visited the Gordonville farm several times. Driven out from the city by a grandson, he would climb out of the car and converse with the grandfather of the Stoltzfus family that owns the property today. Neither house nor barn is that which McCaskey had known as a child; those burned down in the late 1850s.[35] Perhaps, as the old men talked, McCaskey looked out across undulating fields and years, striving to conjure up childhood scenes and tender moments and listening for fiddles and singing.

Music in the curriculum was a major topic of discussion across the state in the early years of the common schools. The *Journal*, in its earliest issues from the 1850s, published many articles advocating music instruction. Miss N. Howe, at the Huntingdon County Teachers' Institute in 1853, wondered: "Need it be asked, if Music is of sufficient importance to be introduced into our schools as a part of the education of the young? The question is easily solved, when we take into consideration, its *powerful influence*, its *reforming effects*, and that it is one of Nature's provisions throughout her wide domain."[36] Early articles expounded on many aspects of music: its history from the earliest times and among the most primitive of people; its innateness; its universality of appeal and usage among all peoples; its soothing effect on evil spirits; its power to promote national pride; its presence in nature, and its ability to connect humans to the Divine.

Music, one contributor wrote, had a "moralizing and harmonizing influence . . . upon children, as well as grown persons . . . [for it] softens boisterous and unruly dispositions and dispels hatred and anger; and in place of revengeful feelings, implants kindness, charity, and an earnest desire for each other's happiness."[37] Music attracts children to school; they learn to love its discipline; it develops a child's hearing and voice; it strengthens a child's organs (those involved in singing); it serves as a mnemonic tool; it is used to help children learn spelling, the math tables and geography; it is relaxing; it "gives inclination for order and morality," and, finally, it refreshes the mind, so that the student is ready for new studies.[38]

Lancaster needed no such convincing. Music instruction was included in its curriculum as early as February 1839, when the school board resolved ". . . to introduce vocal music as a regular branch of teaching" immediately.[39] A variety of resolutions for music instruction appeared in the board minutes over the next decade. Both vocal and instrumental music were offered.[40] At one point, the pupils paid one cent for each hour-long lesson, for the school board was not responsible for the instructor's remuneration.[41]

In 1866, 16 teachers at the high school and secondary schools petitioned the Superintending Committee to provide "scientific" vocal training (theory), as opposed to singing by ear. A competent instructor was recommended to teach students on Tuesdays and Thursdays and interested teachers one evening a week. Singing by ear was valuable because it was relaxing and had a "refining influence on the minds of pupils." However, music theory would have more permanent value and be a source of lifelong gratification. This would be money well spent, the petitioners argued: "[N]o money can be expended to better advantage upon the public schools than that which goes toward the salary of a faithful, thoroughly competent instructor in vocal music." The first signatory was J. P. McCaskey.[42]

To a critic who opposed music education, saying that the common schools were "designed to feed the people upon merely common fare," McCaskey retorted: "The Common Schools are meant to feed the common people upon the very bread of life; and music is no mean slice of the precious loaf wherever it is found." To another, who scoffed at musical training for the poor, saying it was only for the rich, McCaskey exclaimed: "For shame! Who are the rich? Who are the poor? The pauper schools belong to the past of our history. The Common School knows no privileged class. It recognizes but one test of merit—that of brains and heart, the courage that dares, and the will that achieves results."[43]

McCaskey brought his students into the campaign to hire a vocal teacher: "[In 1871 or '72], in the old building on Mulberry street, we talked the matter over with the boys, and thought we wanted singing in the High School."[44] They appealed to the board, and the chairman said they could have a professional teacher if they paid his salary. When several board members visited the school and heard the boys singing, they "were so well pleased that the engagement was made permanent" and paid for by the district.

Instruction was extended to Girls' High and then to the secondary and primary schools.[45]

William B. Hall, who performed often at Fulton Hall, was that first instructor. He had been recommended by McCaskey, as were the next two vocal teachers. Carl Matz, a German-trained musician, replaced Hall at the high school. John B. Kevinski, "a lover of music and a rare friend of children,"[46] was assigned to the secondary and primary schools. Kevinski played a violin to accompany the children's singing as he moved from classroom to classroom, school to school: "For twenty-six years," McCaskey wrote, "[Kevinski] came and went, a familiar presence in these schools, where thousands of children at the appointed hours of singing awaited the coming of [Kevinski] and his violin with eager expectancy. From morning till evening, day by day, through ten months of the year, wherever he appeared the air was vocal with melody—the voice of the violin and the voice of song."[47]

With the vocal music program securely in place, McCaskey launched his fight for free instrumental instruction. It was time, he contended in that 1888 Arbor Day speech. The orchestra performing that day was comprised of boys already receiving private instruction. McCaskey had canvassed all his students about their interest in learning to play an instrument: "Fifty-six additional boys," he said, "have reported to me during the past day or two, that, if instruction in instrumental music were made as free as Latin and German, they would be glad to take lessons, on condition that each of them should provide his own instrument and the necessary music."[48]

In January 1893 McCaskey asked the school board to provide an instructor in instrumental music at the high school for the rest of the year.[49] A capable instructor was available, and McCaskey wanted him: Carl Thorbahn, another German-trained musician, was competent in clarinet, violin, and other instruments. He crafted violins, violoncellos, and double basses and had led orchestras in Montreal, Boston, and Ohio. He was hired.

Thorbahn related how the orchestra began: "*I started the orchestra with my private pupils . . . Among these were Walter and Donald, [sons of McCaskey] . . . and Hiram [McCaskey's nephew] . . . Meeting Dr. McCaskey one morning, he asked me if I could not have my pupils come to the high school for occasional practice with the large chorus under Prof. Carl Matz. . . . So I got the boys together for several mornings before school opened, and we rehearsed the songs. A week later we played with the singing, supporting the fine chorus. . . . Dr. McC., being more than pleased with the result, thought it would be an excellent thing to have a permanent orchestra connected with the school, and asked me if I would become the leader of it at a fixed salary if he would have the city school board to agree to such an arrangement . . . He presented the matter to the board, which body voted in favor of it, and in consequence any boy or girl while in the high school can take any orchestral instrument free of cost, except for instrument and music book.*"[50]

Just as McCaskey had made sure that all students would have a tree or shrub to plant on Arbor Day, so, too, he made sure all had instruments: "To encourage the pupils to take hold of this new work," Thorbahn recalled, "Dr. McCaskey bought two dozen violins, which he gave to such as wished to take lessons but could not afford to buy an instrument."[51] In addition, McCaskey "kept a small backlog of just such musical instruments and loaned them out to the boys until they earned money to buy their own instrument. He was even known on a few occasions to make outright gifts to a needy boy by giving him an instrument of his choice."[52]

The orchestra began in 1887 with about 50 boys and girls, most playing violin, and doubled in size by 1903. Lessons were from 8 to 9 a.m. and 4 to 6 p.m. daily in the high school building. Students were expected to practice an hour a day at home. The high school orchestra, for advanced students, drilled on Thursdays from 7 to 8:30 p.m., followed by "the orchestral school" from 8:30 to 10 p.m. Students in the latter group had been promoted from the orchestra and played "a higher grade of music, that is, more difficult operatic selections, overtures and symphonies," Thorbahn explained.[53]

McCaskey listened to those sessions: "Sometimes when detained in the evening, I sit at the flat desk on the low platform of our attractive study hall, the fine bank clock . . . ticking quietly, suggestive pictures everywhere upon the wall, the Virginia Creeper . . . hanging its rich drapery of green about the windows without, and within the graceful festoons of Christmas laurel from the pillars to the walls, I linger on to hear the boys at practice in different rooms upon their instruments. Here a violin, there a flute or clarionet, or both, it may be, in duet, yonder a trombone or cornet. This lad, a novice, is

Lancaster High School orchestra, 1904. (Photo courtesy of LancasterHistory.org.)

trying to keep time, another plays with more skillful touch, a third makes music worth hearing as it fills the air, and I think: 'Well! who knows? It is surely not the regulation work, but it may be a good curriculum after all!' It is such a school as I would like to live in if I were a boy again."[54]

Students organized their own groups, practiced in private homes, and performed independently. Richard Douglas McCaskey, McCaskey's second son and an 1883 Boys' High graduate, reported to the Alumni Association in 1900 that two of the current classes "have their own private little orchestras, which manage themselves because of the training they have received.[55] Some graduates became professional musicians. Alumni returned, on occasion, to perform with the orchestra.[56]

Lancaster High School was the first school in Pennsylvania (and, Thorbahn thought, perhaps, even in the country) to offer free instrumental instruction to its charges. Thorbahn asserted: "There should be more such schools, and there will be more of them when the men who make the school curriculum have grown wise enough to make school life include the few great things best worth knowing, among them music."[57] McCaskey did his part to promote free instruction across the country; he sent the 1904 photograph of Lancaster High's orchestra, which had been displayed at the St. Louis World's Fair, to city, county, and borough school superintendents throughout the U.S., along with a description of the orchestra's work and how it was organized.[58] Historian H. M. J. Klein maintained that Lancaster was considered the forerunner of all American cities in this area, being the first to pay the instructor's salary from the public school treasury.[59]

Hundreds of boys and girls sang in the chorus, and many participated in the instrumental instruction and orchestra. They performed throughout the year for Arbor Days, patriotic occasions, commencement, and Christmas. Small groups from the orchestra—trios, quartets, quintets, sextets, or septets—were featured, as were vocal duets and piano, violin, cornet, or clarinet solos.

Among McCaskey's 1906 class of students, many sang in the peer-directed Glee Club. Others sang in the chorus. They were tenors and basses; one had a "rumble-rumble-rumbling big bass voice." A few played instruments, including one who "play[ed] the piccolo in the orchestra when he [felt] like it." Another played a banjo. A third "had a drum and was in the High School Band, but the neighbors talked of the police and now he is out of practice and out of the orchestra." Several played the violin, like James Lane, the musician of the class. He worked on his for years; it was "one of Professor Thorbahn's best instruments, who not only makes the fiddle but also makes the artist-fiddler." And the favorite song of one of the rascals in this group was "Wait Till the Sun Shines, Nelly."[60]

When McCaskey pled the case for free instrumental instruction in the schools, calling forth the violins of Enoch Lytle and Johnny Wilson, he pondered the violins' value to his mother and himself: "What were those violins worth to her during all her long life? What have those violins of sixty or seventy years ago been worth to me? Put against them any bank in Lancaster—aye, all the banks—and I would still take the old violins. They mean more in the way of true riches."[61]

And what riches they have led to in the Lancaster city schools, where the tradition of fine vocal and instrumental work continues.

Chapter 14

Christmas All Year Long

"For thirty-three years we have given the day its blessed emphasis. With laurel and holly and reading and song it has been a joyous season to us all. The Christmas spirit has been in the air, and it has helped to put the 'Christmas all year long' into our hearts and our lives. We do not forget it; we will not forget it."[1]

If the genealogists in the McCaskey family are correct, mother Margaret's line can be traced all the way back to eighth-century Europe and Charles Martel, his son Pepin the Short, and to Pepin's son Charlemagne.[2] Charlemagne was crowned the first emperor of the Holy Roman Empire on Christmas Day, 800, by Pope Leo III, an act which established a church-state connection of enduring significance on the European continent.

A millennium later in Lancaster: John P. McCaskey loved Christmas. Granted, tracing that love via his pedigree to a dramatic event so far in the past is inordinately far-fetched, but he did love Christmas. He relished the holiday, calling it his favorite, and he imparted his enthusiasm to his students. The spirit of Christmas imbued the man, and he was a gift-giver of great magnitude throughout his life in philanthropic and charitable actions.

At the high school every December, students and staff decorated the study hall, rehearsed songs of the season, and prepared for the Christmas program. As McCaskey had done in the *Journal* for Arbor Day, he campaigned for Christmas festivities in the Commonwealth schools,[3] albeit not as intensely nor as long. December 25th approached, and Dr. McCaskey read Dickens' beloved narrative or "some other good thing" to his classes.[4] *A Christmas Carol* was "the story that Jack was accustomed to read to his boys, lessons having been laid aside during the school week preceding Christmas."[5] McCaskey recalled: "[H]ow [the boys] sang at Christmas time and how they laughed at Christmas time when Latin verbs and equations were buried hopelessly beneath red holly berries and best wishes."[6]

Preparations for the celebration began weeks earlier. Son Donald remembered that "[Father] always sent the senior class to the woods in teams the kids would dig up from some livery stable—and we'd gather laurel."[7] Diffenderffer wrote of the tradition: "Each year, during early December, the Senior or First Class, was permitted to take time off from school work to set out for the hills of Lancaster County to secure a supply of laurel and other greens. Then during later winter nights this class gathered in the spacious gymnasium 'to tie the greens.' Long festoons were made, tied to a stout string, and the night before the big event the boys hung the greens in the Study Hall, twining them among the tall Corinthian columns supporting the ceiling and around the windows. When the school assembled the next morning they viewed a fairy land of charm."[8] The swags, captured in a photo of the study hall,[9] remained in place until June every year.[10] Sometimes, the four numerals of the new year, such as 1-8-9-5, were fashioned in laurel and placed on the wall behind the teachers' desk.[11]

And there was the tree. Addressing alumni and students in 1904, McCaskey spoke of it: "You may talk of trees and forestry and Arbor Day, but, after all, what tree outranks the Christmas tree? Trees of all sorts, trees of all sizes, trees of all climes, trees for ornament, trees for shade, trees for fruit- . . . but tonight we all know that the greatest of all trees is the Christmas tree, . . . It is a tree of Life, and, like that of Paradise, it is 'for the healing of the nations.'"[12]

The boys and teachers gathered in the morning of the school day closest to Christmas for their own party, and the formal program for Lancaster

High School was held later on. For the latter, there were recitations such as "There's a Song in the Air" and "Calm on the Listening Ear of Night," and readings by individual students, like "Papa's Letter," "The Stranger at Christmas Eve," "Yule Log and Mistletoe," and "The Wise Men." McCaskey sometimes read the story of the nativity from the New Testament. The chorus and orchestra performed, and solos and duets were rendered. Alumni came; some participated in the musical offerings.

There were gifts for the students. Once they were given pictures from McCaskey's *Lincoln Art Series, The Doctor* for the boys and *The Better Land* for the girls.[13] At the close of every celebration, "heavy clothes-baskets, containing the familiar bags of choice fruits, nuts, and candies were brought in."[14] McCaskey distributed the bags. "Upon one side . . . the recipient was wished 'A Merry Christmas and a Happy New Year,' and upon the other was printed a pretty poem [such as] 'Christmas Bells.'"[15] Donald and his cohorts didn't just eat the contents: "We kids would throw the nuts and grapes at each other—AFTER THE DISTRIBUTION."[16]

There were gifts for the teachers, too, "except Miss Mary Martin, who would never accept a gift."[17] Mr. Gable received "fine pictures, beautifully framed"[18] one year. Mr. Thorbahn got "a very fine parlor lamp,"[19] and another year a cherry wood cabinet.[20] Dr. Matz received "a fine gold-headed cane"[21] and "a Meerschaum pipe and tobacco."[22] A turkey, once a "much be-ribboned" one,[23] went to Casper A. Weitzel, the school janitor, every year.

One time McCaskey was presented with a "beautiful mahogany table, finely finished," to which he responded with emotion as he spoke of the close relationship between teacher and student.[24] The next December a mahogany bookcase[25] complemented the table. Another year he got two rugs.[26] In 1905 up the aisle came a "handsome oak chair" carried aloft by several boys. It was for McCaskey, who expressed his thanks, saying the chair would last longer than he would, it was a very useful gift, and he liked "to sit about and take it easy," to which Matz was heard to utter, "Yes, you do!"[27]

The morning parties were quite boisterous. Loud cheers interrupted McCaskey's readings as other teachers arrived. Holiday singing stopped and started as gifts were paraded up to the teachers. Each item was presented with words of appreciation and admiration to which the recipient responded with sentiments both tender and jocular. Then the students resumed singing until there were no more seasonal songs left and "there sprang up quite a vocal rivalry. The seniors start[ed] with several of the class yells, at once followed by the other classes. Each did their best to out-do the other." Matz, the music man, was the arbiter of volume. The party ended with students and teachers exchanging Christmas greetings.[28]

The festivities were "a glorious occasion," student Diffenderffer remembered. "How we did sing the old familiar songs and carols. We really raised the rafters in our enthusiasm. . . . It was indeed a blessed memory. Who can forget it?"[29]

The 1890 Christmas season was blemished by an accident. In early December, while showing the third-floor gymnasium to a state education department official, McCaskey climbed a ladder and fell from the top rung (a distance of 40 feet, Donald claimed).[30] As a result, he was laid up at home and a teacher named Miss Musselman read his address at the holiday program on the 24th. In it, McCaskey greeted the students heartily and rued not being able to look into their eyes and see the joy of the season on their faces. The accident, unanticipated (for he had regarded himself as invincible, he explained), had started his holidays early. "I've done these ladders hundreds of times, never fell, never thought of falling, did not know that I could fall. It had been some time since I had tried to climb, and in the interval, weight had increased, and a good grip lost something of its certainty and staying power. All went well enough up to the last rung, when, the reach being a little short, the right hand slipped, the weight thrown suddenly on the left tore it away also, and down I went to a twisted ankle and a broken and badly bruised leg. Good friends, Dr. McCormick and Dr. Bolenius, were on the spot, fixed me up, and got me home; other good friends, Dr. Metzgar and Dr. Time, have been helping on the work of recovery."[31]

McCaskey, 53, was growing tired of being at home in "an easy chair that is losing somewhat of its attraction from being occupied too long." The holidays were not turning out as he had planned. However, the pain, weariness, and disability would pass, he insisted with characteristic optimism, and he would someday count them as a blessing. He was "so grateful, however, for what was escaped, that what is suffered seems of little account, and mars, in small degree even, the glad season of the Christmastide."[32] He even forgave the ladder: "As to the ladders and the gymnasium, do I stand by them as firmly as ever? Certainly, more firmly indeed, if that were possible."[33]

At the end of the program that afternoon, all the students walked down the hill to McCaskey's home and sang carols, accompanied by the orchestra.[34] Lancaster High School would not neglect its beloved principal, recuperating at home in the Christmas month!

In 1904, some alumni decided to honor McCaskey at his second-to-last Christmas program. There was a sense of urgency about it. After all, he was 67 years old and had been teacher and principal for 48 years. "It has been deemed best to hasten the collection of voluntary contributions, and go ahead with this matter while we have 'Jack' with us to appreciate our well-wishing."[35] Graduates, scattered from Maine to California, had been solicited for at least 50 cents towards a surprise for "their honored preceptor, Dr. J. P. McCaskey, as a token of personal esteem and appreciation." Money and congratulatory notes attesting to their teacher's indelible impact flowed in.[36]

The evening began with the tap of a bell at 8 p.m. Holiday songs were sung; orchestra music filled the air. The exuberance grew and "reverberate[d] through the old familiar halls."[37] Speeches were laced with superlatives for the principal and nostalgia for by-gone school days. "The exercises of the evening throughout partook of the nature of one long paean of unalloyed praise."[38] A paean it was, indeed.

McCaskey was ready with his own speech, for he had been tipped off by a friend that there was going to be a surprise.[39] As he went to the podium, all rose, applauding and cheering. He reminded his former students of what they had gained in that place: "Here it was that you lived and worked, or loafed and dreamed, got a fact now and then and picked up an idea now and then—ideas, you know, were always 'worth a dollar apiece,' much more than ordinary facts—or, what was more important still, got an impression of truth and duty—and slowly grew in weight physical, intellectual and spiritual."[40]

The surprise was a Loving Cup, and Frank B. McClain, a future mayor of Lancaster and Lieutenant-Governor of Pennsylvania, presented it, commenting: "On behalf of my fellow alumni, I present to you this beautiful Cup as a token of our esteem and of the appreciation we have for you. It tells its own story." McCaskey replied: "This loving cup is more than silver fretted with gold, more than gold studded with precious stones. It is of the immortal things that money cannot buy nor time destroy."[41]

The Loving Cup, today in the care of a great-great-grandson, is a finely crafted chalice of "solid silver, with ivory handles, and lined with gold."[42] It is inscribed with these words: "To John Piersol McCaskey—'Jack'—From 'Jack's Boys'—Lancaster High School—1855-1904. And thus he bore the grand old name of gentleman. We'll take the cup o' kindness yet—for Auld Lang Syne."[43]

The Loving Cup presented to McCaskey by his students in December 1904. (Photo courtesy of Megan McCaskey Johnson.)

At program's end, McCaskey stood again to speak. The tributes, he declared, were more unexpected than the Loving Cup, and he deflected all the praise that had rained down upon him that evening: "Men! How mistaken you can be! Your generous enthusiasm passes all bounds. Your kind hearts give credit for more than I have ever been or done. I have not done all that you have said. . . . But I am glad, all the same, to know that you feel like saying some of these things. You are very kind. I thank you out of a full heart, just as if what you say were all true. God bless you!"[44]

As the evening waned, all rose to sing "Auld Lang Syne." Then, McCaskey and his colleagues, Gable, Matz, and Thorbahn, just as they had done December after December in the study hall, received the boys on the old raised platform.[45]

December 1905 marked the last Christmas festivities over which McCaskey would preside. That evening, he expressed poignantly his and colleagues' love of the season and the school: "For thirty-three years we have given the day its blessed emphasis. With laurel and holly and reading and song it has been a joyous season to us all. The Christmas spirit has been in the air, and it has helped to put the 'Christmas all year long' into our hearts and our lives."[46]

Perhaps, an historian has suggested, McCaskey's enthusiasm for the holiday sprang from his childhood memories of gathering greens when he was enrolled at Oak Hill Academy in Paradise.[47] McCaskey recalled a day in December 1848 when he and Jim, James Buchanan's nephew, were given the task of fetching box-wood clippings from the school grounds for decorating All Saints' Episcopal Church, a mile away. The shuttling back and forth in a horse-drawn wagon undoubtedly made for some merry moments, with Jim doing the driving: "[D]idn't he drive 'like Jehu'—that boy? And didn't I enjoy it—backwards and forward again and again?"[48]

Then, again, perhaps it was already in his genes. . .

"Jolly Old Saint Nicholas" was often sung at the high school Christmas programs. Still popular today, it is heard everywhere—in schools, shopping malls, on the radio, television, and the internet. Lancastrians have long been convinced that McCaskey wrote the words and Dr. Matz the music.[49] However, the names McCaskey and Matz are not printed with the piece in any of the popular songbooks which McCaskey compiled. He never credited himself as the song's lyricist nor Matz as composer, which he did for works they collaborated on.[50] Rather, he sometimes gave "Anonymous" the nod and usually noted that he had obtained permission to print the song from S. Brainard's Sons, publisher of *School Chimes*, the publication in which the music and lyrics first appeared in 1874. Over the next 130 years or so, "Anonymous" has allowed for speculation (outside of Lancaster) that the lyricist was Benjamin R. Hanby, who wrote "Up on the Housetop," because of the texts' similarities. The composer was most likely James Ramsey Murray.[51]

The truth is that neither Hanby nor McCaskey penned the words. Emily Huntington Miller, an author, poet, hymnist, and editor of *The Little Corporal* and *St. Nicholas*, children's publications, wrote the text, a poem entitled "Lilly's Secret." Published in December 1865 in *The Little Corporal*, the words remain basically the same today:

"LILLY'S SECRET"

Jolly old St. Nicholas,
Lean your ear this way!
Don't you tell a single soul
What I'm going to say.
Christmas Eve is coming soon!
Now, you dear old man,
Whisper what you'll bring to me;
Tell me if you can.

When the clock is striking twelve.
When I'm fast asleep,
Down the chimney broad and black,
With your pack you'll creep.
All the stockings you will see
Hanging in a row;
Mine will be the shortest one—,
You'll be sure to know.
Johnny wants a pair of skates.
Susy wants a dolly,
Nelly wants a story book—
She thinks dolls a folly.
As for me, my little brain
Never was the wisest.
Choose for me, old Santa Claus,
What you think is nicest.[52]

The belief that McCaskey wrote the words for "Jolly Old St. Nicholas" was most likely spawned in a 1967 Lancaster newspaper article, "100-Year-Old Secret." In it, son Donald was quoted as saying that "one Christmastime, while they were singing the song, he asked his father who wrote the words, and McCaskey responded, 'Donald, I did.'" The reporter also identified the three persons—Johnny, Susy, and Nelly—named in the song as familiar to McCaskey.[53] A 1970 article added Matz as the composer.[54] Repetitions of this information have been published in the local papers and biographical sketches of McCaskey ever since.

During the 1960s, Donald, who was living in California, and Lancastrian Harold F. Diffenderffer, both octogenarians, exchanged lengthy letters about McCaskey. Life-long friends, the two were 1894 graduates of Boys' High and therefore throwers-of-candy and belters-out-of-songs at the Christmas festivities. Their correspondence reveals a compulsion to preserve McCaskey's reputation. Donald had prepared a four-page biographical sketch of his father, "The Untold J. P. McCaskey Story," which he sent to "Diffy."[55] This may have inspired Diffenderffer to write "Life and Times of John Piersol McCaskey," an invaluable 11-page sketch published in the *Lan-*

caster County Historical Society Journal in 1963 and cited often in this book. Up to that point, it was the only account of McCaskey other than those published half a century or more previously, two authored by McCaskey himself.

Donald, regarded as an eccentric by his grandnieces and grandnephews,[56] was effusive in his letters, adventurous and quirky in his life. Townsend, his son, did not fall too far from that tree of adjectives, either. However, while most of the facts they recorded have been substantiated, Donald's claim of McCaskey's authorship of the Christmas ditty was more wishful thinking than anything else. The leap from Donald's claim to certainty among McCaskey descendants and Lancastrians was fueled by several coincidences. McCaskey's love of Christmas was well known, and he had a propensity for self-deprecation, but this was not unusual for the times. Emily Huntington Miller's persona does, too: Santa will recognize the persona's stocking because it is the shortest one, and Santa will have to choose a gift for the child because his or her brain "isn't very bright." Additionally, the names Susy, Nelly, and Johnny were commonplace then. McCaskey knew a Susy, who was a niece of his secretary, Elizabeth McVey, and Nellie was his sister-in-law. And Johnny, who wants a pair of skates? He was John Sidney McCaskey, fourth child of McCaskey and Ellen.

Of their seven biological children, McCaskey and Ellen lost three to early deaths, two in the same summer. Helen Wilson McCaskey died in her infancy in July 1875; the next month Johnny died at age seven. Elsie Piersol McCaskey lived 23 years and died in 1904.

When Johnny died, McCaskey said in 1896, he went away to "that better school where, for twenty years or more, he has known angelic training and association."[57] On another occasion, McCaskey spoke of a time when Johnny was still alive: "There was hung for a long time in my room [a picture of] a beautiful head of a child, to which years ago I would sometimes address a familiar greeting, much to the surprise of my sturdy little boy, who couldn't understand why I should speak so to 'Winnie' [the picture]. His [Johnny's] great, truthful eyes look into those of the angels now, but the picture hangs there still, and while I live will hang, recalling [Johnny] more tenderly than even his life-like portrait not far away."[58]

Elsie was attended in her dying by her mother. In a 1901 letter to Nellie, McCaskey wrote: "Elsie is quite an invalid. Poor girl, she has a hard fight of it, and it looks like a failing fight, but she is brave and patient through it all. She and her mother send love and best wishes to you all. Ellen is a famous nurse. Elsie could not have a better."[59]

The surviving children were Edward William, Richard Douglas, Walter Bogardus, Donald Gilbert, and a foster son, William Solomon (Sol) Gordon. At McCaskey and Ellen's 50th wedding anniversary celebration, McCaskey spoke to the men about their deceased siblings: "And you have lost a brother, a sturdy lad of seven summers, to whom everybody was attracted because of his unconscious individuality and amiable disposition. He is now forty-two years old. What a man he will be for us to meet and to know on that other side!"[60] About the girls, McCaskey said, "Your two sisters have passed beyond; one of them long since in babyhood, the other but yesterday, it seems, as she stood upon the threshold of womanhood. And both of them, now, we fondly believe, are in the bloom of immortal youth in that better land of which we talk and dream!"[61]

Christmas in Song, Sketch, and Story, edited by McCaskey and published in 1891 by Harper and Brothers, New York, was his homage to the holiday he loved above all others. With over 300 pages, it is a large, sumptuous volume bound in red buckram with gold ornamentation on the front cover and spine. The work contains nearly 300 Christmas songs nestled within seven lengthy prose selections by Charles Dickens, Henry Ward Beecher, Berthold Auerbach and others. Twenty-two illustrations by masters such as Raphael and Murillo and contemporary artists like Thomas Nast grace separate pages throughout the book. The extravagant publication sold for $2.50. It was hailed in superlative terms ("luxurious," "elevating," "ex-

McCaskey's Christmas book. (Photos courtesy of B. David Wagner.)

quisite," "astonishing amount of material," "selections judiciously made," "the true spirit of Christmas expressed in song, in art, and in prose") in secular and Christian publications from Boston, New York, Philadelphia, Chicago, and elsewhere.[62]

McCaskey's "hobby," as he called it, of collecting and publishing favorite songs[63] preserved Christmas carols for the American public, according to an historical paper from 1939: "If one man, more than another, has made a lasting contribution to the joys of Christmas in America, it is Dr. J. P. McCaskey. In . . . his [songbooks] . . . there are to be found practically all the finest Christmas carols in the language . . . and there are few of us who did not first learn 'Deck the halls with boughs of holly,' 'Carol, carol, Christians,' 'Christmas bells are sounding clear,' 'Christ was born on Christmas Day,' and many others from his pages. They might all have eventually found their way into our schools and homes from other sources, but it seems certain that they would not have reached us in such bountiful profusion if 'Old Jack' had not been so eager a collector of melodies."[64]

McCaskey's name is correctly linked to "Jolly Old St. Nicholas" because of his inclusion of it in almost every one of his songbooks.

Ten years before the Christmas tome, the first of an eight-volume set of songbooks compiled by McCaskey came out. Just as he had recognized the absence of textbooks, or "readers," for memory work and therefore produced them, so, too, he realized the need for songbooks. He explained in the introduction: "The only apology for this Song Collection which the Compiler presents is that he has wanted some such book, and, not finding it, has tried to make it."[65] Entitled the *Franklin Square Song Collection: Two Hundred Favorite Songs and Hymns for Schools and Homes, Nursery and Fireside*, it was an expansion of his *Pennsylvania Song Collection*, printed in Lancaster in 1875, which itself was the result of needing to fill a void.[66]

Convincing Harper and Brothers, a New York firm, to publish the first of the series was a hard sell: "So little interested were the Harpers in the book when he offered it to them—the plates all ready for press, and costing at that time about seven dollars each—that they refused to publish

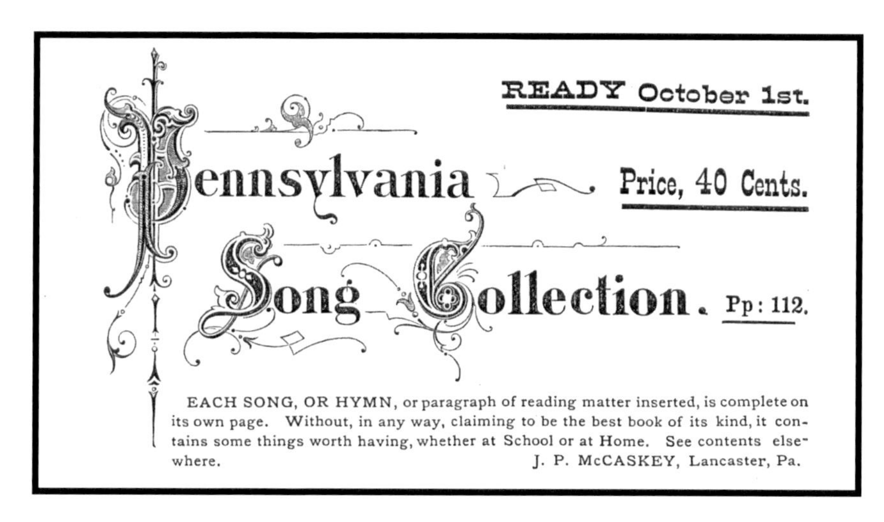

Ad for McCaskey's first songbook in The Pennsylvania School Journal, *October 1875.*

it on any terms, saying their music books had always been a failure. He was resolved to put the book on their list . . . and finally did so on agreement that they should pay him *one cent* royalty on each book sold! The retail price of the book was forty cents, paper cover. They sold *sixty thousand* copies at this rate on which he was paid but six hundred dollars. The copyright royalty was then made more equitable."[67] The remaining seven volumes appeared over the next decade, the last in 1892. The first several were published by the reluctant Harper and Brothers, later ones by the American Book Company.

Publication by a large house guaranteed that the books would be sold and distributed all over the country, and sell they did by the hundreds of thousands.[68] By McCaskey's accounting, he made "about 5,000 music plates of octavo size, 5 ¼ x 8 ¼ inches,"[69] many of which were stored in the vaults of the Wickersham and New Era printing companies in Lancaster.[70] He used the plates over and over again, e.g., in subsequent songbooks, song booklets for the Teachers' Institute meetings, and monthly issues of the *Pennsylvania School Journal.*

The songs were scored for piano in four parts, and each fit on one page. McCaskey filled spaces above and below the songs with reading material, "additional matter of interest and value."[71] The music plates were recycled, and so were these texts. They were written by theologians, scientists, poets, writers, historians, philosophers past and contemporary, and others. McCaskey penned some entries himself, employing the rhetorical convention of "we" rather than "I". He also included the stories behind the songs, information he gathered from the lyricists or composers themselves such as Samuel F. Smith, author of "America."[72] Topics ranged from overcoming shyness to education, nursery rhymes to mythology, health to evenings at home, patriotism to art, nature to religion, history to courtesy, and from human failings to money and immortality. While most are informational or didactic, some are humorous and a few quite poignant. In a subsequent publication in 1899, *Favorite Songs and Hymns for School and Home*, over 120 of the 175 items treat music in some way; McCaskey authored 71.

Between 1903 and 1906, McCaskey published the *Flag of the Free Song Collection* himself, of which 250,000 copies were sold all over the United States.[73] He also published his last songbook series, *A Treasury of Favorite Song, Songs and Hymns of the Millions of Yesterday, To-Day and To-Morrow*, in Lancaster in 1916. The three volumes are hardbacks of excellent quality, with an olive green cloth cover and gilt lettering on the spine; they include over 1,860 songs and hymns. At the end of Volume I, as in most of the previous songbooks, are "Elements of Music," eight pages of music theory. These are 100 points divided into three areas: "Rhythmics: Length of Tones," "Melodics: Pitch of Tones," and "Dynamics: Power of Tones." Music theory was not to be ignored.

Fourteen years later, in 1930 when McCaskey was 93 and still publishing *Treasury of Song*, he sought a publisher to continue the work, for he could not "much longer continue to enjoy this delightful 'hobby.'" He was willing to allow a title change and additions, for "this work should be carried on for generations and such a Cyclopedia should be within reach of any who wish it."[74] It had been his joy, he wrote, in "bringing together the old songs and hymns of the millions."[75]

McCaskey's joy in music had begun under the spell of his mother's beautiful voice and the violins on the farm so many years before. The first volume of *Treasury of Song* begins with a moving tribute to Margaret Piersol McCaskey and credits her with giving "impulse to the successive numbers of the *Franklin Square Collection* . . . and to other song books and music pamphlets that have afforded pleasure and benefit." She would, he wrote, "be glad to know of these books."[76]

Middle class Victorians had both the leisure time and money to make music at home, and songbooks compiled by McCaskey perched on pianos all over the United States and in other countries, too. Many of the selections were "parlor songs," and he painted a "joyous picture of domestic happiness": a family gathered around the piano, singing.[77] Music in the home, he maintained, created a healthy environment and kept the children out of trouble: "The blending of the voices of parents and children in song strengthens the ties that bind them together and the love that centres [sic] about the home fireside. It renders home attractive, interesting, and beautiful; and . . . there will be found a greater freedom from all those discords and inharmonious contentions that render so many parents miserable and their children anxious to find a more congenial atmosphere elsewhere."[78]

The blending of instruments and voices filled the large brick house at 304 West King. Donald played violin and cornet; Walter and Elsie violin; and nephew Hiram the flute. At the end of the 50th wedding anniversary party, the family adjourned to the parlor and "the merry company sang over and over again, to the lead of the violin and piano, a golden wedding song with ringing chorus: 'Put on your old gray bonnet/ With the blue ribbons on it,/ While I hitch old Dobbin to the shay;/ We will drive up to Dover/ On our golden wedding day.' And many another good old song came after."[79]

The great-grandchildren remembered music at 304. McCaskey, by the 1930s, spent much of his time in his second floor bedroom, and young

Kay McCaskey Adelman and her brother James McCaskey, often went there in the evenings to listen to singing from the parlor beneath them. In the bedroom floor was a grate through which heat from the potbelly stove below ascended. The two would remove the grate to hang their heads down in the opening and see the people gathered around the piano. Kay said, "Everybody used to come and everybody sang, but I particularly remember the choir [which included her parents] from St. Mary's [Roman Catholic Church]. . . . J. P. might have been sleeping," Kay thought.[80] Maybe he wasn't.

Kay and James had Christmas memories from 304, too. Kay played hide 'n seek with her friends among the December evergreens that were being sold from the terraced property at the back of the house.[81] Also, up in great-grandfather's room, the pair peered through the same grate opening and watched as grownups placed presents under the Christmas tree, thereby putting an end to the children's belief in Santa Claus.[82] James recalled their father playing guitar and piano and singing in a "strong and beautiful voice" during the holiday season.[83]

Grandson Townsend, too, remembered Christmas eve in his grandparents' home: the music box, his Uncle Ed playing the piano, and "greens from a dozen fir trees" that hung "behind each picture in that old house making it smell like a pine forest and then the Christmas carols at that time [and] sometimes there were 40 people in the house with the . . . doorbell ringing all the time as citizens came by to pay their respects to J.P."[84]

"Getting and giving are the rule of Christmas time," McCaskey said, "but getting without gratitude and giving without gladness have, in neither of them, the spirit of the Christmas Gift. Giving is better than getting."[85] All right, then, how much should one give? "[O]ur giving should be to the limit of our means and opportunity."[86]

McCaskey certainly gave to the limit of his means and opportunities. He spent several hundred dollars each year on the Christmas bags.[87] He bought instruments to loan or give to his students. He subsidized, in order to keep the student ticket price low, a week-long exhibition at the Fulton on world travel and art, including the final evening's display of over 100 statues and busts.[88] For the Star Club, he paid part of the cost of an astronomy lecture at the Fulton and the entire cost for a second one.[89] In 1912, he sent 1,000 volumes to the Marble, Colorado, library.[90]

McCaskey intervened when a lecture by Henry Ward Beecher, a prominent American minister and supporter of the abolition of slavery and other causes, was about to be canceled at the Fulton in 1875. Reputed to be a womanizer, Beecher had been on trial that summer for adultery, a trial which resulted in a hung jury and a more tarnished reputation. McCaskey, who admired Beecher and had attended his lectures and heard him preach at Plymouth Church in Brooklyn, New York, acted to keep the evening scheduled. He bought up some of the tickets,[91] advertised the event in the newspapers, and used his printing skills to make up large posters and circulars for display in the city and county. Over 1,000 tickets were sold, so many that extra seats had to be set up on the stage.[92] McCaskey took great satisfaction in having given Beecher such a large audience, for he believed Beecher to have been "foully maligned."[93]

On memorial committees of the Pennsylvania State Teachers' Association, McCaskey made up the difference when contributions fell short of the costs, a deficit that amounted to more than $3,000.[94] He donated pictures from his *Lincoln Art Series* and portraits of William Penn, George Washington, Benjamin Franklin, Abraham Lincoln, and Thaddeus Stevens to schools, St. James, and also the YWCA in honor of his mother.[95]

McCaskey and Ellen welcomed several of his brothers, an aunt, in-laws, and his secretary as permanent residents at 304. Family members and sometimes entire families who lost everything in the Great Depression moved in and out, sleeping three to a bed.[96] In 1889, the couple also took in Sol Gordon, a teenager from Russia, whom they raised along with their children, encouraging him to practice his own faith and helping him to finish high school and attend college and law school. Great-grandson Edward recalled the story:

"When Grandpa was Principal of the High School, the janitor brought him a youngster he found sleeping near the furnace. Grandpa asked him why he slept there and the young fellow replied that in Odessa (Russia) the Shul (school) was the seat of learning. When he came to America and had no place to stay, he

thought he might learn something if he slept in the High School. Grandpa was so impressed that he took the boy home and raised him with his own children. His name was Solomon (Sphoont). Grandpa couldn't call him Solomon McCaskey, so his name was changed to William S. Gordon. Grandpa not only raised him, but insisted that he tend to his religious duties as a Jew. Uncle Sol went to Yale, Yale Law School, and became a prominent attorney in New York City."[97]

McCaskey's generosity extended to strangers, as well. He owned properties in the city and did not evict tenants if they fell behind in their rent.[98] On West King Street, at 304, when the main meal of the day was about to be served at noontime, Olive Carpenter, the McCaskeys' housekeeper, would often answer a knock at the front door to find a hungry man waiting on the stoop. McCaskey would rise from the table, escort the stranger in and, with a sweep of his arm, direct him to the unoccupied place at the table, next to his own, and say: "My good man, can't you see we've been expecting you?"[99]

For McCaskey, it wasn't just Christmas all year long, it was Christmas his whole life long.

Chapter 15

THE BEST GOOD OF ALL

"Is this politics? It is the high-water mark of the best politics I know. It is the ideal towards which high-souled men are striving everywhere: The best good of all."[1]

"Gentlemen: Though little conscious of failing vigor, either mental or physical, I decided two years ago to retire from the school work at the end of fifty years' service. Election since then to the office of Mayor changes resolve into duty. My work at the Boys' High School is done."[2]

So began McCaskey's letter of resignation to the school board. Regret for not having done his job better, gratitude for the opportunity, and a Biblical connection between himself and St. Paul was followed then by his estimation that the measure of life and work depended solely on the quality of each: "The gauge of life is not the number of its years, but what the years have been; and in this school they have been to me both many and good. . . . Nothing is left but our work, and that is worth leaving only as it is worthy."[3]

In 1906, McCaskey stepped out of 50 years at Boys' High and into the next four at City Hall.

It had not been McCaskey's intention to seek political office. He had not thought of becoming mayor, had not lain awake at night waiting for some sign to do so, nor had he contemplated ways to gain "distinction of any sort."[4] His retirement plans included travel and then more work before his demise. He told the Young Men's Republican Club in early February 1906 that he "had been dreaming quietly of going beyond the sea for a brief holiday, the first in forty years, to ease up the pull upon the collar, to live for a while carefree as to clock or almanac . . . and to visit some places abroad in which I have long been interested. . . . Then to push on for another ten or twenty years—so I have been dreaming—broadening upon certain lines of work for which thus far time has been wanting, and slowly 'getting my house in order' for the end of earth."[5]

However, former students had urged him to run. They were so adamant that they formed an organization called "Jack's Boys."[6] He acquiesced: "But good friends, especially old High School boys, have urged me to follow the High School with a term in the mayor's office. I care as much to oblige the boys as to be elected Mayor. . . . [T]he call comes to me at a time when I can heed it, and I do so, believing it a call of duty."[7] He had actually warmed to the challenge, he admitted, like his ancestors, whose blood stirred in him still: "The fact is, I believe I like it. My ancestors of five or six generations ago were from the brave hill country and rugged mountains of Scotland and Wales and Switzerland. They were all fighting men upon occasion, and the fire has not yet—not all of it, at least—died out of their quick red blood."[8]

Several days before the February 20 election, an "imposing street parade,"[9] organized by "Jack's Boys" took place. The Iroquois Band led the procession from the Wheatland Hotel and headed through Center Square and on to the Swan Hotel and the Plow Tavern. The ranks swelled along the way as members of the Citizens' Club, the Young Republicans, and the nine city ward clubs stepped into the lines. A drum corps fell in near the last pick-up spot. Then the entourage turned down West King Street, "handsomely illuminated with red lights."[10] All in all, a spectacle of sound and sight to behold.

When the participants reached 304 West King, they sent up three hearty cheers. McCaskey came out on his stoop and delighted them "by stepping with the agility of one much younger to the head of the procession and treading with his admirers" to Fulton Opera House where a grand rally followed,[11] this a loud, enthusiastic riposte to the Democrats' charge that Jack's boys were not supporting him.[12]

★ Song by Dr. McCaskey ★

"Flag of the Free."

Flag of the Free! all turn to thee,—
Golden thy stars in the blue of their sky:
Flag of the brave! onward to save!
Crimson thy bars floating gaily on high!
* * * * * *
All hail, "Old Glory!" hearts leap to see
How from the nations the world looks to thee.
[Air: Wedding March from Lohengrin, page 2.]

"E Pluribus Unum."

Forever float that standard sheet! Where breathes the foe but falls before us,
With Freedom's soil beneath our feet, and Freedom's Banner streaming o'er us.

Grand Rally at Fulton Opera House,
FRIDAY EVENING, FEBRUARY 16, 1906,
Of High School Boys of many classes in honor of Dr. J. P. McCaskey, their old-time Teacher, in support of his candidacy for Mayor of Lancaster, at the close of Fifty Years of service in the Lancaster High School. Addresses by High School "Boys" and others.

Prof. Carl Matz will direct the Singing by the Old Boys of the High School.

Cover of the program for the rally at the Fulton, February 16, 1906.

The old theater house, with seats for over 900, was packed "from pit to roof;" hundreds more could not squeeze in. The stage was decorated with greens, the American flag, and festoons of red, white, and blue bunting. Enthusiasm ran high. The evening was filled with "[h]ilarious ovation[s] . . . tumultuous cheering . . . walls reverberat[ing] with the mighty choruses" sung by the audience.[13] Among the attendees were a few women; McCaskey family members occupied one of the boxes. Distributed were "button-hole flags and handsome souvenir programmes" which contained a "fine likeness of the candidate," a prior speech of his, and the songs for the evening: the "Star Spangled Banner, "Flag of the Free," (lyrics written by McCaskey set to the tune of the "Wedding March" from Wagner's *Lohengrin*), "We'll Rally Round the Flag," the "Battle Hymn of the Republic," and "Auld Lang Syne."[14]

On election night large crowds, equipped with noise-makers, gathered downtown. Returns from the wards, chalked on blackboards outside newspaper offices, see-sawed between candidates. Of the 11,000 registered voters, 10,247 cast ballots that day, the most ever in Lancaster elections, including presidential races.[15] At 10 p.m. on February 20, 68-year-old J. P. McCaskey was declared the winner, defeating Milton T. Garvin by only 73 votes.[16] Apparently, the Democrats among Jack's Boys yielded to party rather than teacher. The margin was narrow, but it was a victory, nonetheless, and that evening "McCaskey enthusiasm broke loose and ran rampant over all the city." Bands, once again, led cheering admirers to the McCaskey home.[17]

Addressing the throng from the marble stoop, McCaskey expressed his humility at being elected and a recognition that he was about to embark on an unfamiliar course. However, he would try to do his best, and he acknowledged his faith in his party: "Well, the old party is good enough for us. I voted for Abraham Lincoln in 1860, and for the noble line of Republican Presidents since his time down to Theodore Roosevelt, the peerless leader of today in our American political life."[18]

McCaskey embraced political parties and different perspectives: "We need parties, and a wide latitude in the expression of opinion must always

Mayor McCaskey to the left of door; unidentified man in the center; Howard Wilson to right of door; Lancaster Central Market building to the right of City Hall. (Photo courtesy of LancasterHistory.org.)

The former City Hall, now functioning as a visitors' center. (Photo courtesy of the author.)

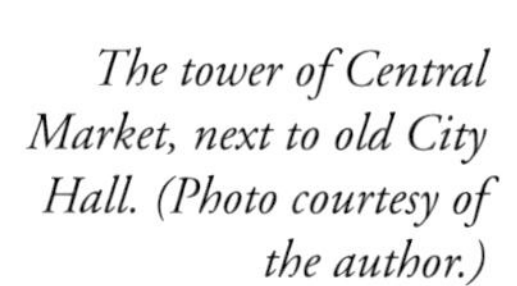

The tower of Central Market, next to old City Hall. (Photo courtesy of the author.)

be encouraged, [so] that mistaken views may be corrected and abuse of opportunity in public office checked and punished."[19] Criticism was beneficial: "We need good men to manage our municipal affairs, . . . There has never been a time when everybody was content with civic conditions. Criticism and condemnation are always to be looked for, and are often most helpful."[20] City politics had other requirements, as well: "We need good temper and good sense, good purpose, good will, good friends, and good foes."[21] Among McCaskey's foes was the *Intelligencer Journal*, which labeled him "a blameless blind man"[22] and over the next four years made him out to be a puppet for the "bosses" William W. Griest, H. L. Trout, and Ex-Mayor Cummings.[23]

The morning after the 1906 election, Mayor-elect McCaskey went around the corner and five minutes up the Mulberry Street hill to the high school, as he had on his ambles of the past 30 years. The study hall was decorated with flags and bunting, and on his desk was a "large box of beautiful daffodils," behind it his picture. The boys congratulated him and cheered and sang patriotic songs.[24]

That study hall, where Christmas songs and holiday wishes and violins and voices had filled the space, where 40 Arbor Day programs had transpired, where maxims for living reminded the boys to be of good character, where portraits of presidents and educators kept vigil . . . that study hall was full of laughter and congratulatory cheers.

McCaskey's new ten-minute morning walk would lead from his front door east down hilly West King Street for a block and then up two more to City Hall, a strong brick building that anchors yet the northwest corner of Penn Square (formerly Center Square) and serves today as the Lancaster Visitors' Center.

Lancaster's 23rd mayor, John Piersol McCaskey, was sworn into office April 2, 1906, at 12 noon, in City Hall before council members, family, and close friends.[25] In his inaugural address he thanked his Republican predecessor, Mayor Cummings, for installing a water filtration plant that brought "pure, clean, wholesome water" to every household in the city. He praised Lancaster: "Where can you find a better, or safer, or more home-like, or more comfortable town in all the land in which to live? We do have a cyclone, a landslide, or an earthquake at times in the way of a strenuous election, but our good temper survives it, our good markets survive it, and the Conestoga brand of water, one of the best in the world, when at its best, is just as good after such a roiling as before it."[26]

In the speech, McCaskey tracked the city's growth in population (over 4,000 in 1800 to an estimated 50,000 in 1906) and property values (five times greater than in 1855). He listed all the mayors from 1818 to 1906 and noted that in 10 of the 31 races since 1856, including his, the winner won by fewer than 100 votes, one by a single vote.[27] (McCaskey did much better in his 1908 re-election, defeating opponent Charles M. Howe by 1,607 votes.[28]) He listed issues he would deal with while in office, including water, lighting, street improvements and extensions, transportation into and out of the city, expanded city limits, the school system, and city parks. He promised to do his best and not disappoint. In conclusion, he apologized for mistakes he might make, offering the solace of brevity: "For mistakes and shortcomings I ask your indulgence in advance. Those of my fellow citizens to whom these may seem to be serious will be consoled by the reflection—that it is not for long."[29]

In his second inaugural address, McCaskey acknowledged that he had not accomplished a lot in his first term: "Things about us are much the same." He laid the blame at the feet of an underfunded city treasury. However, he said, "the ordinary work of the city has been carried along with efficiency, good-will and right purpose. We are getting something done."[30]

Among the "ordinary" work of the city that he and the councils tended to was the safety of her citizens. The new water filtration system, which had made Lancaster's water safe—the number of typhoid cases was down—was costing too much. McCaskey, after his first year in office, wondered, "What good citizen of Lancaster would be willing to go back to the raw water of the Conestoga, and take the chances of the stream, as we did until within the past fifteen months?"[31] And yet, citizens were paying less for their water than it cost the city to provide it. McCaskey's remedy was conservation achieved by raising the price: "Our rates should be such as to encourage the habit of saving water, just as we save gas and electricity, by shutting it off when it is not needed." Each of the 50,000 city residents (including children) was using two hogsheads (about 126 gallons) per day, a total of six million gallons or more city-wide. The mayor suggested a reduction to one and a half hogsheads, thereby saving citizens money while increasing the revenue to operate the water works.[32]

The mayor's call to conserve went unheeded. He requested another review of the rates in 1908. Citizens were still consuming two hogsheads daily for bathing, cooking, laundry, washing horses and carriages or horseless carriages, and whatever else they did with the liquid while the cost remained 5 cents per 1,000 gallons. Spigots, evidently, were not being shut off. By 1909 nearly 7 million gallons of water were being pumped, thus exceeding two hogsheads per person, but the cost stayed the same, and the city was still losing money.

At one point, McCaskey was accused of planning to privatize the water system by selling it to the Susquehanna Railway, Light and Power Company. This he denied: "I have no knowledge of any design or purpose looking to the transfer of the city water works to private or corporate control. . . . I am sure the people of Lancaster would not tolerate any such move, and this fact has been so well established that I regard any mention of such a proposition as highly ridiculous. Nor is there any necessity for raising funds in that way."[33] The water system was not privatized.

The fire department needed upgrading. When McCaskey began as mayor, it could have used a newer fire truck with 85-foot extensions to be set in place more quickly than the old Hayes truck from 1882 with its 65-foot ladder.[34] In fact, the department needed an overhauling of all its equipment and more men to stay at the engine houses. It needed more men, period.[35] It had 5 steamers, 5 hose carts, 1 antiquated hook and ladder truck, 17 horses, and 48 men. A sixth fire company, for the northern part of the city, should be added.[36] When the mayor gave his final annual message, the department was still without a truck with 85-foot ladders, additional men, or a sixth firehouse.[37]

McCaskey was concerned with Lancastrians' safety on the streets and sidewalks. He urged the police to enforce the speed limit of 10 miles per hour;[38] automobiles nationwide were traveling too fast and maiming and killing pedestrians. He had 100 blue "No Spitting" signs placed around town: "$1 fine for spitting on walks. Please avoid it." Repeat expectorators were to be arrested.[39] Before the 1906 Fourth of July, the mayor reminded citizens about the law prohibiting sale or use of explosives, including trick matches, and he cautioned boys not to put caps on the trolley tracks. The boys might enjoy it, he said, but not everyone did.[40]

Citizens committing petty crimes were judged and sentenced by their mayor in police court, e.g., city garbage collector James Dussinger, who was arrested for disorderly conduct. Dussinger's garbage wagon and team of horses had been commandeered by a young woman, who whipped the horses into a full gallop and went careening from Duke to Walnut to Queen to Lemon and then to Prince before she was finally stopped on Clay Street. The explanation that the girl was known to become "mentally unbalanced at times" did not placate Dussinger, who lost his self-control, and so was hauled before His Honor and fined.[41]

McCaskey's celebrated "morning talks" at Boys' High morphed into lectures to the scallywags brought before him. Twelve young men, ages 15-27, had been hanging around near a coal yard playing craps and insulting passersby. Warned by younger boys serving as their pickets, they hooted and jeered when the police arrived. McCaskey gave the perpetrators "a scathing lecture on their conduct" and imposed fines and costs.[42] Sometimes, the penalty was waived if offenders could recite the Ten Commandments. Unfortunately, four rowdy F&M students were not able to do so, and, besides, they didn't know Latin and Greek, either.[43]

"Laws and ordinances are still disregarded, as they have always been. . . . The commands of the Decalogue are still violated, notably the first, third, ninth—and the rest of them," McCaskey lamented.[44] Undaunted, he pressed for enforcement. He ordered arcade shows to be stopped and morally offensive posters to be removed from the city streets.[45] Licentiousness was being delivered through the mail, and McCaskey appealed to local members of the National Letter Carriers' Association to be more vigilant in their handling of the mail. Acknowledging that they handled a large volume each day, he said, "But now and then a foul thing, mailed in violation of the law of the land, as well as of common decency, slips through your hands."[46]

The fourth of the Ten Commandments, keeping the Sabbath day holy, was the rationale behind the Blue Laws in the state; these prohibited sales and conducting business on Sundays. Early in McCaskey's first term, some cigar vendors, grocers, butchers, druggists, and confectioners in the city were flouting the law, which prompted a contingent of clergy to prevail upon the mayor to do whatever he could for enforcement.[47] Saying that he would prefer no business or work of any sort on Sundays, McCaskey promised to help the ministers as he could. The *Intelligencer Journal*, reporting on this, made him out to be an old fool who wept at the thought of merchants being open on Sundays.[48] In its coverage of the same event, the *Daily New Era*, always a McCaskey supporter, made no mention of tears from the mayor.[49]

McCaskey was unable to halt the inevitable, but he decided in November 1908 to draw the line for the center of town. He issued a statement about a Greek merchant in the first block of North Queen Street who "persisted in doing business on Sunday in violation of city ordinances."[50] Acknowledging that some businesses did Sunday trading, he accepted that precedent, leaving it up to the conscience of the individual and the guild (trade organization) to which the person belonged. However, he would fine anyone doing business on the "principal streets," King and Queen, in the center of the city.[51] The offender, confectioner John Roumanis, contended that he needed the trade to help cover his rent, and so paid $6.87 in fines and costs every week, doing so "cheerfully."[52] Neither mayor nor candy vendor relented. By September 1909, Roumanis had paid $6.87 fifty-nine times.[53] The *Intelligencer* kept track. The *New Era* did not.

McCaskey had referred to the Blue Laws as "sky blue," appropriate, he asserted, because the color suggested looking upward in gratitude and aspiring to life eternal beyond the blue dome.[54] The *Intelligencer* pounced on "sky blue" and printed a poem mocking the self-righteous, weepy (yet again!) mayor:

A WARNING TO ST. PETER

"Our mayor is such a pious man," said Jackboy to Skyblue;
"He goes to church on Sunday and sits in a front pew;
He's such a Christian gentleman, he always says his prayers:

'Give us this day our daily bread and forgive our trespasses.'
And the way he used to lecture us, when we were boys at school,
About the Ten Commandments and the shining golden rule,
And doing to our neighbors as we'd like to be done by,
Oft brought deep sorrow to our hearts and tear drops to his eye."

"Oh! the mayor is such a funny chap," said Skyblue to Jackboy;
"I think his piety must be ninety-nine percent alloy.
If he has so much religion, why does he persecute the Greek
For selling Tutti Fruitti on the seventh day of the week,
And overlook the beer clubs that are holding forth all day
And all the other places where they neither fast nor pray?
Yes, the mayor is so religious that when he goes to heaven,
If St. Peter opens the gates on Sunday—he'll be fined six-eighty-
seven."[55]

McCaskey died, in fact, on a Thursday, thus enabling St. Peter to conduct business as usual.

Censorship also figured into McCaskey's work as mayor. *The Clansman,* a 1905 play by Thomas Dixon set in the Reconstruction era which maligned African Americans and Thaddeus Stevens, had set off protests in 490 American cities. In several venues the production was blocked. On November 12, 1906, a delegation of local African Americans prevailed upon Mayor McCaskey to stop the play's impending performance at the Fulton Opera House. Having seen it several months previously in Philadelphia, McCaskey judged it to be "a drama justifying Ku Klux outrage, discrediting and dishonoring Thaddeus Stevens, and representing the negro in authority as a shrewd villain without conscience or any proper sense of decency."[56] It would have the effect of inflaming race relations and stirring up old antagonisms, but he had decided that banning it in Lancaster would create more, not less, interest. When he discussed the situation with the Fulton manager, Charles A. Yecker, McCaskey promised not to interfere, but the meeting with the African Americans and opposition from a number of whites convinced him that the performance should be stopped. He sent Yecker a letter asking him to halt the production. The show was cancelled, and McCaskey was accused of obstructing freedom of the stage.[57]

A film version of *The Clansman* entitled *Birth of a Nation,* released in 1915, was banned in Lancaster by Mayor Harry Trout.[58]

A paucity of green spaces within Lancaster prompted McCaskey to outline a plan for parks to compensate for James Hamilton's omission of them in the 1700s. Frequent visits to Buffalo, New York, exposed him to the comprehensive park system created there by Frederick Law Olmstead. In addition, McCaskey's intimate familiarity with the hills and woods surrounding Lancaster, gained from Tucquan Club excursions and field trips with his students, made it easy to identify sites for park development. He had already outlined his vision for a unified park system almost 20 years earlier in two Arbor Day speeches, in which he spoke of a network along the Conestoga River.[59] Coursing in wide loops to the east and south of the city and bordered by hilly terrain and meadowland, the river was the obvious location. The hillsides would need to be replanted and the primeval forest at Rocky Springs preserved. Roads on both sides of the river would provide "delightful drives . . . corresponding to the famous Wissahickon drive near Philadelphia." Small parks would dot the drive here and there, and many foot bridges would cross the water. This would be "within easy reach, by railroad or street car lines, of Lancaster . . . [or] within a few minutes' walk of the centre of the city."[60]

In the 1892 speech, McCaskey said that on the west side of town, Wheatland, President Buchanan's home, had been suggested as a park venue. With more than 25 acres and a grove of native forest trees, it "would be the pride of the city."[61] Wheatland, in fact, had also been considered as a cemetery site, which was, McCaskey noted, "our Lancaster substitute for a park. Death is a pleasant thing to think of, and a quiet, well kept cemetery is an attractive place." Even though there was need for one in the western part of town to "meet the growing demand for graves," McCaskey preferred the alternative, cremation: "I hold cremation to be better than earth burial, but the crematorium . . . [is] in little favor as yet." Grave sites were still needed until they would pass "out of fashion, as may be the case before the year 2000 of the Christian era," he said. Wheatland became neither park nor cemetery.[62]

In his 1906 annual message, McCaskey reiterated his dream of a park system along the Conestoga, for "water is the soul of a landscape. No park satisfies without water."[63] He noted that west of the city 70 acres, donated by Catharine H. Long, were being transformed into a park, H. S. Williamson had given land near Rockford to the city, and there were other suitable locations. Completing the dream would take 100 years, and by then the population of Lancaster would be 250,000. He called for a park commission and a fund of $250,000 to develop such a system. He himself was prepared to contribute $5,000.[64]

McCaskey's projection of a much bigger population and his hope for an extensive, contiguous park system have not been realized. Lancaster's citizens currently number approximately 60,000, only 10,000 more than in 1906, and there have been more parks created, some along the Conestoga, but not to the extent he envisioned.

In 1908 Lancaster was experiencing its biggest building boom ever.[65] That year, labor unions and fraternal organizations demanded that the city employ American workers over "aliens" in contracted work. McCaskey countered that, as long as enough Americans were available for such work, they would be employed, but if not, then immigrants would be hired, for "the work must be finished."[66] The city was growing.

From his office on the second floor of City Hall, the mayor looked out on Center Square. He saw a tangle of telegraph, telephone, and trolley lines and wires crisscrossing above the streets and steel tracks gleaming below. In 1884 trolleys had begun replacing stage coaches. By the first years of the new century, the Conestoga Traction Company expanded its system to include 13 routes throughout the county, with Center Square as its bull's-eye. "Trolleys ran to and from every point in the county every hour. In 1908 as many as 798 cars per week day and 904 on Saturday departed from Center Square. Cars were able to depart from this hub every two minutes."[67]

The bustle of activity below got McCaskey thinking: "Out of these front windows we look down upon what is and always must be the central station or terminus of our city and county trolley system. People come here daily by thousands, sometimes by tens of thousands. There is no other spot in Lancaster county more easy of access or that is so familiarly known to so many of our people."[68] That was it! Lancaster needed a public building for meetings and conventions, similar to Boston's Faneuil Hall. The Pennsylvania Legislature had just passed a law for memorial halls to be built in the county seat of those counties with populations over 150,000. These edifices were to contain a large auditorium and meeting rooms for military and patriotic groups, educators, historical and agricultural associations, religious organizations, and for conventions. Additional rooms would house a county historical society, with displays and relics of past wars, and a museum of natural history.[69]

McCaskey knew where to put it: "Out of these north windows . . . we have an ideal spot on which to build this great central public hall of Lancaster city and county."[70] He was looking at the Central Market House, a whisper away. Keep the first floor for a public market, and so build up, not out. Add a second floor for the rooms for museums, meetings, and record-keeping, and a third floor for the auditorium.[71]

He knew what to name it: "'The Soldiers' Memorial Hall of Lancaster County,' that it may stand for generations an object-lesson of patriotism—a worthy reminder of a heroic age—and closely associated in the thought of our own and of future generations with our beautiful [Sailors' and] Soldiers' Monument."[72]

The Central Market building did not bulge upward to become a public meeting place. It has undergone renovations and remains solely a public farmers' market and thrives, attracting tourists and supplying loyal locals with fresh produce, meat, fish, breads, dairy, handicrafts, candy, flowers, ethnic foods, and many other items every Tuesday, Friday, and Saturday. Kitty-corner from Central Market and old City Hall is a building on Penn Square that does answer McCaskey's call, 100 years later, for a public meeting facility: the Lancaster County Convention Center. Opened in 2009, the complex offers spacious meeting and convention areas and two large ballrooms; it includes a hotel, restaurant, and the Thaddeus Stevens & Lydia Hamilton Smith Historic Site.

In almost every speech McCaskey gave as Lancaster's spokesperson to local conventions or at events out of town, he included much of the city's history, particularly the Revolutionary War era and her most famous citizens: James Buchanan, Thaddeus Stevens, General John Reynolds, Robert Fulton, Thomas Burrowes, and sometimes John Wise, the local aeronaut whose balloon liftoffs in the 1850s attracted the schoolboys, McCaskey among them.[73]

In April 1907, when the tricentennial celebration of the founding of Jamestown, Virginia, was being planned, participating municipalities were asked to provide their flag. Lancaster did not have one, and so McCaskey chaired a flag committee of three.[74] The result, only slightly varied, is still visible today around the city. Look down and there is the circular center design, the city seal, on old manhole covers. Look ahead and there it is on the sides of municipal vehicles and on some trash cans. Look up and see a six-foot diameter metal version on the front of the new police station, or see the whole flag floating in front of City Hall.

The flag features the seal at the center of a royal blue field. Near the circle's outer edge, two concentric circles of blue dots unite Lancaster to its British namesake. Arcing in the upper half within the circles are the words "Lan-castra, Britannia" in bright red, old English font. This was the Roman name for Lancaster, England, and means "the Lan camp." "Lancaster Pennsylvania" fills the lower half. Separating the halves are two roses, and below each is a year: 1730, the year the town was laid out, and 1907, the year the flag was adopted.[75]

Inside the circles is a two-layered red rose patterned on the House of Lancaster's heraldic badge. At the rose's center is a modification of the coat of arms of the mother city, outlined in gold. A golden crown is at the top. Below it on a light blue background is a Conestoga wagon, representing transportation, under which are three silver globes on black in a gold-bor-

Center design of Lancaster's flag.

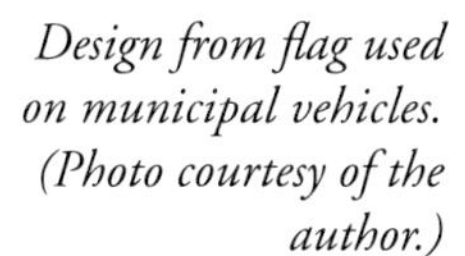

Design from flag used on municipal vehicles. (Photo courtesy of the author.)

Manhole cover. (Photo courtesy of the author.)

Mayoral campaign coin. (Photo courtesy of B. David Wagner.)

dered rectangle. Taken from William Penn's coat of arms, the globes might represent faith, hope, and charity, McCaskey conjectured, or virtue, liberty, and independence. At the bottom, also on light blue, are three sheaves of wheat, representing agriculture.[76]

Recumbent beneath the circle is a bright red rose in full bloom on a stem with several buds and green leaves. A red rose signified the English House of Lancaster, a white one the House of York, hence the name, the Wars of the Roses, for the series of wars the two enemies waged with one another between 1455 and1485. Lancaster is often referred to as the Red Rose City, and York, its neighbor west of the Susquehanna, as the White Rose City. On New Year's Eve, a red rose is dropped in Penn Square.

When McCaskey sought re-election in 1908, he ordered 6,000 copper and bronze medals, about 1¼ inches in diameter, from the United States Mint.[77] The seal was used on one side; McCaskey's visage, encircled by "J. P. McCaskey Mayor Fifty Years A Teacher 1908," is on the other.

McCaskey's last full year as mayor, 1909, was bookended by two significant historical events: the Abraham Lincoln commemoration in February and a Robert Fulton celebration on September 21, 1909. Fulton was a famous inventor, particularly of nautical devices and boats. His steamboat, the *Clermont*, the first commercially successful steam-powered vessel, made her maiden voyage up the Hudson River 100 years earlier, carrying passengers 150 miles from New York City to Albany in 32 hours.

Fulton was born in 1765 on a farm in Little Britain Township (since renamed Fulton Township), southern Lancaster County, and lived there until he was six when the family moved to Lancaster. It was to that farm, located near the Conowingo Creek, that 5,000[78] spectators traveled on that early autumn day by "automobiles, buggies, carriages, railroad trains, on foot and one party even came in an ox-cart. School children came in a large hay wagon drawn by six fine gray mules." The Lancaster, Oxford, and Southern Railroad handled the largest crowds in its history,[79] and extra trolley cars from Lancaster to Quarryville were put into service.[80] McCaskey and son Donald were among the distinguished guests, who included Governor Stuart, ex-governor Pennypacker, and Fulton descendants; they traveled in a 25 vehicle motorcade from Lancaster in cool, clear air.[81]

Now Fulton Elementary School, this building was Boys' High School from 1918 until 1938. (Photo courtesy of Noah Brundin.)

Governors and poets spoke from the stage, and a replica of the *Clermont* issued forth smoke from its stack and even sounded a hoarse steamboat whistle.[82] The event lasted all day, with the Conowingo not too far away, a stream where "the heaven-gifted boy" had sailed his tiny boats and watched the water wheels of the mills turning, or so a poet for the occasion said.[83] Fulton's home is open today as an historic site.

Lancaster continues to honor Fulton and his achievements. Named for him are the Fulton Opera House (opened in 1851 as Fulton Hall), a bank, a street, and an elementary school at Orange and Mulberry Streets. A

Fulton Opera House. (Photo courtesy of the author.)

massive and stately structure built in 1916, the school originally replaced the older building for Boys' High where McCaskey had reigned from 1876 to 1906, when he ended his walks up Mulberry and began them down King.

As amusing as some of the stories from McCaskey's mayoral years seem, he and the city councils did their work in earnest. Their reality was a burgeoning Lancaster with all of its issues and needs. For McCaskey, politics had to do with generosity and doing good, a life value and goal he had expressed repeatedly in his teaching. Of politics, he said: "Not what we give, but what we share—not so much the good we do as that we help others to do and enjoy doing—not what we have and hold and hoard for ourselves and for our own, but what we use generously, helpfully, wisely, recognizing the fatherhood of God and brotherhood of man—these are the things that count for most and best, both here and hereafter. Is this politics? It is the high-water mark of the best politics I know. It is the ideal towards which high-souled men are striving everywhere: The best good of all."[84]

Chapter 16

A Reverence for Things Sacred and Divine

"What more blessed thing for a child than to be brought up in an atmosphere of regard for truth and purity, and a reverence for things sacred and divine?"[1]

Eighty-nine roses. McCaskey received 89 roses at a testimonial dinner in his honor on October 9, 1926, his birthday. Twenty years after he had left the high school, his "boys," almost 300 of the 743, came to honor him. The celebration was broadcast via radio station WGAL from the Brunswick Hotel,[2] the same site as former hotels where Lincoln, other nationally prominent figures, and McCaskey himself had addressed the citizens of Lancaster. The men praised him, thanked him, and adored him. Just as they had at Christmas parties and mayoral campaigns, they cheered, applauded, shouted and sang, accompanied by a small orchestra made up from their own number. And more than $600 had been raised to establish a McCaskey prize fund for future graduates.[3]

Their teacher, a man rarely without words who expected students and grandchildren to know lots of words, was so moved he could not deliver his prepared speech. When he did speak, "[h]is voice faltered just a bit, perhaps, and was just a whit more husky than in the old days."[4] Bearded as he had been since the Civil War, (it had turned white many years before), he wore a heavy coat,[5] fending off the cold of old age. He laid aside the prepared text and said: "Boys, God bless you! I never thought I was doing the work you say I did. My advice tonight is this: Play the game hard, win what we can fairly, and then let it all go. Soon we will all pass into another stage of existence where, I think, we pass upward and onward if we have lived right here. This is a great meeting—I thank you with all my heart for it. If you got any good out of the old high school, I am glad. And I got as much as you did. If I did some good I was led to it by a wise providence, and I thank God for it."[6]

In the R.S.V.P.s and the speeches that night, the recurring theme was McCaskey's influence on his students' character development, a fitting tribute to a man whose favorite piece for memorization had been a brief paragraph, "Enduring Influence."[7] He had "taught his boys that character and honest living are worth more than mere book learning, and . . . laid the foundation for their success in the business and professional world."[8] He himself had been an example, as one alumnus wrote: "[T]he good and noble deeds he did for so many of his scholars, as well as other poor and worthy ones, were so deeply impressed on my mind as a boy."[9] Others said that "Mr. McCaskey himself was about the best friend many and many a boy ever had"[10] and "Who ever understood boys as he did?"[11]

In his thank-you, McCaskey spoke of the opportunities the life of a teacher provided: doing and getting good; pleasant and grateful memories; and living among the "boys," who were always young and had kept him young.[12] The relationship between teacher and students had been mutually beneficial.

In the speech he did not give, he had planned to tell them that he would like to read something to them and talk about it, think about it, as they had done so often. Instead, he would give them a one-sentence speech from Dickens: "Boys, just do all the good you can, and don't make any fuss about it." He would have spoken of Zook School, true wealth, the soul and dying, another textbook he was ready to publish, Lancaster High School and its graduates, star study, botanizing, memory work, music, Arbor Days, Christmas programs, and trips they took with him to the great cities. And he would have talked about the teachers, all the boys' teachers. They, after all, made the school: "It is not the school curriculum, nor the studious habit, nor the spirit of inquiry, nor high rank in class room or at graduation, that means most in school life. All these things are desirable and important, but the great thing—the greatest thing of all—is the personality of the teacher. In these teachers you have had that resolutely ennobling personality."[13]

Testimonial Dinner at the Hotel Brunswick. (Photo courtesy of LancasterHistory.org.)

His had certainly been an ennobling personality, and they had come to thank him. "Jack's boys" filed past the head table to shake his hand one last time, and the evening ended.[14]

Missing from the festivities were the girls. Even so, McCaskey included them in his remarks that evening. He had long advocated for co-education, an issue that appeared in the *Journal* from its very earliest days in the 1850s and was debated and considered there and in other educational forums. McCaskey in 1888 expressed his regret that girls were not among his students. He rejected the notion that they "have less average good sense than boys and are therefore harder to manage," saying that his experience with females was that they were "the very best people—the most patient, the most unselfish, the most royal-hearted, the most unwearied in well-doing, I have ever known."[15] Several years later, concluding a lengthy speech to an audience that included women, he demonstrated his awareness of the sexist nature of English: "I have said 'man' all the way. The term is generic, and includes her also who is the 'better man' because, I think, nearer the kingdom of God."[16]

Speaking to the Alumni Association in 1896, McCaskey said, "Ladies, I wish I could talk to you as to old friends. But I don't know you. We have never had the pleasure of mutual acquaintance." He told them that "had the present High School building been planned—as it should have been—for recitations by boys and girls in the same class-rooms, there would have been greater good to both." Also, it was not good that the girls had only female teachers and the boys male teachers. A mixing of genders would model home life.[17]

In fact, Boys' High already had a woman on its faculty. Many years before, McCaskey had succeeded in getting one hired. He knew Mary Martin was *the* teacher to fill a vacancy that required someone "good in Latin and German and English literature and certain branches of natural science, who could talk well and write well, who was in love with learning, and a strong personality to interest, attract and influence students." She was "worth a half dozen ordinary male teachers, all in one, who could be had for the salary offered." Martin agreed to accept the offer, if extended, but would not campaign for it. McCaskey, finding "much prejudice against the election of a lady-teacher" twisted some arms. One board member said that he knew Miss Martin well: "She is a little Napoleon. But I am against it." McCaskey asked him to vote for her "in the interest of the school" and as a personal favor. She was hired in January 1884.[18]

The high school at Orange and Mulberry was becoming crowded. In December 1905 the Thaddeus Stevens High School for Girls, two short blocks from the old school, was dedicated. Until then, boys and girls had shared the same buildings but separate floors, the "Male Department" on the second and the "Female Department" on the first. McCaskey expressed his hope in April that the new school would be co-educational—there was such a movement—and he suggested the current building be converted into a manual training school.[19] While he had been able to bring about other things he wanted, such as vocal and instrumental music, a gymnasium on the school's third floor, the hiring of Howard W. Gilbert, Mary Martin, John Kevinski, Carl Matz, and Carl Thorbahn, this was not to be. The school board voted against co-education that June.[20]

McCaskey had urged years before, when talk about a separate building for the girls first began: "Let it have the best location the town can afford; let it be a noble structure, broad in plan and complete in equipment, worthy to stand for a hundred years the pride of the city, the crown of her educational system."[21] His aspirations notwithstanding, the new building, designed by architect C. Emlen Urban, was regarded far less favorably when it was completed, scorned at the time as a "yellow elephant" and a "garish pile of tasteless architecture."[22]

Stevens School is a magnificent building. Facing west on Charlotte Street, it was added to the National Register of Historic Places in 1983 and functions today as an apartment building. Its orangish brick and brownstone exterior, trimmed with terra cotta designs, has been competently preserved. The three-story structure, with a slate mansard roof edged in copper now aged green, rises atop a hill several blocks northwest of downtown. Tulip poplars, as old as the building they shade, tower far above the side of the building, stretching its appearance ever higher. On one of "the best locations the town can afford," it is positioned so that early morning light, sometimes intense sunrise red, orange, gold, purple, or pink, passes horizontally through the large, softly arched windows of the auditorium (now a ballroom) on the top floor and across the expansive room to flood the western windows, fleeting moments of exquisite beauty.

Forever hopeful, McCaskey kept the prospect of co-education open. Speaking to the Alumni Association in June 1906 about his retirement, he said: "The time is out, the labor done, and I welcome the holiday. ... If I could—after a season of rest and refreshment—I would gladly go back to work in the school room for another fifty years, far better than the first. But this time it should be where boys and girls are educated together."[23] Two years after his death, boys and girls walked together through the same entrances of John Piersol McCaskey High School and sat next to one another in the same classrooms.

As much as McCaskey loved teaching—it was "the best business going—"[24] he did not regard it as his greatest accomplishment. In fact, he ranked it third, his songbook collections second and *The Pennsylvania School*

Girls' High School (Stevens High School). U.S. National Register of Historic Places.

Stevens' School for Girls. (Photo courtesy of Noah Brundin.)

Journal first.[25] For the latter two, his youthful impulse to learn the printing trade proved inordinately worthwhile. *The Journal* originated in the Lancaster County Educational Society in 1852, with Thomas H. Burrowes, the society's president, as its first editor. Along with the *Ohio Educational Monthly*, it was the oldest such periodical in the country.[26] In 1854 it became the publication for the Common School Department, later named the "Official Organ of the Department of Public Instruction." McCaskey, in the 1860s, a decade already demanding much from him personally and professionally, became assistant editor at Burrowes' request, which he initially refused: "In 1865 Dr. Burrowes, needing some one to assist him on *The Pennsylvania School Journal*, offered me the position, and urged my acceptance of it, but made the requirement that I stop teaching. I declined the place, telling him that I would do for him what work I could but I would not leave the schoolroom. That was not satisfactory to him then, but a year later, meeting him in Centre Square, he hailed me and said, 'I'll take you on your own terms. But you must stop teaching night school, as I don't want to write your obituary.'"[27]

From then on, McCaskey became the driving force behind the magazine, gradually becoming its general editor (Pennsylvania State Superintendents of Public Instruction were, for the most part, nominally the editors-in-chief), business manager,[28] publisher, and owner. With the exception of one year while mayor,[29] he "made up and put through press every number since April, 1866,"[30] and continued this amazing effort until he was 84. In 1921, 56 years

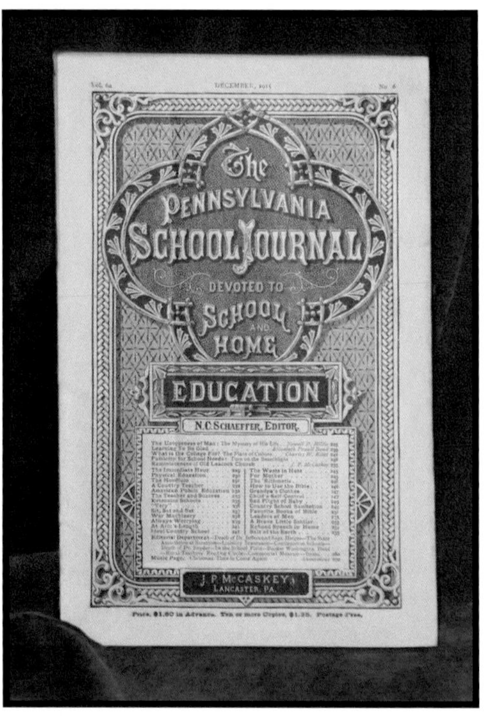

The Pennsylvania School Journal, *December 1915. (Photo courtesy of B. David Wagner.)*

after Burrowes had sought him out, he sold the *Journal* to the Pennsylvania State Education Association.[31] For 56 years, McCaskey, through his selection of articles and topics and his editorials, influenced and shaped public education. It is no wonder that he deemed this his greatest work or that he was praised posthumously as a "nationally significant figure."

Printed and mailed from Lancaster, the monthly periodical averaging 45-50 pages per issue was going out by the end of McCaskey's ownership to 2,600 Pennsylvania school districts, 2,000 school directors, and to all county, city, borough and township superintendents. It was provided gratis to editors, clergymen, and superintendents of public instruction in other states.[32] Copies went to Canada and across the Atlantic to the education departments of France, Spain, Italy, England, Ireland, Switzerland and other countries.[33] As the official publication of the Department of Public Instruction, it included all the reports of state, city and borough superintendents, and school boards. The *Journal* proved particularly important as such a repository, for a fire in the capitol building in Harrisburg in 1897 destroyed all departmental records from 1854 until then.[34]

Additionally, the *Journal* printed reports of the annual sessions of the Pennsylvania State Teachers' Association, a perfect fit for McCaskey, who was for 66 years a member of the association, 54 years as its secretary. He attended his first meeting in 1855 in Pittsburgh when he was 17 years old.[35] The association's memorial committee, which he chaired, planned and raised funds for tombstones, plaques, and memorial booklets to preserve the contributions of leading educators like E. E. Higbee and Thomas Burrowes.

Memorials honoring Burrowes can be found at St. James' Episcopal Church, where both he and McCaskey worshipped. McCaskey and his committee raised funds, including pennies from schoolchildren and teachers all across the state, for an interior black onyx memorial tablet and an imposing granite tombstone in the graveyard. It was, after all, Burrowes who had created "order from chaos" in the organizing of the Common Schools in the schools' early years.[36]

Thomas Burrowes' tombstone in St. James' Episcopal Church graveyard. (Photo courtesy of Mary Alice Gerfin.)

As if two memorials were not enough, McCaskey also wanted to install a stained-glass window in Burrowes' honor above the pulpit of the church. However, the vestry on which he was serving ultimately rescinded its approval, for the tablet and tombstone seemed sufficient. McCaskey, undeterred, appealed for placing the window in the south wall of the church, which the vestry also rejected, suggesting that he turn instead to the local Y.M.C.A., which was about to build a new structure,[37] and he did so.

McCaskey commissioned the window, "Cross and Crown," and dedicated it to both Burrowes and Higbee. Costing $1,000 dollars, it weighed almost half a ton and measured 12' x 9.5'. In the center is a Maltese cross, set in brilliant jewels above an ecclesiastical crown composed of gemstones. A spectacular arrangement of stained glass and 1,000 jewels, it was manufactured by Redding, Baird, & Co. of Boston, where it was viewed by thousands prior to shipment.[38] It was installed in 1901 above the landing of the main staircase of the then new Y on Orange Street. When that building was demolished in 1965, the piece was stored until 2009 and then refurbished and installed in the new Y.M.C.A. on Harrisburg Pike.[39]

The "Cross and Crown" at the Lancaster City Center Y.M.C.A. (Photo courtesy of the author.)

The fifteenth rector at St. James', the Reverend Clifford Gray Twombly, arrived in Lancaster when McCaskey was in his second year as mayor, 1907. The new pastor's views on morality reflected the mayor's. Their association continued until McCaskey's death. Twombley "believed in social action and in the influence of environment for good or evil." He recognized the disparity between what young people were learning about living a decent and religious life and their exposure to moral evil and vice,[40] of which there was plenty in Lancaster: 45 houses of prostitution, burlesque shows with nude scenes at the Fulton Opera House, lewd dancing, 72 saloons and 50 beer clubs, objectionable movies, gambling, and cockfights.[41] Churches and synagogues numbered 62 that same year, 1913.[42]

Twombley bucked the prevailing custom among clergy of the era not to get involved in the "objectionable features in the life and customs of the community they served."[43] He preached about social action and politics from the pulpit, to the consternation of even his vestry.[44] He spoke against child labor but for a living wage for women, a shorter workday, and a curfew, among other things. In 1912, the activist minister formed a "Law and Order Society" to fight vice in Lancaster. McCaskey, certainly galled by the existence of a house of prostitution across from Boys' High,[45] was among the

McCaskey's plaque in St. James'. (Photo courtesy of the author.)

St. James' Episcopal Church in Lancaster. (Photo courtesy of the author.)

society's members. Over the next 20 years, when society members and then hired agents investigated places where illicit activities were taking place and when the police began enforcing laws they had once ignored, much of the vice was eradicated.[46]

Twombley and McCaskey shared a very close relationship, and in his final 15 years on St. James' Vestry, McCaskey served as the "Rector's warden." When still able, he attended services, clad in a dark overcoat even on hot, humid Lancaster summer days.[47] Elected to the vestry in 1867, he served until his death in 1935, a record of 68 years. St James' placed a plaque to his memory directly below Burrowes' and near the pew in which McCaskey reportedly regularly sat.[48]

Along with his work at St. James', McCaskey continued his publishing, churning out the *Journal* month after month and producing his final collection, *Treasury of Song*, in Lancaster in 1916 and selling it until 1933. In 1927 he advertised his final work, *The Teacher's Assistant*, a compilation of material on memory work, music, star study, and Arbor Day. However, there is no evidence of the book ever having been published.

In his lifetime, besides songbooks, textbooks, the *Lancaster School Mottoes*, and the *Lincoln Art Series*, McCaskey made and lost money from investments in various local printing companies, in the enterprise that became Hamilton Watch Company, and in the Yule Marble Company, in which he had invested $30,000.[49] He also invested in real estate locally and in Florida.[50] The *Journal*, as well, had not been lucrative for him.[51] He estimated that he lost well beyond $100,000 in his lifetime.[52] When he died during the Great Depression, his estate was valued at $273.11.[53]

However, acquiring wealth was not important to McCaskey, for one could be "money-drunk as well as drunk on brandy," he asserted.[54] A Sanskrit proverb he selected for the large family grave marker in Greenwood Cemetery stands as a permanent testimony to his view of wealth: "All you can hold in your cold dead hand is what you have given away." The real wealth, then, was in the giving, not having, which McCaskey demonstrated again and again.

Real wealth was also in family. At his and Ellen's 50th wedding anniversary, he said that he regarded himself as a "millionaire in sons," and asked, "What are banks and farms compared to that?" He and Ellen had been blessed with "worthy parenthood," and he praised their four adult sons and foster son.[55] In a 1901 letter to sister-in-law Nellie, McCaskey congratulated her and Will on their successful sons and daughters, for "that's wealth of great account." He continued: "I've often thought that I'm the richest man in Lancaster . . . with my six boys, one of them a young man of thirty or more in the great company of saints and angels beyond and another a foster son of splendid ability and purpose and as loyal to me as one of my own, and four who stand with their work like men. That's wealth beside which the childless millionaire or the man of millions who has but poor unworthy sons makes but a cheap showing. For the best thing in the world is a noble man or woman."[56]

McCaskey, hewing the honor-one's-parents' line, encouraged Nellie to continue giving advice to her adult children, just as his mother had done: "As when they were young you forbade, and compelled if necessary, so through all your life hold your place. When you see what you would condemn 'go for it' with directness and force. It may stir anger sometimes but it will usually do good. Sincerity and earnestness of well-directed purpose are the things that most impress our children. We all blunder more or less, old and young, and need to feel the check rein. One of the best things I know of our own mother is that we never grew beyond her criticism."[57]

Health was wealth to him, as well, "for what is money when weighed against the blessing of health and vigor?"[58] Of the seven male cousins all named John after their grandfather, McCaskey, as a very young child, was the weakest, and the assumption was that he would not survive beyond several years.[59] His mother's "loving care by day [and] by night, ... her constant prayer," and his "strong ancestry on a dozen lines," he believed, pulled him through.[60] When he was seven, his father snatched him from certain death under a threshing machine.[61] Several accidents, including the December fall from the ladder in the gymnasium, marred his adulthood, but he did not suffer from illnesses.

1892 or 1893 picture of the McCaskey family. Standing left to right are sons Donald, Richard, Edward, and Walter, with McCaskey in the middle. Seated left to right are Ellen, Bert (Richard's wife), Kate (Ed's wife), unidentified woman (perhaps Aunt Margaret McCaskey White), McCaskey's mother with baby, unidentified child, and Edna (Walt's wife). Two unidentified children on ground, with daughter Elsie in the middle. (Photo from a private collection.)

1902 picture of McCaskey and Ellen's family, taken in the backyard at 304 West King Street. Standing with McCaskey are sons Donald (left) and Richard (right) with grandson Jack. Seated left to right are granddaughter Mary, daughter Elsie, secretary Elizabeth McVey, "Aunt Bert," Ellen, daughter-in-law Kate with grandson Walter standing in front of her, son Edward; on the grass left to right are grandchildren Catherine, Hugh, Richard, Donald, and Edward. (Photo from private collection.)

Left: McCaskey, 1907. Right: Ellen, 1907. (Photos from private collection)

In 1914, he narrowly escaped having his feet and lower legs crushed in an elevator,[62] and in 1926 he fell down some stairs, which resulted in broken ribs and a hospital stay, but the 89 year old recovered within several months and was "back again on the job, and pushing the work about as usual."[63]

The good health McCaskey experienced in his lifetime, along with his personal discipline, enabled him to be exceedingly productive. He wrote a column a day for the *Journal*,[64] worked late into the evenings,[65] and combined work with vacation,[66] often at Ocean Grove with the family. Work for him was essential: "To have plenty of work worth doing, and time and strength to get it done, are the great things," he believed.[67]

Always a proponent of physical education, McCaskey included articles on the topic in the *Journal*. As a young professional, he addressed the Lancaster County Teachers' Institute in 1862 on "Physical Training in the Public Schools,"[68] enlisting Manny Pehrson and other students to demonstrate Indian clubs.[69] He strove to be physically fit and, when he was 97, he attributed his good health and longevity to a "one-ton weight-lifting machine and two 50-pound dumbbells."[70] The machine, which was McCaskey's own modification of one invented by Dr. George Winship and then another by a Dr. Riley,[71] consisted of a frame with 20 large iron plates laid on top of one another, to be added in increasing number until the person working out had found his maximum lifting strength. The machine and dumbbells were requested by Harvard University, but the McCaskey family chose to keep them at Boys' High School. [72]

In his final years, McCaskey remained "keen eyed and alert," and on the occasion of his 95th birthday, he presided over a family dinner with all his sons present and greeted the many well wishers who came to 304 West King Street that Sunday.[73] President Herbert Hoover had sent a letter of congratulations, and letters, telegrams, cards, and flowers had descended from all over the country. Yellow gladioli and blue delphinium graced the dining table. Bowls and baskets of roses, dahlias, gladioli and orange geraniums filled the house. [74]

McCaskey, in his public note of thanks, admitted that he was "not very strong these days—have been confined to the house during the past year as a half-invalid, and taken breakfast in bed, about seven o'clock in the morning—the best I have ever known—a tumbler of ordinary whey (on the doctor's advice), a cup of ordinary postum, or other cereal, and a tumbler of canned peaches from one of the Pacific States ... the choicest fruit I know."[75] His penchant for sharing the good things in life with others had not atrophied, for he added that people could get the peaches "at any good grocery store, and if you are not familiar with them in your homes, it would be well to make their acquaintance."[76]

McCaskey died on a Thursday in September 1935. The next day flags at the high school and city hall were lowered to half-staff, his portrait was draped in black and placed on the dais in the school's auditorium, a special assembly was called, a faculty committee was appointed to draw up resolutions, the pep rally for the first football game of the season was canceled, and at the game, taps were rendered and the high school band played "special music as a tribute to the man who brought music to the public schools."[77] Thousands paid their respects to the family at 304 West King the next evening,[78] and on Sunday the Reverend Twombley conducted the funeral liturgy in front of a packed St. James' Church, while more than 100 persons stood outside.[79] Three hundred continued along to the cemetery[80] where McCaskey's cremains were interred. After Twombley read the burial service, members of the Free and Accepted Masons conducted a Masonic ritual.[81] Among those in attendance at the gravesite was devoted student Harold Diffenderffer: "We laid his body to rest in Greenwood Cemetery one mild September day, full of years and good works! The bright Autumn sun cast flickering shadows through the trees over God's Acre that received his tired body."[82]

For McCaskey, life was inextricably and joyously tied to death, for it was in death that he would begin a life in eternity, a belief he expressed both publicly and privately all his life. He and his contemporaries spoke clearly and frequently of their religious beliefs and, like other educators, McCaskey did not shirk from imbuing teaching with faith. He shared with Friedrich W. Froebel, a 19th-century educator famous for the concept of the kindergarten, the belief that religion must be at the heart of education.

McCaskey had been steeped in the Christian faith from his earliest days on the farm in Gordonville, where his family attended alternately Old Leacock Presbyterian Church, just a mile or so from the family farm on Route 340 west of Intercourse, and All Saints' Episcopal Church in Paradise. It was to Old Leacock that McCaskey often asked in his old age to be taken, and in October 1915, when he was 78, he spoke at the church's 175th anniversary. Standing in the cemetery, he began with an allusion to "Haunted Houses," a poem by Henry Wadsworth Longfellow. The "blessed dead . . . may have come from far to be with us here to-day amid these familiar surroundings,"[83] McCaskey suggested. He did not intend this as something macabre; rather, the presence of both the Church militant (those still alive) and the Church

Old Leacock Presbyterian Church. (Photo courtesy of the author.)

The cemetery behind Old Leacock church. (Photo courtesy of the author.)

triumphant (those in Heaven), he explained, made for a very fitting memorial to the place.

He named many buried in the churchyard, among them grandparents John and Margaret and other McCaskeys. He told of feeling the wooden benches against his back inside the stone church or aching with frozen feet on the hunt for a rabbit or meandering along the dirt road kicking up dust on the way to school or lying under the grand oaks in the cemetery and gazing up at a summer's sky of blue and dreaming about going away to school.[84] And so McCaskey recalled his childhood as he spoke on the grounds of a graveyard, an old man gathering up his past for himself, his audience, and us.

Old Leacock provided social and community ties, but its doctrines and spirituality also penetrated McCaskey's soul. "This old church is a temple to me, as it has been to many another," he said.[85] He made no apologies about the importance of religion in his life, and he elevated, to the highest degree, his immersion in it: "What more blessed thing for a child than to be brought up in an atmosphere of regard for truth and purity, and a reverence for things sacred and divine? What more helpful habit for a child than the morning and evening readings and prayer at the mother's side or the mother's knee, and the regular attendance at the services of the church?"[86]

Faith permeated his entire life; it emanated from him in everything he did, said, and taught. He credited Old Leacock with impressing upon him the magnitude of that faith which surpasses and transcends this world. "Here [Old Leacock] I think I first came to feel something of the mighty thought that 'the fashion of this world passeth away.'"[87] His parents carried the Sunday lessons back to the farmhouse, solidifying the message. Life was not boxed into the sacred on Sundays and the secular the rest of the week. "My parents required that I should read [the Bible], and read, and read. I became interested, and knew every story in the Old and New Testaments and in the Apocrypha. I knew every noted man and woman in the Book, good or bad. I knew its history, and was strangely impressed by its poetry and prophecy. What a book it is for youth and age!"[88]

Immersion in the Scriptures. Daily readings and prayers at his mother's knee. Sunday afternoon recitations of answers to questions from the Presbyterian Shorter Catechism, marked by a rivalry among the children as to who knew it best,[89] all of these extended the teachings at Old Leacock

McCaskey and grandchildren. (Photo courtesy of LancasterHistory.org.)

into the home. This was, however, not rote memory without comprehension or inquiry. Discussions of the preacher's sermons took place, and McCaskey was expected to know what the preacher had said and be able to locate in the Bible "any references that came up for question or discussion."[90] This, he said, was "the best that I have ever learned from books. I would not exchange it for any university training in the wide world that should exclude the Bible. And in this relation I think always of my mother and of this old church."[91]

McCaskey's dedication to the Bible and constant return to it continued throughout his life, and he sought to impart the value and wisdom of it to all his offspring, including great-grandchildren, who played in his bedroom when he was an infirmed old man, waiting to die. "Bring me the Good Book," he would instruct a very young Kay McCaskey Adelman. And he, her great-grandfather, would recite passages from memory that he wanted her to know.[92]

End Notes

Chapter 1

As the Years Pass His Memory Grows in Fragrance

1. McCaskey, John P., *Lincoln Literary Collection*, 3
2. Eshleman, 55-56
3. Ibid., 65
4. "Reception of Mr. Lincoln," 2
5. Ibid.
6. Ibid.
7. Eshleman, 66
8. "The President Elect," 3
9. Young, 64
10. "All Lancaster Celebrates," 8
11. Ibid.
12. Eshleman, 68
13. "All Lancaster Celebrates," 8
14. "Reception of Mr. Lincoln," 2
15. Eshleman, 70
16. "Reception of Mr. Lincoln," 2
17. Eshleman, 66
18. Ibid., 71-74
19. "Reception of Mr. Lincoln," 2
20. Ibid.
21. "All Lancaster Celebrates," 1
22. Ibid., 8
23. "Where Lincoln Stood," 5
24. "All Lancaster Celebrates," 8
25. Ibid.
26. Ibid.
27. "Visit to Cemetery Hill," 58
28. Ibid., 60
29. Ibid., 59-60
30. McCaskey, John P., "Life in a High School," 69
31. "All Lancaster Celebrates," 8
32. Schindle, 7-9
33. McCaskey, John P., *Lincoln Literary Collection*, 3
34. Ibid.
35. "Our Lamented Chief," 2
36. Alexander, "A Nation Mourns," 1
37. Ibid.
38. "Our Lamented Chief," 2
39. "The Passage of the Presidential Funeral Train," 2
40. Ibid.
41. Ibid., 3
42. Ibid.
43. Ibid.
44. Eshleman, 76
45. "Our Lamented Chief," 2
46. "The Martyred President," 2
47. "Our Lamented Chief," 2
48. "All Lancaster Celebrates," 8
49. Ibid.
50. Ibid.

Chapter 2

A Dog, a Cane, an Education

1. John P. McCaskey to Will and Nellie McCaskey, 1 September 1895
2. "Dr. J. P. McCaskey Dies of Pneumonia," 1
3. Klein, *Lancaster County Pennsylvania a History*, 971
4. Riddle, 3
5. Klein, *Lancaster County Pennsylvania a History*, 971-972
6. Ibid., 972
7. Riddle, 6
8. Klein, *Lancaster County Pennsylvania a History*, 972-974
9. Riddle, 14-15
10. Ibid., 16
11. Klein, *Lancaster County Pennsylvania a History*, 975
12. Harsh, "One-Room Schools in Leacock Township before 1844"
13. Ibid.
14. John P. McCaskey to Will McCaskey, 20 March 1891
15. United States Federal Census for 1880
16. Riddle, 3
17. Klein, *Lancaster County Pennsylvania a History*, 97
18. Wickersham, "Historical Sketch of Education in Pennsylvania," 209
19. Evidence for this is seen in vouchers submitted for "Poor Law" expense recovery. Harsh, "One-Room Schools in Leacock Township before 1844"
20. Mombert, 463
21. Wickersham, "Historical Sketch of Education in Pennsylvania," 209
22. Riddle, 21
23. Mombert, 463
24. Riddle, 21-22
25. Klein, "The Reverend William Augustus Muhlenberg," 98
26. Riddle, 22
27. McCaskey, "Dr. Burrowes' Memorial Elms," 18
28. Klein, *History of St. James*, 98
29. Riddle, 28-32
30. Board Minutes, August 10, 1838, 21
31. Klein, *Lancaster County Pennsylvania a History*, 981
32. Ellis, 410
33. Winship, 298
34. Ibid., 297
35. McCaskey, John P., "After Forty Years," 40
36. "John Piersol McCaskey, A.M., Ph.D.," 171
37. "John McCaskey," 117
38. John P. McCaskey to Will and Nellie McCaskey, 1 September 1895
39. Harsh, "One-Room Schools in Leacock Township after 1844"
40. McCaskey, John P., "An Address That Was Not Read," 7
41. "John Piersol McCaskey, A.M., Ph.D.," 171
42. McCaskey, John P. "Thomas H. Burrowes, LL.D.," Volume 19, 283
43. Burrowes, *State-Book of Pennsylvania*

44. McCaskey, John P., "Mayor after Fifty Years," 76
45. McCaskey, John P., "Fifty-four Years in the High School," 56
46. McCaskey, John P., "Reminiscences," 258
47. "Oak Hill Academy," 3
48. McCaskey, John P., "The Health Lift," 33
49. "Oak Hill at Public Sale," 3
50. "Christmas Loving Cup," 87
51. "Oak Hill Academy," 3
52. Witmer, 157
53. "Oak Hill Academy," 3
54. Ibid.
55. Ibid.
56. McCaskey, John P., "Christmas Loving Cup," 87
57. McCaskey, John P., "Fifty-four Years," 55
58. John P. McCaskey to Will and Nellie McCaskey, 1 September 1895
59. McCaskey, John P. "After Forty Years," 40
60. Ibid.
61. Ibid., 41
62. "A Busy Life on Varied Lines Through Sixty Years," 231
63. McCaskey, John P., "An Address That Was Not Read," 8
64. Kay Adelman in discussion with the author, 27 July 2009
65. Ibid.
66. Joann Kersch in discussion with the author, October 2009
67. McCaskey, Edward, *Ed McCaskey Tells Stories*
68. F&M Board of Trustees Minutes, 1853-1881, 419
69. F&M Faculty Minutes, 1853-1892
70. "Commencement," 70

When the Sands of the Hour-glass Ran Gold

1. McCaskey, John P., "Life in a High School—Fifty-two Years," 101
2. McCaskey, John P., "Some Reminiscences of 'Old Leacock,'" 257
3. Klein, *Lancaster County Pennsylvania a History*, 994
4. McCaskey, John P., "Fifty-four Years," 54
5. Board Minutes, Book 2, 197
6. "Serenaded the Mayor," 1
7. United States Federal Census records for 1850
8. Board Minutes, Aug. 1, 1838, 20
9. Riddle, 96-97
10. Ibid., 142-143
11. Board Minutes, July, 1849, 180-182
12. Riddle, 171-172
13. McCaskey, John P., "Fifty-four Years," 54
14. "The Old Boys' High School," 222
15. Board Minutes, Book 2, 1849,196-197, 504
16. Riddle, 161-162

17. Ibid., 159
18. Board Minutes, Book 2, September, 1854, 508
19. "Lectures in the High Schools," 2
20. Board Minutes, 1849, Book 2, 200
21. Chapman, 7
22. Ibid., 17
23. Ibid., 18
24. Landis, 130
25. McCaskey, John P., "Life in a High School—Fifty-two Years," 101
26. Ibid.
27. "The Old Boys' High School," 222
28. McCaskey, John P., "Fifty-four Years," 55
29. Magerl
30. "The Old Boys' High School," 222
31. McCaskey, John P., "Fifty-four Years," 55
32. Board Minutes, Book 2, 315-320
33. "The Old Boys' High School," 222. McCaskey may have provided the copy for the article.
34. McCaskey, John P., "Life in a High School, Fifty-two Years," 101
35. Ibid.
36. Ibid.
37. Riddle, 148
38. McCaskey, John P., "Life in a High School, Fifty-two Years," 101
39. Ibid.
40. "Serenaded the Mayor," 1
41. McCaskey, John P., "Fifty-four Years," 57
42. McCaskey, John P., "A Busy Life on Varied Lines through Sixty Years," 243
43. "Serenaded the Mayor," 1
44. Ibid.
45. McCaskey, John P., "A Busy Life on Varied Lines through Sixty Years," 243
46. McCaskey, John P., "Life in a High School, Fifty-two Years," 101
47. McCaskey, John P., "A Busy Life on Varied Lines through Sixty Years," 243
48. McCaskey, John P., "Life in a High School, Fifty-two Years," 102
49. McCaskey, John P., "Dr. Higbee, Greetings!" 429
50. Ibid.
51. McCaskey, John P., "Life in a High School, Fifty-two Years," 101-102
52. Ibid., 102
53. Ibid.
54. Ibid.

Chapter 4
Was Ever June Day More Beautiful?

1. McCaskey, John P., "After Forty Years," 39
2. Leacock Township Tax Records for 1852
3. United States Federal Census for 1860, 1870,1880
4. "Sad Suicide," 2
5. McCaskey, John P., "Fifty-four Years," 55
6. Ibid.

7. McCaskey, John P., "After Forty Years," 39
8. "Lancaster Savings Institution," June 19, 1855, 2
9. "Lancaster Savings Institution," June 26, 1855, 2
10. Diffenderffer, 110
11. McCaskey, John P., "Fifty-four Years," 55
12. Ibid.
13. McCaskey, John P., "Dr. Higbee, Greetings!," 429
14. Riddle, between 172 and 173
15. "John Piersol McCaskey," 117
16. Board Minutes, Book 2, 581
17. Board Minutes, August 28, 1857, Book 3 (not paginated)
18. McCaskey, John P., "Fifty-four Years," 56
19. Ibid.
20. Ibid.
21. "Serenaded the Mayor," 1
22. McCaskey, John P., "Fifty-four Years," 56
23. Smith, 446
24. "One Way to Get a Position," 116
25. McCaskey, John P., "Mayor after Fifty Years," 70
26. McCaskey, John P., "Fifty-four Years," 56
27. McCaskey, John P., "After Forty Years," 39
28. Ibid.
29. Klein, *Lancaster County Pennsylvania a History*, 898
30. Board Minutes, Book I, 39
31. Ibid., 389
32. Board Minutes, Book 2, 510
33. Klein, *Lancaster County Pennsylvania a History*, 989
34. Board Minutes, Book 3, March 13, 1863, (not paginated)
35. Board Minutes, Book 2, 354
36. Board Minutes, Book 3, July 8, 1858; July 7, 1859
37. McCaskey entered Boys' High in 1850 as a student and retired in 1906. He did not attend school in 1852-53, did not complete the 1854-55 school year, and did not teach for the school year 1857-1858, so the total is 52 years.
38. Board Minutes, Book 2, 503
39. Ibid.
40. Ibid.
41. Ibid., 185
42. Board Minutes, Book 3, Oct. 6, 1859, (not paginated)
43. Ibid.

Chapter 5
Out of the Window Yonder

1. McCaskey, John P., "Thaddeus Stevens," 262
2. "Serenaded the Mayor," 1
3. Clark, "Lancaster County's Relation to Slavery," 51
4. Hensel, 7
5. Whitson, 78-81
6. Slaughter, 20-42
7. Whitson, 81-83
8. Hensel, 16
9. Klein, *Lancaster County Pennsylvania a History*, 603

10. Alexander, "Law empowered slave catchers," A5
11. Hensel, 11
12. "The Sadsbury Murder," 2
13. Slaughter, 69
14. Ibid., 77-78
15. "Christiana's Notable Day," 2
16. Slaughter, 79
17. The riot was first called the "Sadsbury Murder" or the "Sadsbury Outrage" because it took place in the township so named. The town of Christiana was about two miles away from the farmhouse, and it became known as the Christiana Riot. Today, historians refer to the event as the Christiana Resistance.
18. "The Riot of 1851," 4
19. "The Christiana Treason Cases," 1
20. Hood, 285
21. Hensel, 128
22. McCaskey, John P., "Samuel Breck, Thaddeus Stevens," 192
23. McCaskey, John P., "The Inaugural Address," 14
24. Brubaker, A11
25. "Return Home of Hon. Thaddeus Stevens," 2
26. "Thaddeus Stevens," 184
27. McCaskey, John P., "Samuel Breck, Thaddeus Stevens," 192
28. *High School News*, June 1906, 1
29. Bordewich
30. Harris, 1
31. Hood, 286
32. "Thaddeus Stevens. Memorial Day Tribute at His Tomb," 28
33. McCaskey, John P., "Thaddeus Stevens," 263
34. Ibid.
35. McCaskey, John P., "Samuel Breck, Thaddeus Stevens," 193
36. McCaskey, John P., "Thaddeus Stevens," 262
37. Hood, 289
38. McCaskey, John P., "Samuel Breck, Thaddeus Stevens," 192
39. Hood, 281
40. Bordewich
41. Alexander, "Buchanan Heads Nation Headed to Crisis," A9
42. Inglet lecture
43. "All Lancaster Celebrates," 8
44. Ibid.
45. With plans to retire from public life, Buchanan had just purchased Wheatland, in Lancaster, for his residence. Alexander, "Buchanan Heads Nation Headed to Crisis," A9
46. "A Proclamation," 2
47. "The National Fast," 2

Chapter 6
Goodbye to Mr. Reigart and Mr. McCaskey

1. Kieffer, "A Lancaster Schoolboy," 29
2. McCaskey, John P., "A Busy Life on Varied Lines through Sixty Years," 239
3. Diffenderffer, 110
4. Kay Adelman in discussion with the author, 27 July 2009
5. "A Proclamation," 2
6. "The Fast Day," 2. Restaurants and taverns were not closed and did "a smashing business, from

which, [a local paper inferred] that the fasting part . . . was the exception, not the rule of the day."

7. "At Home," 2
8. "Reception of President Buchanan," 2
9. Young, 15
10. "Proceedings of Court," 3
11. "The Old Guard Has Spoken," 2
12. Ibid.
13. Young, 16
14. "The Flag Raising in Centre Square," 2
15. Ibid.
16. "The War Excitement," 2
17. Chapman, 3
18. "The War Excitement," 2
19. Many years later, McCaskey recalled that "[t]he Jackson Rifles and Lancaster Fencibles were the distinctively Lancaster companies that went to the front at the outbreak of the Civil War. We saw them start within a week after the fall of Fort Sumter . . ." McCaskey, John P., "Remarks of Mr. McCaskey," 192
20. Hank Chapman in discussion with the author
21. Chapman, 4
22. Ibid., 7
23. Ibid., 8
24. "The War Feeling—Arrival of the Ohio Volunteers," 2
25. "War Fervor," 2
26. Ibid.
27. McCaskey, John P., "Remarks of Mr. McCaskey," 192
28. Chapman, 3
29. Ibid., 9
30. "Teachers and the Draft," 129
31. Board Minutes, July 7, 1859, and July 3, 1862
32. Chapman, page 38
33. "Honoring Themselves," 261-262
34. "The Keystone of the Arch," 504
35. Kieffer, "A Lancaster Schoolboy," 31-34
36. Ibid., 20-23, 26-27
37. Ibid., 23
38. Ibid., 27-28
39. Ibid., 29

Chapter 7
Steel to the Hilt

1. Chapman, 38
2. Young, 24
3. "Rosencrans," 2
4. Chapman, 72
5. Ibid., 15-16, 18
6. Ibid., 19
7. Ibid., 89
8. Ibid., 31
9. Ibid., 82
10. Ibid., 42
11. Ibid., 79
12. Ibid., 69
13. Ibid., 71
14. Ibid., 34
15. Ibid., 71
16. Ibid., 83
17. Ibid., 28, 30
18. Ibid., 37
19. Ibid., 79
20. Ibid., 70

21. Ibid., 16
22. Ibid., 8
23. Ibid., 35
24. Ibid., 16-17
25. Ibid., 19
26. "Copperheads," 2
27. Chapman, 19
28. Ibid., 18
29. Ibid., 38
30. Ibid., 46
31. "The Contrast," 2
32. Chapman, 38
33. Ibid., 5
34. Ibid., 12
35. Ibid.
36. Ibid.
37. Crane, 199-200
38. Chapman, 80
39. Ibid., 13, 3, 84
40. Ibid., 29, 46
41. Ibid., 46
42. Ibid., 85
43. Hank Chapman said in a November 6, 2009, phone conversation that McCaskey exaggerated the number of battles Will fought in. The number was closer to 15.
44. "Col. William Spencer McCaskey," 123
45. Chapman, 46
46. Ibid., 90, 92
47. Farioli, 37
48. Donald McCaskey to Will McCaskey, 1 March 1903
49. Ibid. In fact, by May 1918, two of McCaskey's sons, three grandsons, two nephews, and two grand-nephews, were all U.S. Army officers; two nieces were married to army officers. "Eleven M'Caskeys Serve as Officers," *Evening Sun* May 17, 1918. (city and page number not identified) In William S. McCaskey papers at lancasterhistory.org

Chapter 8
Times of Tribulation

1. William S. McCaskey to J. P. McCaskey, 24 December 1863
2. Chapman, 16
3. Ibid.
4. Young, 32
5. "Defenses of the City," 2
6. Knight, 169-170
7. Caledonia State Park has preserved that history.
8. Young, 60
9. "Local Department," 2
10. Chapman, 29
11. Banner lecture
12. Young, 40
13. Ibid., 19
14. Chapman, 31
15. "The Flag Raising in Centre Square," 2
16. Chapman, 29
17. Ibid., 27
18. McCaskey, John P., "The Health Lift," 33
19. Chapman, 7
20. Ibid., 30
21. "Civil War Draft Days"
22. "The Enrollment," 2
23. "List of Drafted Men," 2
24. Chapman, 31

25. Sener/Sehner Collection
26. "The Conscription," July 28, 1863, 2
27. Chapman, 31
28. "Exempts From the Draft," 2
29. William S. McCaskey to J. P. McCaskey, 24 December 1863
30. Ibid.
31. Board Minutes, Book 4, May 7, 1863
32. Ibid., July 2, 1863
33. Ibid., August 13, 1863
34. Ibid.
35. "Educational Events in Penna.,"197, 230
36. Board Minutes, July 15, 1864, Book 4, page 42
37. William S. McCaskey to J. P. McCaskey, 26 July 1864. This information is in three sentences deleted from Chapman's book, page 46, but included in a photocopy of the original letter Chapman sent the author.
38. Ibid., 69
39. Board Minutes, July 22,1869, Book 6, page 46
40. Chapman, 47
41. "From the Seventy-Ninth," 2
42. Chapman, 76
43. Ibid., 22
44. Ibid., 22-23
45. Ibid., 26
46. William S. McCaskey to J. P. McCaskey, 24 December 1863
47. Ibid., 38
48. Ibid., 77
49. James Marshall to J. P. McCaskey, 13 September 1864
50. James Marshall to J. P. McCaskey, 18 December 1864
51. Chapman, 35
52. "'Colonel Miles' Experiences in 'Dixie'," 2
53. Chapman, 69
54. Slaugh, "Better Know an Officer"
55. Harris, 263
56. "'Boys' of the '79th' in Annual Reunion," 1
57. Chapman, 77
58. "The Conscription," June 7, 1864, 2; "Get Ready for the Draft," 2; "The Draft," September 22, 1864, 2
59. Chapman, 89
60. Ibid., 89
61. Ibid., 83
62. Ibid, 95

Chapter 9
The First Great End of Education Is Character

1. McCaskey, John P., "Life in a High School," 69
2. Hersh, 9-13
3. Ibid., 12-13
4. Ibid., 9-14
5. Ibid., 14
6. McCaskey, John P., "Life in a High School," 69
7. Ibid.
8. Ibid.
9. Ibid.
10. Ibid.
11. McCaskey, John P., "One-Third of a Century," 179
12. Riddle, 39
13. Ibid., 39-40

14. Ibid., 40-42
15. Ibid., 85
16. Ibid., 126-127
17. Board Minutes, Book 2, Feb. 1848, 81
18. McCaskey, John P., "Commit to Memory," 360-361
19. J. P. McCaskey to Margaret McCaskey, 23 October 1892
20. McCaskey edited a book about Penn: *William Penn, the Illustrious Founder of Pennsylvania*
21. Burrowes, *State-Book of Pennsylvania*, 6
22. McCaskey, John P., "Commit to Memory," 241
23. McCaskey, John P. "Life in a High School," 69
24. "A Christmas Loving Cup," 90
25. *High School News, 1906*, 45
26. "A Christmas Loving Cup," 90
27. McCaskey, John P., "Life in a High School," 69
28. McCaskey, John P., "Commit to Memory," 241
29. McCaskey, John P., "Life in a High School," 69
30. Ibid.
31. Diffenderffer, 112
32. McCaskey, John P., "Commit to Memory," 241
33. Ibid.
34. McCaskey, John P., *Lincoln Literary Collection*, 3-4
35. McCaskey, John P., "Life in a High School," 69
36. McCaskey, John P., "Commit to Memory," 360
37. McCaskey, John P., "Methodical Memory Work in Literature," 24
38. McCaskey, John P., "Life in a High School," 69
39. Ibid.
40. Ibid.
41. Ibid.
42. McCaskey, John P., "Commit to Memory," 361
43. Ibid.
44. McCaskey, John P., "Good Memory Work in Literature," 30
45. McCaskey, John P., "Commit to Memory," 359
46. "Autumn Arbor Day," V. 46, 226. The poem was "Forget-Me-Not" in three stanzas of four lines each by Emily Bruce Roelofson.
47. "Spring Arbor Day," 508
48. Ibid.
49. Ibid.
50. Donald McCaskey to Townsend McCaskey, undated.
51. McCaskey, John P., "Good Memory Work," 223

Chapter 10
The High-Souled Teacher

1. McCaskey, John P., "Dr. Burrowes' Elms," 235
2. Riddle, 178
3. Ibid., 178-179
4. Ibid., 179-181
5. Untitled, "Flogging school-boys," 84
6. Board Minutes, Book 1, 398-399, and Book 2, 517
7. Board Minutes, Book 1, Dec. 1845, 389

8. Diffenderffer, 114
9. Kay Adelman in discussion with author July 27, 2009
10. Townsend McCaskey to Tom and Betty McCaskey
11. Townsend McCaskey to Edward McCaskey
12. Ibid.
13. Ibid.
14. Chapman, 38
15. McCaskey, John P., "A Busy Life on Varied Lines through Sixty Years," 243
16. McCaskey, John P., "Some Reminiscences," 256
17. Gordon, 30
18. "Discussion," 99
19. Ibid.
20. Ibid.
21. Ibid.
22. Ibid., 100
23. McCaskey, John P., "Good Memory Work," 223
24. Ibid., 223-224
25. Ibid., 224
26. A complete set of *The Lancaster School Mottoes* is preserved in the library of the Winterthur Museum, Delaware
27. *The Lancaster School Mottoes*
28. McCaskey, John P., "A Busy Life on Varied Lines through Sixty Years," 243
29. Ibid.
30. McCaskey, Patrick K.
31. Michael Adelman in discussion with the author
32. Townsend McCaskey to Tom and Betty McCaskey, 28 November 1981
33. This can be seen in an undated picture in the School District of Lancaster's files at LancasterHistory.org. It shows McCaskey, other teachers, and all the boys in the large study hall. School District of Lancaster Records, 1838-1947
34. "Mercy's Dream," 573
35. "The Picture on the Wall," 228
36. McCaskey, John P., "Life in a High School," 72
37. McCaskey, John P., "Dr. Burrowes' Elms," 235
38. McCaskey, John P., "Life in a High School," 69
39. Hersh, 13
40. Groff
41. McCaskey traveled a great deal: Florida, Louisiana, South Carolina, Colorado, Boston, Chicago, St. Louis, New York, Philadelphia, and Canada, among other places. The family vacationed in the summers at Ocean Grove, New Jersey.
42. Gordon, 29
43. Diffenderffer, 114
44. McCaskey, John P., "Life in a High School," 71-72
45. Ibid., 73
46. Ibid.
47. Ibid.
48. Ibid.
49. Ibid.
50. "Nearly 300 Former Pupils Pay Tribute to Dr. McCaskey," *Testimonial Dinner to Jack McCaskey, 6*

Chapter 11
Teach the Children to Love the Trees

1. De Goey, 20
2. Untitled, "Hon. J. S. Morton," 196
3. Anderson, 32
4. Ibid., 33
5. Stetson, 109
6. Ibid., 90
7. Ibid., 101
8. Ibid., 64-65
9. Untitled, "We remember well…" 180
10. McCaskey, John P., "A Busy Life on Varied Lines through Sixty Years," 242
11. McCaskey, John P., "Life in a High School, Fifty-Two Years," 104
12. Ibid.
13. "Oak Hill at Public Sale," 3
14. McCaskey, John P., "Fifty-Four Years in the High School," 57
15. McCaskey, John P. "A Busy Life on Varied Lines through Sixty Years," 243
16. This is in Lancaster County Central Park. An historical marker commemorates the location as a site of Indian burials.
17. "Our Ninth Arbor Day," 392
18. McCaskey, John P., "Fifty-four Years in High School," 57
19. "Our Educational Fathers," 3
20. "Memorial Addresses," 126
21. "School Excursion to Chiques," 3
22. Diffenderffer, 116
23. Ibid.
24. Ibid.
25. Diffenderffer Family Papers
26. "A Lad Meets a Sad Fate," 1
27. Ibid.
28. Ibid.
29. Diffenderffer Family Papers
30. Ibid.
31. "A Lad Meets a Sad Fate," 1
32. Diffenderffer Family Papers
33. James McCaskey in discussion with author, December 17, 2009
34. Diffenderffer, 116
35. Hersh, 9
36. McCaskey, John P., "An Address That Was Not Read," 9
37. "Talk on Trees," 1
38. Lant, M. W., *Directory*, #21, 135
39. "The Linnaean Society," 128
40. Lant, M. W., *Directory* #21, 135
41. Mombert, 577
42. McCaskey, John P., "The Scotch Broom," 15
43. Ibid., 15-16
44. Ibid., 16
45. Anderson, 32
46. For example: "The Day We Celebrate," 462, and "Spring Arbor Day," Volume 44, 507
47. "Arbor Day in a High School," Journal, V. 53, 182
48. Untitled, "The Arbor Day League…," 174
49. Egleston
50. Untitled, "The space given…," 452
51. "Swinging 'Neath the Old Apple Tree," 470
52. "Woodman, Spare That Tree," 424

53. McCaskey provided its context: In the novel *Heart of Midlothian* by Sir Walter Scott, as the lord of an estate lay dying, he offered advice to his son, advice he said he himself did not follow: "Jock, when ye hae naething else to do, ye may be aye stickin' in a tree; it will be growin', Jock, when ye're sleepin."("Our Fall Arbor Day," 174).
54. "Editorial," *High School News,* June, 1902, 30
55. "Our Spring Arbor Day," 504
56. Untitled, "To spend a day…," 365
57. "The January Cover," 172
58. De Goey, 20
59. Ibid.
60. "Planting Trees," 202-203, and "Arbor Day in Pennsylvania," 320
61. Untitled, "Have you ever…," 184
62. "Planting Trees," 203
63. Ibid.
64. "Arbor Day in the Schools-Circular," 165
65. Drybred, 25
66. "Our School Arbor Day," 243
67. "Fall Fashions," 3
68. "Protect the Birds," 611
69. "Our Spring Arbor Day," 503
70. McCaskey, John P., "An Address That Was Not Read," 8-9
71. McCaskey, Edward W., "Star Study in the Old High School," 32
72. "Stars and Star Groups," 223-224
73. "John Piersol McCaskey, A.M., Ph.D.," 173
74. "Study of the Stars," 21-22
75. Ibid., 21
76. McCaskey, John P., "Yule Marble," 4
77. James McCaskey in discussion with the author, February 23, 2010
78. McCaskey, Edward, 4
79. "Study of the Stars," 21
80. "Stars and Star Groups of Our Winter Heavens," 224
81. Thoreau, 182

Chapter 12
A Miracle of Bloom

1. "Our Sixth Arbor Day," 198
2. "Arbor Day," 416
3. "Memorial of Roses," 547
4. "Arbor Day at Lancaster," 490
5. Untitled, "There are very many good men…," 196
6. "Arbor Day at Lancaster," 490
7. "Arbor Day," 413
8. "Spring Arbor Day," 507
9. "Arbor Day at Lancaster, Millersville, and Elsewhere," 427
10. "Autumn Arbor Day" V. 35, 250
11. "Arbor Day Proclamation," 398
12. "Our Sixth Arbor Day," 198-199
13. "Trees Must Be Planted, 374
14. McCaskey, John P., "Annual Message" 1906, 13
15. "Our Spring Arbor Day," 506
16. "La Fayette Arbor Day," 235
17. Ibid., 237
18. James Bowers in discussion with author, March 31, 2015

19. "La Fayette Arbor Day," 237
20. Ibid.
21. "Autumn Arbor Day," V. 35, 250
22. "Our Sixth Arbor Day," 199
23. James Bowers in discussion with author, March 31, 2015
24. "Dr. J. P. McCaskey is 96 Years Old," 2
25. "Our Ninth Arbor Day," 392
26. "Arbor Day at Lancaster, Millersville, and Elsewhere," 428
27. "Arbor Day at Lancaster," 490
28. "Arbor Day Friday, April 22," 411
29. "Our Spring Arbor Day at Lancaster High School," 498
30. "Memorial of Roses," 547
31. "Our Seventh Arbor Day," 420
32. Donald McCaskey to Townsend McCaskey
33. "Nineteenth Arbor Day," 500
34. Ibid., 503
35. "Pleasures That Are Not Sought," 433
36. "Arbor Day at Lancaster, Millersville, and Elsewhere," 422
37. "Arbor Day," New Era, 1
38. Schaeffer, 183
39. "Our Sixth Arbor Day," 199
40. "Autumn Arbor Day," V. 35, 250-251
41. Ibid., 250
42. "Our Sixth Arbor Day," 198
43. Ibid.
44. "Our Eighth Arbor Day," 178
45. J. P. McCaskey to Nellie McCaskey, 19 January 1930
46. Ibid.
47. Michael Adelman in discussion with author
48. Kay Adelman in discussions with author, July 31
49. Ibid.
50. Michael Adelman in discussion with author
51. McCaskey, Edward "304", 2

Chapter 13
The Charm of Old Enoch Lytle's Fiddle

1. McCaskey, John P., "One-Third of a Century," 180
2. J. P. McCaskey to Nellie McCaskey, 3 October 1901
3. J. P. McCaskey to Will and Nellie McCaskey, 1 September 1895
4. Ibid.
5. McCaskey, John P., "A Busy Life on Varied Lines through Sixty Years," 240
6. Ibid.
7. "Preface"
8. "Dr. McCaskey, the Man," 6
9. "The Douglas Family," 1507
10. J. P. McCaskey to Nellie McCaskey, 5 October 1922
11. "The Douglas Family," 1507-1508
12. J. P. McCaskey to Will and Nellie McCaskey, 1 September 1895
13. Ibid.
14. Ibid.
15. "The Douglas Family," 1509
16. "Jenkins Davis," 1519
17. J. P. McCaskey to Will and Nellie McCaskey, 1 September 1895

18. Ibid.
19. "The Douglas Family" 1507
20. J. P. McCaskey to Will and Nellie McCaskey,1 September 1895
21. "Romantic Story of Ancient Church," 8
22. Ibid.
23. Information from caption of a photograph of the oldest tombstones in St. John's Cemetery. Picture in private collection.
24. "A New Cemetery Dedicated," 2
25. Ross, 9
26. "Romantic Story of Ancient Church," 8
27. McCaskey, John P., "One-Third of a Century," 180
28. "The Douglas Family," 1509
29. Ibid.
30. McCaskey, John P., "One-Third of a Century," 180
31. "Jenkins Davis," 1520
32. McCaskey, John P., Treasury of Song, Volume I, 3
33. Diffenderffer, 117
34. McCaskey, John P., "One-Third of a Century," 180
35. Stoltzfus Family in discussion with the author
36. Howe, 239
37. "Vocal Music in Common Schools," 332
38. Perrot, 294
39. Board Minutes, Book 1, Feb. and March, 1839
40. Board Minutes, Jan. 30, 1862
41. Board Minutes, Sept. 10, 1844
42. Riddle, 249-250
43. McCaskey, John P., "One-Third of a Century," 179-180
44. Ibid., 180
45. Ibid.
46. "Music in a High School," 111
47. "Christmas at the High School," 62
48. McCaskey, John P., "One-Third of a Century," 180
49. Board Minutes, Book 8, 497-498
50. "Music in a High School," 113
51. Ibid.
52. Diffenderffer, 115
53. "Music in a High School," 113-114
54. McCaskey, John P., "Life in a High School," 72
55. McCaskey, Richard D., "Alumni Address," 34
56. "Music in a High School," 114
57. Ibid.
58. McCaskey, John P., "An Address That Was Not Read," 10
59. Klein, *Lancaster County Pennsylvania, a History*, 995
60. Hersh, 10-13
61. McCaskey, John P., "One-Third of a Century," 180

Chapter 14
Christmas All Year Long

1. McCaskey, John P., "Christmas Cheer," 319
2. Information from *The Hereditary Register of the United States of America 1978*, pages 618-620, according to photocopies in private collection.
3. "Christmas Festival, Tribute to Dr. Higbee," 267

4. "Of Christmas Cheer," 330
5. Diffenderffer, 111
6. "An Ambrosial Night," 1
7. Donald McCaskey to Townsend McCaskey, undated
8. Diffenderffer, 115
9. Undated photo in the School District of Lancaster Records, 1838-1947
10. McCaskey, John P., "Life in a High School," 72
11. "Christmas at High School," 61
12. "Christmas Loving Cup," 84
13. "Christmas at High School," 63
14. "Of Christmas Cheer," 330
15. "Christmas Exercises," 42
16. Donald McCaskey to Townsend McCaskey, undated
17. Diffenderffer, 115
18. "Christmas Entertainment," 1
19. Ibid., 2
20. "Christmas Exercises," 42
21. "Christmas Entertainment," 2
22. Diffenderffer, 115
23. "Christmas at High School," 63
24. "Christmas Entertainment," 1
25. "Christmas with the Boys," 32
26. "Christmas Exercises," 42
27. "Christmas at High School," 62-63
28. "Christmas Entertainment," 2
29. Diffenderffer, 115
30. Donald McCaskey to Townsend McCaskey, undated
31. McCaskey, John P., "Spirit of Christmas," 308
32. Ibid.
33. Ibid.
34. Ibid.
35. "Christmas Loving Cup," 92
36. Ibid.
37. Ibid., 83
38. Ibid.
39. Ibid., 86
40. Ibid., 84
41. Ibid., 86
42. Ibid., 91
43. Ibid.
44. Ibid.
45. Ibid.
46. "Christmas Cheer," 319
47. Kieffer, "Christmas Customs of Lancaster County," 178
48. Landis, 130
49. "Jolly Old St. Nicholas," 54
50. "Scrapbook, 1880-1912"
51. Murray may have done so, for he edited a school songbook in which the poem, set to music, appeared. "Hymns and Carols of Christmas"
52. Ibid.
53. Lestz, 10
54. "Jolly Old St. Nicholas," 54. The 1967 and 1970 articles also claimed that McCaskey had sketched an original picture of Santa Claus with a sprig of holly in his hat to be printed with the song, further proof of his connection to "Jolly Old St. Nicholas." However, the sketch is very similar in style to other Santa Claus pictures by artist Thomas Nast. Many of them feature a holly sprig in Santa's hat. McCaskey had used a Nast illustration in his Christmas volume.
55. Donald McCaskey to Harold F. Diffenderffer, 17 July 1961
56. Kay Adelman and James McCaskey in discussions with the author
57. McCaskey, John P., "Life in a High School," 72
58. "The Picture on the Wall," 228

59. J. P. McCaskey to Nellie McCaskey, 3 October 1901
60. McCaskey, John P., "A Busy Life on Varied Lines through Sixty Years," 239-240
61. Ibid., 239
62. From ads in *The Pennsylvania School Journal*, Volume 41, after p. 226
63. McCaskey, John P., *A Treasury of Song, Volume I*, 2
64. Kieffer, "Christmas Customs of Lancaster County," 178
65. McCaskey, John P., *Franklin Square Song Collection, Volume 1*, 2
66. "The Song Collection," 150
67. McCaskey, John P., "A Busy Life on Varied Lines through Sixty Years," 234
68. McCaskey, John P., *Favorite Songs and Hymns*, 2
69. McCaskey, John P., *A Treasury of Song*, Insert
70. McCaskey, John P., "A Busy Life on Varied Lines," 47
71. McCaskey, John P., *Favorite Songs and Hymns*, 2
72. "Of Thee I Sing"
73. "Dr. McCaskey, the Man," February 2, 6
74. McCaskey, John P., *A Treasury of Song*, Insert
75. Ibid.
76. Ibid., Volume 1, 3
77. McCaskey, John P., *Favorite Songs and Hymns*, 10
78. Ibid., 156
79. McCaskey, John P., "A Busy Life on Varied Lines through Sixty Years," 241
80. Kay Adelman in discussion with author, August 12, 2009
81. Ibid., June 20 and July 27, 2009
82. James McCaskey in discussion with author, February 23, 2010
83. Ibid.
84. Townsend McCaskey to Tom and Betty McCaskey, November 28, 1981.
85. McCaskey, John P., "Spirit of Christmas," 308
86. Ibid., 309
87. Donald McCaskey to Townsend McCaskey, undated
88. McCaskey, John P., "A Busy Life on Varied Lines," 50
89. "Dr. McCaskey, the Man," February 5, 6
90. "The Marble Booster." The books included 500 volumes for general reading, which included the Harvard Classics in 50 volumes; 10 volumes of Thackeray, five of the World's Greatest Events, five of Short Story Classics, among others. Additionally, McCaskey included 300 reference books for teachers.
91. McCaskey, John P., "Be Good to Live With," 149
92. McCaskey, John P., "A Busy Life on Varied Lines," 50
93. McCaskey, John P., "Be Good to Live With," 150
94. "Dr. McCaskey, the Man," February 2, 6
95. Ibid.
96. Kay McCaskey Adelman in discussion with author, July 27, 2009
97. Edward McCaskey to Susan Garofola
98. Kay McCaskey Adelman in discussion with author, July 31, 2009
99. Ibid., June, 2009

Chapter 15
The Best Good of All

1. "Mayoralty Campaign," 68
2. "Retirement of Dr. McCaskey," 6
3. Ibid.
4. "Mayor of Lancaster after Fifty Years," 487
5. Ibid., 488
6. Schaeffer, 42
7. "Mayor of Lancaster after Fifty Years," 488
8. Ibid.
9. Ibid., 490
10. "Jack's Boys Hold Their Final Grand Rally," 1
11. Ibid.
12. "The Sentimental Candidate," 4
13. "Jack's Boys Hold Their Final Grand Rally," 1
14. "Mayor of Lancaster after Fifty Years," 490
15. "McCaskey Elected," 1
16. Ibid.
17. Ibid.
18. Ibid. Two years later on his second election night, speaking from the same spot, McCaskey told another cheering crowd that in his childhood years, he had been a Democrat. "All about us were Whigs, but my father's family were all good Democrats. When James K. Polk and Henry Clay were rival candidates for the Presidency in 1844, and the long lines of farm wagons going to the Whig mass meetings at Lancaster passed up the 'Old Road,' with their banners and bells, and cheering thousands, as it seemed, dragging behind them great bundles of poke (Polk) through the dust and mud, in contempt of our candidate, we Democratic lads were all on fire at the indignity. I remained a Democrat until nearly twelve years of age." ("Serenaded the Mayor," 1)
19. "Mayor of Lancaster after Fifty Years," 489
20. Ibid., 493
21. Ibid.
22. "The Sentimental Candidate," 4
23. "Stops the Clansman," page 1
24. "McCaskey Elected," 1
25. "Mayor McCaskey Inducted into Office," 1
26. Ibid.
27. McCaskey, John P., "The Inaugural Address," 14-15
28. "McCaskey's Great Sweep," 1
29. "Mayor McCaskey Inducted into Office," 1
30. McCaskey, John P., "Mayor's Inaugural Address," 440-441
31. McCaskey, John P., "Annual Message of John P. McCaskey," 1907, 7
32. Ibid., 7-8
33. "A Bald Campaign Lie," 1
34. McCaskey, John P., "Annual Message of John P. McCaskey," 1906, 6
35. Ibid., 1907, 6
36. Ibid., 1908, 5
37. Ibid., 1909, 6
38. "Mayor McCaskey Gives Advice to Policemen," 1
39. "Warning to Spitters," 1
40. "A Warning about Fireworks, 2
41. "An Exciting Incident," 2

42. "Nice Crowd before the Mayor," 1
43. "Hadn't Learned It," 1
44. McCaskey, John P., "Mayor's Inaugural Address," 440
45. "Let the Good Work Go On," 4
46. "Letter Carriers' Banquet," 2
47. "Sabbath Observance," 1
48. "Mayor Favors Blue Laws," 1
49. "Sabbath Observance," 1
50. Diffenderffer, 117
51. "Sunday Observance," 2
52. Diffenderffer, 117
53. "It Has Cost Him $409.33," 1
54. "Sunday Observance," 2
55. "Greek Passes the $200 Mark," 2
56. "Stops The Clansman," 1
57. Ibid.
58. "Mayor Stops the 'Birth of a Nation'," 1
59. Other community leaders, such as J. P. Wickersham, also called for public parks. "Our School Arbor Day," 249
60. "Our Ninth Arbor Day," 392
61. "Our Spring Arbor Day," 506
62. Ibid. Also, McCaskey was a stockholder, member of the board of the Lancaster Cremation and Funeral Reform Society, and one of the leaders of the movement for cremation, according to articles in the *New Holland Clarion* between 1884 and 1895.
63. McCaskey, John P., "Annual Message of John P. McCaskey," 1906, 15
64. Ibid., 14
65. "Lancaster City Enjoys Its Biggest Building Boom," 1
66. "The Issue Over City Labor," 2
67. Denlinger, 126
68. McCaskey, John P., "Mayor's Inaugural Address," 1908, 443
69. Ibid., 443-446
70. Ibid., 444
71. Ibid., 446
72. Ibid.
73. "The Mayor's Welcome," 7. "We schoolboys knew [Wise] well, and were all awake when he was at work on a new balloon in his pleasant yard on Lime street, and more than ever when he announced the date of his next trip among the clouds. … I remember well seeing him come home from his last successful ascension, and hearing him tell the story of it. He had started from St. Louis and landed somewhere in Ohio or New York. He left St. Louis on another trial trip, it being his purpose to attempt to cross the Atlantic if he should reach the coast on this trip. But neither he nor his balloon was ever seen or heard of again."
74. "The Flag of Lancaster," 163
75. Ibid.,164-165
76. Ibid., 165-166
77. "It Was a Happy Campaign Thought," 3
78. "Fulton Celebration Splendid Success," 1
79. "Report of Committee Which Arranged the Robert Fulton Celebration at Fulton House," 194-196, 219-220
80. "Pleasant Weather Only Thing Needed," 1
81. "Report of Committee Which Arranged the Robert Fulton Celebration at Fulton House," 194-196
82. Ibid., 209-210
83. Ibid., 211-213
84. "Mayoralty Campaign," 68

Chapter 16

A Reverence for Things Sacred and Divine

1. McCaskey, John P., "Some Reminiscences of 'Old Leacock,'" 257
2. "Nearly 300 Former Pupils Pay Tribute to Dr. McCaskey," 6-7
3. Ibid.
4. "'Boys' from 45 Classes Gather," 16
5. Donald McCaskey to Harold F. Diffenderffer, 17 July 1961
6. "'Boys' from 45 Classes Gather," 1
7. Diffenderffer, 118. The text includes these lines: "Every morning, when we go forth, we lay the moulding hand upon our destiny; and every evening, when we have done, we leave a deathless impression upon our characters. We touch not a wire but vibrates in eternity,—we breathe not a thought but reports at the Throne of God."
8. "Nearly 300 Former Pupils Pay Tribute to Dr. McCaskey," 5
9. "Some Extracts From Letters," 16
10. Ibid., 14
11. Ibid., 15
12. "To the 'Old Boys': Greeting," 3
13. McCaskey, "An Address That Was Not Read," 7-10
14. "'Boys' from 45 Classes Gather," 16
15. McCaskey, John P., "One-third of a Century," 179
16. McCaskey, John P., "Life in a High School," 73
17. McCaskey, John P., "After Forty Years," 41
18. Untitled, "We have heard …," 120
19. "Spring Arbor Day," 502
20. "Co-Education Defeated," 1
21. McCaskey, John P., "After Forty Years," 42
22. "Our Yellow Elephant," 4
23. McCaskey, John P., "Address of Dr. McCaskey," 114
24. John P. McCaskey to Will and Nellie McCaskey, 1 September 1895
25. "John Piersol McCaskey," 120.
26. Wickersham, "The Rise of the Teachers' Profession," 655
27. McCaskey, John P., "After Forty Years," 39
28. McCaskey, John P., "Fifty-Four Years in the High School," 54
29. "The January Cover," 172
30. "Transfer of Ownership," 550
31. "The January Cover," 172
32. McCaskey, John P., "A Busy Life on Varied Lines through Sixty Years," 236
33. Wickersham, "An Era of Growth," 575
34. "John Piersol McCaskey," 120
35. Untitled, "Our first visit …" 197
36. McCaskey, John P., "Thomas H. Burrowes, LL.D.," Volume 39, 236
37. *St. James' Church Vestry Book*, July 31, 1895; January 3, 1896; April 10, 1896; April 20, 1896
38. "Dr. McCaskey, the Man," February 2, 6
39. Van Ingen, 1-2
40. Klein, "The Reverend Clifford Gray Twombly," 220
41. Cobey, 112-113
42. Loose, 105
43. Klein, "The Reverend Clifford Gray Twombly," 220

44. St. James' Vestry Minutes, October 1, 1920, page 202, and November 3, 1922, page 230. See also vestry's call for investigation of Law and Order Society, October 5, 1928, page 315.
45. Loose, 108
46. Betts, 222
47. Leo Shelley in discussion with the author
48. Ibid.
49. McCaskey, John P., "Yule Marble," 10
50. Garrison McCaskey to Margaret McCaskey
51. "No. 600," 303
52. McCaskey, John P., "A Busy Life on Varied Lines through Sixty Years," 239
53. Archives Division
54. "Mayor Favors Blue Laws," 1
55. McCaskey, John P., "A Busy Life on Varied Lines through Sixty Years," 239-240
56. John P. McCaskey to Nellie McCaskey, 3 October 1901
57. Ibid.
58. McCaskey, John P., "The Health Lift," 34
59. Ibid., 33
60. Ibid.
61. Ibid., 35
62. "Dr. McCaskey Hurt," 573
63. "Some Extracts from Letters," 11
64. Note in McCaskey's handwriting on back of photo of his son Walter, 1902
65. John P. McCaskey to Nellie McCaskey, 3 October 1901, and John P. McCaskey to Eleanor McCaskey, 15 September 1916
66. "Dr. McCaskey's Candidacy," 4
67. "John Piersol McCaskey," 121
68. "McCaskey, John P., "Physical Training in the Public Schools"
69. Kieffer, "A Lancaster Schoolboy Views the Civil War," 32
70. "McCaskey's Exerciser Permanently on View," 1
71. "The Health Lift," 33-34
72. "McCaskey's Exerciser Permanently on View," 1
73. "President Greets Dr. M'Caskey on 95th Anniversary," 1, 5
74. Ibid.
75. Ibid., 5
76. Ibid.
77. "Rites Sunday for Dr. M'Caskey," 1, 8
78. "Throngs Pass M'Caskey Bier," 3
79. "Hundreds Attend Last Rites Held for Dr. M'Caskey," 1
80. "Throngs Pass M'Caskey Bier," 3
81. McCaskey had been a member of the Masons' Lodge No. 43 in Lancaster for over 70 years, according to "Rites Sunday for Dr. M'Caskey."
82. Diffenderffer, 119.
83. McCaskey, "Some Reminiscences of 'Old Leacock'," 256
84. Ibid., 257
85. Ibid.
86. Ibid.
87. Ibid., 258
88. Ibid.
89. Ibid.
90. Ibid.
91. Ibid.
92. Kay McCaskey Adelman in discussion with the author, August, 2009

Bibliography

Adelman, Kay (Katharine) McCaskey (great-granddaughter), in discussions with the author, Lancaster, Pennsylvania: June, July, and August, 2009.

Adelman, Michael (great-great-grandson), in discussion with the author, Lancaster, Pennsylvania: October, 2009.

"Address That Was Not Read, An," *Testimonial Dinner to Jack McCaskey*, Lancaster, Pennsylvania (1926): 7-10.

Alexander, Larry, "Buchanan Heads Nation Headed to Crises." *Intelligencer/New Era* (Lancaster) May 3, 2011: A9.

———, "(A) Nation Mourns," *LNP* (Lancaster) April 21, 2015: 1, A10.

———, "Law Empowered Slave Catchers," *Intelligencer/New Era* (Lancaster) March 29, 2011: A5.

"All Lancaster Celebrates Abraham Lincoln Centenary," *Intelligencer Journal* (Lancaster) February 12, 1909: 1, 8.

"Ambrosial Night, An," *Testimonial Dinner to Jack McCaskey*. Lancaster, Pennsylvania (1926):1-3.

Anderson, Byron, "Julius Sterling Morton," *Forest History Today* Fall 2000: 31-33. www.foresthistory.org/pu

"Arbor Day," *New Era* (Lancaster) April 16, 1885: 1.

"Arbor Day," *The Pennsylvania School Journal* 33, no. 10 (1885): 413-416.

"Arbor Day at Lancaster," *The Pennsylvania School Journal* 34, no. 12 (1886): 490-493.

"Arbor Day at Lancaster, Millersville, and Elsewhere," *The Pennsylvania School Journal* 33, no. 11 (1885): 421-428.

"Arbor Day, Friday, April 22," *The Pennsylvania School Journal* 35, no. 10 (1887): 411.

"Arbor Day in Pennsylvania," *The Pennsylvania School Journal* 33, no. 8 (1885): 320.

"Arbor Day in the Schools- Circular," *The Pennsylvania School Journal* 34, no. 4 (1885): 165-166.

"Arbor Day Proclamation," *The Pennsylvania School Journal* 34, no. 10 (1886): 398.

Archives Division, Records and Archives Services Office. Lancaster County Courthouse, Lancaster, Pennsylvania. Photocopy in private collection.

"At Home," *Lancaster Examiner and Herald* (Lancaster) March 6, 1861: 2.

"Autumn Arbor Day," *The Pennsylvania School Journal* 35, no. 6 (1886): 248-251.

"Autumn Arbor Day," *The Pennsylvania School Journal* 46, no. 5 (1897): 226-229.

"Bald Campaign Lie, A," *New Era* (Lancaster) February 17, 1908: 1.

Banner, Glenn, "The Burning of the Columbia-Wrightsville Bridge 150 Years Later," Lecture at LancasterHistory.org June 27, 2013.

Betts, Peter J., "A History of the Lancaster Law and Order Society." *Journal of the Lancaster County Historical Society* (Lancaster) 69 (1965): 215-239.

Board Minutes, School District of Lancaster Records, 1838-1947 Manuscript Group, LancasterHistory.org.

Bordewich, Fergus, "Digging into a Historic Rivalry," *Smithsonian Magazine*. February 2004. http://www.smithsonianmag.com/history/digging-into-a-historic-rivalry-106194163/.

Bowers, James (City Arborist Lancaster, Pennsylvania) in discussion with author, Lancaster: March 2013 and 2015.

"'Boys' from 45 Classes Gather to Pay Tribute to Ex-Teacher." *Sunday News* (Lancaster) October 10, 1926: 1, 16.

Brubaker, Jack, "Stevens' Historic Profile Grows," *Intelligencer/New Era* (Lancaster) April 7, 2012: A11.

Burrowes, Thomas H., *State-Book of Pennsylvania.* Philadelphia: Uriah Hunt and Son, 1847.

Chapman, Hank (great-grandnephew), in discussion with the author, Columbia State Park, California: September, 2012.

——— (ed.), *The Letters of William S. McCaskey: Civil War Letters of the Last Officer to Retire from Lincoln's First Call for 75,000 Troops.* West Conshohocken PA: Infinity Publishing, 2008: 124 pages.

"Christiana's Notable Day," *New Era* (Lancaster) September 11, 1911: 2.

"Christina Treason Cases, The," *Lancaster Examiner and Herald* (Lancaster) November 26, December 3 and 10, 1851: 1-2.

"Christmas at High School," *High School News* (Lancaster) June 1906: 61-63.

"Christmas Cheer," *The Pennsylvania School Journal* 54, no. 7 (January 1906): 319-320.

"Christmas Entertainment," *High School News* I, no. 1 (January 1897): 1-2.

"Christmas Exercises," *High School News* IV, no. 4 (December 1899): 41-42.

"Christmas Festival, Tribute to Dr. Higbee," *The Pennsylvania School Journal* 38, no. 7 (January 1890): 267-269.

"Christmas Loving Cup, A," *High School News* (Lancaster) June, 1906: 83-96.

"Christmas with the Boys," *High School News* II, no. 4 (December 1897): 32-33.

Clark, Martha B., "Lancaster County's Relation to Slavery." *Journal of the Lancaster County Historical Society* (Lancaster) 15, no. 2 (1911): 43-61.

Cobey, Harry S., "The Lancaster Law and Order Society, 1912-1972." *Journal of the Lancaster County Historical Society* (Lancaster) 93 (1991): 112-117.

"Col. William Spencer McCaskey," *Biographical Annals of Lancaster County.* The Reprint Company Publishers, Spartanburg, South Carolina Volume 1: 122-126.

"Co-Education Defeated," *Intelligencer Journal* (Lancaster) June 8, 1906: 1.

"Commencement," *The Pennsylvania School Journal* 37, no. 2 (August 1888): 69-70.

"Conscription, The," *Intelligencer Journal* (Lancaster) July 28, 1863: 2.

"Conscription, The," *Intelligencer Journal* (Lancaster) June 7, 1864: 2.

"Contrast, The," *Daily Evening Express* (Lancaster) June 20, 1864: 2.

"Copperheads," *Lancaster Examiner and Herald* (Lancaster) June 10, 1863: 2.

Crane, Stephen. *The Red Badge of Courage*. New York: The Modern Library, 1993.

"Day We Celebrate, The" *The Pennsylvania School Journal* 35, no.11 (1887): 462-463.

Dedication Exercises of the Boys' High School Lancaster, Pennsylvania. Lancaster PA: The New Era Printing Company, 1919.

De Goey, Roger (trans.), Elizabeth McVey. "Belgium Demands Arbor Day." *The Pennsylvania School Journal* 35, no. 1 (1886): 19-23.

Denlinger, Robert C. (ed.), *Paradise Our Heritage Our Home.* Lancaster County: Paradise Township Citizens, Inc, 1997.

"Departure of the Fencibles," *Daily Evening Express*, (Lancaster) April 19, 1861: 3.

Diffenderffer Family Papers, 1691-1963 Manuscript Group 410, Folder 19, Insert 3, and Folder 20, Inserts 2 and 3. LancasterHistory.org.

Diffenderffer, Harold F. "Life and Times of John Piersol McCaskey." *Journal of the Lancaster County Historical Society* 67, no. 3 (1963): 109-120.

"Discussion," *The Pennsylvania School Journal* 29, no. 3 (September 1880): 98-100.

Donald McCaskey to Harold F. Diffenderffer, 17 July 1961. Diffenderffer Family Papers, Folder 20.

Donald McCaskey to Townsend McCaskey, undated. Private collection.

Donald McCaskey to William S. McCaskey, 1 March 1903. Private collection.

"Douglas Family, The," *Biographical Annals of Lancaster County* Southwest Pennsylvania Genealogical Services, 1987 Volume 4:1507-1511.

"Dr. J. P. McCaskey Dies of Pneumonia, Aged 97, Dean of Pa. Educators," *Intelligencer Journal* (Lancaster) September 20, 1935: 1, 16.

"Dr. McCaskey Hurt," *The Pennsylvania School Journal* 62, no. 12 (1914): 573-574.

"Dr. McCaskey, the Man," *New Era* (Lancaster) February 2, 5 and 6, 1906: 6.

"Dr. McCaskey's Candidacy," *New Era* (Lancaster) January 13, 1906. 4.

Drybred, John, "High School Remembers J. P. McCaskey at 150," *Intelligencer Journal.* (Lancaster) October 10, 1987: 36, 25.

"Editorial," *High School News* VI, no. 1 (June 1902).

"Educational Events in Penna.," *The Pennsylvania School Journal* 11, nos. 7 and 8 (1863): 197, 230.

Edward McCaskey to Susan Garofola (Alumni Coordinator for J.P. McCaskey High School) 12 May 1999. High School Alumni Association office.

Egleston, Nathaniel H., "Tree-Planting- #1-7," *The Pennsylvania School Journal,* Volume 33, nos. 4-10 (1884-85).

"Enrollment, The," *Intelligencer Journal* (Lancaster) July 14, 1863: 2.

Eshleman, H. Frank, "Lincoln's Visit to Lancaster in 1861; And the Passing of His Corpse in 1865." *Journal of the Lancaster County Historical Society* 13, no. 3 (1909): 55-79.

"Exciting Incident, An," *New Era* (Lancaster) August 27, 1908: 2.

"Exempts from the Draft," *Daily Evening Express* (Lancaster) August 7, 1863: 2.

"Fall Fashions." *New Era* (Lancaster) October 22, 1884: 3.

Farioli, Dennis, Ron Nichols and Lee Noyes, *Last Man Standing: William Spencer McCaskey.* Self-published 2014.

"Fast Day, The," *Lancaster Examiner and Herald* (Lancaster) January 9, 1861: 2.

Federal Census Records. AncestryLibrary.com. 1850, 1860, 1870, 1880.

"Flag of Lancaster, The." *Journal of the Lancaster County Historical Society* 11, no. 4 (1907) 162-166.

"Flag Raising in Centre Square, The," *Daily Evening Express* (Lancaster) April 18, 1861: 2.

Franklin & Marshall College Board of Trustees' Minutes,1853-1881; 1882-1897 Franklin & Marshall College Archives, Lancaster, PA.

Franklin & Marshall Faculty Minutes, 1853-1892. Franklin & Marshall College Archives, Lancaster, PA.

"From the Seventy-Ninth," *Daily Evening Express* (Lancaster) August 20, 1864: 2.

"Fulton Celebration Splendid Success," *Intelligencer Journal* (Lancaster) September 22, 1909: 1.

Garrison McCaskey to Margaret McCaskey, 13 February 1887. Private collection.

Gordon, William S., "Tribute from Mr. Gordon." *Testimonial Dinner to Jack McCaskey,* (Lancaster) 1926: 29-30.

Groff, Addison, "Honest Doubt." Undated, unidentified newspaper article in private collection.

"Hadn't Learned It," *New Holland Clarion*, June 6, 1909: 1.

Harris, Alexander, "Hambright, Henry A." *A Biographical History of Lancaster County*. Baltimore: Genealogical Publishing Company Inc., 1977: 262-264.

Harris, Bernard, "Historical Ties Proven." *Intelligencer/New Era* (Lancaster) April 8, 2011: 1.

Harsh, M. Duffield, "Rural One-Room Schoolhouses in Leacock Township, Lancaster County, Pennsylvania." Lancaster County Historical Society. October 31, 2005.

Hensel, William Uhler, "The Christiana Riot and the Treason Trials of 1851." *Journal of the Lancaster County Historical Society* 15, no. 8 (1911): 1-134.

Hersh, Howard M., "Retrospect and Prophecy." *High School News* (Lancaster) June 1906: 9-14.

"High School Graduates." *High School News* (Lancaster) June 1906: 22-31.

"Historical Sketch of Education in Pennsylvania," *The Pennsylvania School Journal* 16, no. 7 (1868): 209-212.

"Honoring Themselves," *The Pennsylvania School Journal* 39, no. 6 (1890): 261-262.

Hood, Alexander, "Thaddeus Stevens." *The Pennsylvania School Journal* 39, no. 7 (1891): 278-289.

Howe, N., "On Music." *The Pennsylvania School Journal* 2, no. 7 (January 1854): 239-240.

"Hymns and Carols of Christmas." www.hymnsandcarolsofchristmas.com/Hymns_and_Carols/jolly_old_st_nicholas.htm.

"Hundreds Attend Last Rites Held for Dr. M'Caskey," *Intelligencer Journal* (Lancaster) September 23, 1935: 1, 12.

Inglet, Thomas, "James Buchanan." Lecture at Chestnut Street Mennonite Church, Lancaster, Pennsylvania. March, 2011.

"Issue over City Labor, The," *New Era* (Lancaster) April 15, 1908: 2.

"It Has Cost Him $409.33," *Intelligencer Journal* (Lancaster) September 22, 1909: 1

"It Was a Happy Campaign Thought," *New Era* (Lancaster) March 7, 1908, 3.

"Jack's Boys Hold Their Final Grand Rally," *New Era* (Lancaster) February 17, 1906: 1, 3.

James Marshall to John P. McCaskey, 13 September 1864. In author's collection.

"January Cover, The," *The Pennsylvania School Journal* 101, no. 5 (January 1953): 172.

"Jenkins Davis." *Biographical Annals of Lancaster County* Southwest Pennsylvania Genealogical Services, 1987 Volume 4:1519-1520.

"John McCaskey," *Biographical Annals of Lancaster County* The Reprint Company Publishers, Spartanburg, South Carolina, 1985 Volume 1: 116-117.

"John Piersol McCaskey," *Biographical Annals of Lancaster County* The Reprint Company Publishers, Spartanburg, South Carolina, 1985 Volume 1:117-122.

"John Piersol McCaskey, A.M., Ph.D.," *Portrait and Biographical Record of Lancaster County*. Southwest Pennsylvania Genealogical Services, Laughlintown, Pennsylvania, 1988: 170-175.

John P. McCaskey to Eleanor McCaskey, 15 September 1916. Private collection.

John P. McCaskey to Margaret M. McCaskey, 23 October 1892. Private collection.

John P. McCaskey to Nellie McCaskey, 3 October 1901. Private collection.

John P. McCaskey to Nellie McCaskey, 5 October 1922. Private collection.

John P. McCaskey to Nellie McCaskey, 19 January 1930. Private collection.

John P. McCaskey to Will and Nellie McCaskey, 20 March 1891. Private collection.

John P. McCaskey to Will and Nellie McCaskey, 1 September 1895. Private collection.

"Jolly Old St. Nicholas." *Sunday News* (Lancaster) December 20, 1970: 54.

"J. P. McCaskey Is 96 Years Old," *New Era (Lancaster)* October 9, 1933: 2.

Kaufman, Jay Warren (ed.), *The Leacock United Presbyterian Church A History 1740-1940.* Lancaster, Pennsylvania: Horting Printing, 1940.

Kersch, Joanne McCaskey (great-granddaughter), in discussions with the author, Wilmington, Delaware: October and November, 2009.

"Keystone of the Arch, The" *The Pennsylvania School Journal* 45, no.10 (1897): 503-504.

Kieffer, Elizabeth Clarke, "A Lancaster Schoolboy Views the Civil War." *Journal of the Lancaster County Historical Society* 54 (1950): 17-37.

———, "Christmas Customs of Lancaster County," *Journal of the Lancaster County Historical Society* 43 (1939): 175-182.

Klein, H. M. J., *Lancaster County Pennsylvania A History* Volumes I and II (1924): 1-544; 547-1172.

Klein, H.M.J., and William Diller, "(The) Reverend Clifford Gray Twombly," In *The History of St. James' Church, 1744-1944*, 219-254. (Lancaster: Published by the Vestry of St. James' Church, 1944).

———, "(The) Reverend William Augustus Muhlenberg," In *The History of St. James' Church, 1744-1944*, 97-110. (Lancaster: Published by the Vestry of St. James' Church, 1944).

"La Fayette Arbor Day." *The Pennsylvania School Journal* 47, no. 5(1898): 234-238.

"Lad Meets a Sad Fate, A." *Intelligencer Journal* (Lancaster) May 18, 1888: 1.

"Lancaster City Enjoys Its Biggest Building Boom," *New Era* (Lancaster) September 5, 1908: 1.

"Lancaster Savings Institution." *Intelligencer Journal* (Lancaster) June 19, 1855: 2.

"Lancaster Savings Institution." *Intelligencer Journal* (Lancaster) June 26, 1855: 2.

Landis, Bertha C., "Rev. Edward Young Buchanan, D.D., Brother of the President." *Journal of the Lancaster County Historical Society* 32 (1928):123-132.

"Lancaster School Mottoes, The." Advertisement in *The Pennsylvania School Journal* 24, no. 5 (1875): At end of issue, not paginated.

"Lancaster to Have a Municipal Flag." *New Era* (Lancaster) April 4, 1907: 1.

Lant, M. W. (compiler), *Lant's Directory of Lancaster City.* Lancaster, Pennsylvania: Cooper, Sanderson, & Co., 1866.

Leacock Township, Lancaster County, Pennsylvania Tax Records. 1847-1859. At LancasterHistory.org.

"Lectures in the High Schools." *Intelligencer Journal* (Lancaster) December 17, 1850: 2.

Lestz, Gerald S., "100-Year-Old Secret." *New Era* (Lancaster) December 20:10.

"Let the Good Work Go On," *New Era* (Lancaster) November 7, 1907: 4.

"Letter Carriers' Banquet," *New Era* (Lancaster) March 13, 1908: 2.

"Linnaean Society, The." *The Pennsylvania School Journal* 15, no. 6 (December 1866): 128

"List of Drafted Men." *Intelligencer Journal* (Lancaster) July 21, 1863: 2.

"Local Department." *Intelligencer Journal* (Lancaster) June 30, 1863: 2.

Loose, John W. W., "A History of Sin and Vice: Lancaster- The Fallen Angel." *Journal of the Lancaster County Historical Society* (Lancaster) 94 (1992): 105-113.

Magerl, Barbara, "Coates, Kersey." 2003 http://www.kchistory.org/cdm4/item_viewer.php?CISOROOT=/Biographies&CISOPTR=38&CISOBOX=1&REC=1 accessed August 27, 2011.

"Marble Booster, The." Private collection.

"Martyred President, The." *The Daily Evening Express* (Lancaster) April 24, 1865: 2.

"Mayoralty Campaign," *High School News* (Lancaster) June 1906: 65-77.

"Mayor Favors Blue Laws," *Intelligencer Journal* (Lancaster) November 26, 1906: 1.

"Mayor McCaskey Gives Advice to Policemen," *Intelligencer Journal* (Lancaster) April 5, 1909: 1.

"Mayor McCaskey Inducted into Office." *New Era*, (Lancaster) April 2, 1906: 1.

"Mayor of Lancaster after Fifty Years in High School," *The Pennsylvania School Journal* 54, no. 11 (1906): 487- 499.

"Mayor Stops the 'Birth of a Nation,'" *Intelligencer Journal* (Lancaster) January 24, 1916: 1.

"Mayor's Welcome, The" *New Era* (Lancaster) September 15, 1908: 7.

McCaskey, Edward, "304." Essay. Private collection.

———, *Ed McCaskey Tells Stories.* Private collection.

McCaskey, Edward W., "Star Study in the Old High School." *The High School NewsJubilee Number* (Lancaster) 1926: 32-33.

"McCaskey Elected," *New Era*, (Lancaster) February 21, 1906: 1.

McCaskey, James (great-grandson), in discussions with the author, Kennett Square, Pennsylvania: December 2009 and February 2010.

McCaskey, John Piersol, "Address at Montreal." *The Pennsylvania School Journal* 46, no. 1 (1897): 25-33.

——— , "Address of Dr. McCaskey." *High School News*, June,1906, 114-117.

———, "(An) Address That Was Not Read." *Testimonial Dinner to Jack McCaskey,* (Lancaster) October 9, 1926: 7-10.

———, “After Forty Years.” *The Pennsylvania School Journal* 45, no. 1 (1896): 37-42.

———, “Annual Message of John P. McCaskey,” *Journal of Select Council.* (Lancaster) June 6, 1906: 3-17.

———, “Annual Message of John P. McCaskey,” *Journal of Select Council.* (Lancaster) June 5, 1907: 3-11.

———, “Annual Message of John P. McCaskey,” *Journal of Select Council.* (Lancaster) June 3, 1908: 3-16.

———, “Annual Message of John P. McCaskey,” *Journal of Select Council.* (Lancaster) June 2, 1909: 3-13.

——— , “(A) Busy Life on Varied Lines,” *High School News*, 1906, 43-54.

———, “(A) Busy Life on Varied Lines through Sixty Years and More.” *The Pennsylvania School Journal* 67, no. 6 (1918): 231-248.

——— (ed.), *Butler's Literary Selections, “Ten-Times-Ten” Series* 3. Lancaster PA: Inquirer P. & P. Co., 1877.

——— (ed.), *Christmas in Song, Sketch, and Story.* New York: Harper & Brothers, 1891.

——— , “(A) Christmas Loving Cup.” *The High School News Jubilee Number* (Lancaster) June 1906: 83-96.

———, “Commit to Memory.” *The Pennsylvania School Journal* 41, no. 6 (1892): 240-242.

———, “Dr. Burrowes' Elms.” *The Pennsylvania School Journal* 43, no. 5 (1895): 235-237.

———, “Dr. Higbee, Greetings!.” *The Pennsylvania School Journal* 29, no. 10 (1880): 429-430.

——— (ed.), *Favorite Songs and Hymns for School and Home.* New York: American Book Company, 1890.

——— , “Fifty-four Years in the High School.” *The High School News Jubilee Number* (Lancaster) June 1906: 54-58.

——— (ed.), *(The) Franklin Square Song Collection.* Harper and Brothers and American Book Company, New York, Numbers 1(1881,184 pages), 2 (1884, 176 pages), 6 (1889, 184 pages), 7 (1890, 184 pages).

———, "Good Memory Work." *The Pennsylvania School Journal* 54, no. 5 (November 1905): 221-228.

———, "(The) Health Lift." *Testimonial Dinner to Jack McCaskey,* (Lancaster) October 9, 1926: 33-35.

———, "(The) Inaugural Address." *Journal of Select Council.* (Lancaster) April 2,1906: 12-17.

———, "(The) Lancaster School Mottoes." Library at Winterthur Museum & Country Estate, Winterthur, Delaware.

———, "Life in a High School." *The Pennsylvania School Journal* 45, no. 2 (1896): 68-74.

———, "Life in a High School, Fifty-Two Years in a Boys' School." *The Pennsylvania School Journal* 53, no. 3 (1904): 100-105.

——— (ed.), *Lincoln Literary Collection.* New York: American Book Company, 1897.

———, "Mayor after Fifty Years." *The High School News* (Lancaster) June 1906: 65-77.

———, "Mayor's Inaugural Address," *Journal of Select Council,* 1908. City Hall, Lancaster: 440-447.

——— , "Methodical Memory Work in Literature." *The Pennsylvania School Journal* 47, no. 1 (July 1898): 17-31.

———, "One-Third of a Century." *The Pennsylvania School Journal* 37, no. 5 (1888): 178-180.

———, "Physical Training in the Public Schools." *The Pennsylvania School Journal* 10, no. 9 (March 1862): 281-285.

———, "Remarks of Mr. McCaskey." *The Pennsylvania School Journa*l 47, no. 4 (1898): 190-192.

———, "Samuel Breck, Thaddeus Stevens, Thomas H. Burrowes." *The Pennsylvania School Journal* 67, no. 5 (1918): 185-203.

———, "(The) Scotch Broom." *The Pennsylvania School Journal* 47, no. 1 (1898): 15-17.

———, "Some Reminiscences of 'Old Leacock'." *The Pennsylvania School Journal* 64, no 6 (1915): 255-260.

———, "Spirit of Christmas." *The Pennsylvania School Journal* 39, no. 7 (1891): 308-310.

———, "Thaddeus Stevens." *The Pennsylvania School Journal* 39, no. 6 (1890): 262-264.

———, "Thomas H. Burrowes, LL.D." *The Pennsylvania School Journal* 19, no. 10 (1871): 281-285.

———, "Thomas H. Burrowes, LL.D." *The Pennsylvania School Journal* 39, no. 6 (1890): 236-240.

———, "Transfer of Ownership." *The Pennsylvania School Journal* 69, no. 12 (1921): 550.

——— (ed.), *(A) Treasury of Song, Volumes I-III.* Lancaster PA: self-published, 1916.

——— (ed.), *William Penn, The Illustrious Founder of Pennsylvania*. Philadelphia: J. B. Lippincott and Company, 1882.

———, "Yule Marble," 1908. Private collection. 16 pages.

McCaskey, Patrick K., "McCaskey High School in Lancaster, Pennsylvania,"Private Collection.

McCaskey, Richard D., "Alumni Address." *The Pennsylvania School Journal* 49, no. 1 (July 1900): 33-35.

"McCaskey's Exerciser Permanently on View," *New Era* (Lancaster) April 20, 1934: 1.

"McCaskey's Great Sweep, An Overwhelming Republican Victory," *New Era* (Lancaster) February 19, 1908: 1.

McCaskey, Seldon Fant, Family Tree. Prepared for William McCaskey Chapman, 14 December 1954. Author's collection.

"Memorial Addresses." *The Pennsylvania School Journal* 30, no. 3 (1881): 123-130.

"Memorial of Roses." *The Pennsylvania School Journal* 43, no. 12 (1895): 546-548.

"Mercy's Dream," *The Pennsylvania School Journal* 54, no. 12 (June 1906): 572-573.

Mombert, J. I., *An Authentic History of Lancaster County.* Lancaster: J.E. Barr and Company, 1869: 614 pages.

"Music in a High School." *The Pennsylvania School Journal* 53, no. 3 (1904): 111-114.

"National Fast, The." *Daily Evening Express* (Lancaster) January 5, 1861: 2.

"Nearly 300 Former Pupils Pay Tribute to Dr. McCaskey," *Testimonial Dinner to Jack McCaskey*, October 9, 1926, Lancaster, Pennsylvania: 5-7

"New Cemetery Dedicated, A" *New Era* (Lancaster) October 12, 1908: 2.

"Nice Crowd Before the Mayor," *New Era* (Lancaster) January 21, 1908: 1.

"Nineteenth Arbor Day." *The Pennsylvania School Journal* 42, no. 11 (1894): 499-504.

"No. 600," *The Pennsylvania School Journal* 50, no. 6 (1901): 301-302.

"Oak Hill Academy." *Lancaster Examiner and Herald* (Lancaster) August 25, 1847:3.

"Oak Hill at Public Sale," *Lancaster Intelligencer and Weekly Advertiser* (Lancaster) November 6, 1849: 3.

"Of Christmas Cheer." *The Pennsylvania School Journal* 47, no. 7 (1899): 330-331.

"Of Thee I Sing," Unidentified newspaper clipping in private collection.

"Old Boys' High School, The" *The Pennsylvania School Journal* 67, no. 5 (November 1918): 222-224.

"Old Guard Has Spoken, The." *Daily Evening Express* (Lancaster) April 18, 1861: 2.

"Old Leacock (Circa 1754)." http://www.leacockpres.org; accessed 2010.

"One Way to Get a Position" *The Pennsylvania School Journal* 52, no. 3 (1904): 116.

"Our Educational Fathers," *Lancaster Daily Examiner* (Lancaster) December 8, 1876: 3.

"Our Eighth Arbor Day." *The Pennsylvania School Journal* 37, no. 5(1888): 176-180.

"Our Fall Arbor Day." *The Pennsylvania School Journal* 39, no. 4 (1890): 173-174.

"Our Lamented Chief." *Lancaster Examiner and Herald* (Lancaster) April 26, 1865: 2.

"Our Ninth Arbor Day." *The Pennsylvania School Journal* 37, no. 11(1889): 387-392.

"Our School Arbor Day." *The Pennsylvania School Journal* 34, no. 6 (1885): 243-251.

"Our Seventh Arbor Day." *The Pennsylvania School Journal* 36, no. 11(1888): 420-422.

"Our Sixth Arbor Day." *The Pennsylvania School Journal* 36, no. 5 (1887): 196-199.

"Our Spring Arbor Day." *The Pennsylvania School Journal* 40, no. 11 (1892): 502-507.

"Our Spring Arbor Day at Lancaster High School." *The Pennsylvania School Journal* 35, no. 12 (1887): 498-501.

"Our Yellow Elephant," *Intelligencer Journal* (Lancaster) April 7, 1906: 4.

"Passage of the Presidential Funeral Train Through the City, The," *Intelligencer Journal* (Lancaster) April 26, 1865.

"Past of the Journal, The," *The Pennsylvania School Journal* 3, no. 11 (May 1860): 322-325.

Perrot, Augustus, "On Vocal Music," *The Pennsylvania School Journal* 2, no. 9 (March 1854): 292-295.

"Picture on the Wall, The." *The Pennsylvania School Journal* 39, no. 5 (November 1890): 227-230.

"Planting Trees." *The Pennsylvania School Journal* 33, no. 5 (1884): 202-204.

"Pleasant Weather Only Thing Needed," *Intelligencer Journal* (Lancaster) September 20, 1901: 1.

"Pleasures That Are Not Sought." *The Pennsylvania School Journal* 41, no. 10 (1893): 433-434.

"Popular Protest, A," *New Era* (Lancaster) November 12, 1906: 1.

"Preface," *Biographical Annals of Lancaster County* The Reprint Company Publishers, Spartanburg, South Carolina, 1985 Volume 1: preface.

"President Elect: His Progress Towards the White House, The." *Lancaster Examiner and Herald* (Lancaster) February 27, 1861: 2-3.

"President Greets Dr. M'Caskey on 95th Anniversary," *Intelligencer Journal* (Lancaster) October 10, 1932: 1, 5.

"Proceedings of Court." *Daily Evening Express* (Lancaster) April 15, 1861: 3.

"Proclamation, A." *Lancaster Examiner and Herald* (Lancaster) January 2, 1861: 2.

"Protect the Birds." *The Pennsylvania School Journal* 45, no. 12 (1897): 611-612.

"Reception of Mr. Lincoln." *Daily Evening Express* (Lancaster) February 22, 1861: 2.

"Reception of President Buchanan." *Daily Evening Express* (Lancaster) March 7, 1861: 2.

"Report of Committee on the Commemoration of the Christiana Riot and Treason Trials of 1851." *Journal of the Lancaster County Historical Society* 15, no. 8 (1911): 237-243.

"Report of Committee Which Arranged the Robert Fulton Celebration at Fulton House," *Journal of the Lancaster County Historical Society* 13, no. 8 (1909):193-228.

"Retirement of Dr. McCaskey," *New Era* (Lancaster) June 8, 1906: 6.

"Return Home of Hon Thaddeus Stevens." *Daily Evening Express* (Lancaster) July 9, 1864: 2.

Riddle, William, *One Hundred and Fifty Years of School History in Lancaster, Pennsylvania.* Lancaster PA: The New Era Printing Company, 1905.

"Riot of 1851, The." *Inquirer* (Lancaster) April 1, 1911: 4.

"Rites Sunday for Dr. M'Caskey." *New Era* (Lancaster) September 20, 1935: 1, 8.

"Romantic Story of Ancient Church." *Daily Local News* (West Chester) September 20, 1929: 8.

"Rosencrans." *Daily Evening Express* (Lancaster) January 7, 1863: 2.

Ross, Chester R., *Two Hundred Years of Church History.* Reprinted 1989, Gordonville, Pennsylvania Print Shop. 178 pages.

"Sabbath Observance," *New Era* (Lancaster) November 26,1906, 1.

"Sadsbury Murder, The." *The Lancaster Examiner and Herald* (Lancaster) September 24, 1851: 2.

"Sad Suicide," *Intelligencer Journal* (Lancaster) January 21, 1884: 2.

Saint James' Church Vestry Book. Vestry Minutes, April 5, 1847- November 29, 1903. St. James' Episcopal Church archives, Lancaster, Pennsylvania. 560 pages.

Saint John's Episcopal Church Compass, www.stjohnscompass.org. Accessed 2011.

Schaeffer, Nathan C., "A Deserved Honor." *The Pennsylvania School Journal* 54, no. 11 (1906): 42.

———, "La Fayette Arbor Day." *The Pennsylvania School Journal* 47, no. 4 (1898): 183.

Schindle, Willis A., "Our Trip to Gettysburg." *High School News Jubilee Number* (June 1906): 7-9.

"School Excursion to Chiques." *Intelligencer Journal* (Lancaster), October 17, 1884: 3.

Scott, Bob, "Think of J.P. McCaskey When You Hear 'Jolly Old St. Nicholas,'" *Intelligencer Journal* (Lancaster) December 24, 1996: B-4.

"Scrapbook, 1880-1912." School District of Lancaster Records, 1838-1947 Manuscript Group, LancasterHistory.org.

Sener/Sehner Collection, 1805-1911 Manuscript Group 112, Folder 2, Insert 1. LancasterHistory.org.

"Sentimental Candidate, The," *Intelligencer Journal* (Lancaster), January 31, 1906: 4.

"Serenaded the Mayor and Heard a Good Speech," *New Era* (Lancaster) February 19, 1908: 1.

Shelley, Leo, (archivist at St. James Episcopal Church) in discussion with the author, Lancaster, Pennsylvania: March 31, 2010.

Slaugh, Vince, "Better Know an Officer." www.lancasteratwar.com. December 12, 2014.

Slaughter, Thomas, *Bloody Dawn: The Christiana Riot and Racial Violence in the Antebellum North.* New York: Oxford Press, 1991.

Smith, Harriet (ed.), *Autobiography of Mark Twain, Volume 1.* Berkeley: University of California Press, 2010.

"Some Extracts from Letters," *Testimonial Dinner to Jack McCaskey*, October 9, 1926, Lancaster, Pennsylvania: 10-17.

"Song Collection, The." *The Pennsylvania School Journal* 24, no. 3 (1875): 150.

"Spring Arbor Day." *The Pennsylvania School Journal*44, no. 11 (1896): 507-508.

"Spring Arbor Day," *The Pennsylvania School Journal*, 54, no. 11 (1906): 499-502.

"Stars and Star Groups of Our Winter Heavens." *The Pennsylvania School Journal* 27, no. 7 (1879): 221-234.

Stetson, Lee (ed.), *The Wild Muir.* Heyday and Yosemite Conservancy, 1994. 211 pages.

Stoltzfus Family in discussion with the author, Gordonville, PA November, 2012.

"Stops the Clansman," *Intelligencer Journal* (Lancaster) November 12, 1906: 1.

"Study of the Stars." *The Pennsylvania School Journal* 29, no. 1 (1880): 20-23.

"Sunday Observance," *New Era* (Lancaster) November 28, 1908: 2.

"Swinging 'Neath the Old Apple-Tree." *The Pennsylvania School Journal* 35, no. 11 (1887): 470.

"Talk on Trees," *New Era* (Lancaster) March 21, 1890: 1.

"Teachers and the Draft." *The Pennsylvania School Journal* 11, no. 5 (1862): 129.

"Thaddeus Stevens." *The Pennsylvania School Journal* 54, no. 4 (1905): 183-185.

"Thaddeus Stevens. Memorial Day Tribute at His Tomb." *The Pennsylvania School Journal* 54, no. 1 (1905): 28-29.

Thoreau, Henry D., *Walden; Or, Life in the Woods*. New York: Dover Publications, Inc. 1995.

"Throngs Pass M'Caskey Bier." *New Era* (Lancaster) September 23, 1935: 3.

"Thursday Evening, July 16." *New Era* (Lancaster) July 16, 1908: 4.

Townsend McCaskey to Edward McCaskey, 25 January 1987. Private Collection.

Townsend McCaskey to Tom and Betty McCaskey, 28 November 1981. Private Collection.

"Trees Must Be Planted." *The Pennsylvania School Journal* 36, no. 10 (1888): 374-375.

"To the 'Old Boys': Greeting," *Testimonial Dinner to Jack McCaskey*, October 9, 1926, Lancaster, Pennsylvania: 3.

United States Federal Census Record for 1860, 1870, and 1880. http://search.ancestrylibrary.com

Untitled, "(The) Arbor Day League..." *The Pennsylvania School Journal* 42, no. 4 (1893): 174.

———, "Flogging school-boys..." *The Pennsylvania School Journal* 1, no.1 (1852): 84.

———, "Have you ever..." *The Pennsylvania School Journal* 47, no. 4 (1898): 184.

———, "Hon. J. S. Morton..." *The Pennsylvania School Journal* 34, no. 5 (1885): 196-197.

———, "Our first visit ..." *The Pennsylvania School Journal* 54, no. 12 (1906): 196-197.

———, "(The) space given..." *The Pennsylvania School Journal* 33, no.11 (1885): 452.

———, "There are very many good men..." *The Pennsylvania School Journal* 34, no. 5 (1885): 196.

———, "To spend a day…" *The Pennsylvania School Journal* 33, no. 9 (1885): 365.

———, "We have heard . . .," *High School News*, June 1906: 120. Lancaster, Pennsylvania.

———, "We remember well…." *The Pennsylvania School Journal* 46, no. 4 (1897): 180.

Van Ingen, Lori, "A Jewel for New YMCA." *Intelligencer Journal/Lancaster New Era* September 21, 2009: B1-B2.

"Visit to Cemetery Hill." *The Pennsylvania School Journal* 15, no. 3 (1866): 58-60.

"Visit to Pittsburgh." *The Pennsylvania School Journal* 45, no. 7 (1897): 338-339.

"Vocal Music in Common Schools," *The Pennsylvania School Journal* 4, no. 10 (April 1856): 331-332

"War Excitement, The." *Lancaster Examiner and Herald* (Lancaster) April 24, 1861: 2-3.

"War Feeling- Arrival of the Ohio Volunteers, The" *Intelligencer Journal* (Lancaster) April 30, 1861: 2

"War Fervor." *Lancaster Examiner and Herald* (Lancaster) May 1, 1861: 2.

"Warning about Fireworks, A" *New Era* (Lancaster) June 23, 1906: 2.

"Warning to Spitters," *New Era* (Lancaster) June 5, 1908: 1.

"Where Lincoln Stood City Will Celebrate." *Intelligencer Journal* (Lancaster) February 11, 1909: 5.

Whitson, Thomas, "The Early Abolitionists of Lancaster County." *Journal of the Lancaster County Historical Society* 15, no. 3 (1911): 69-85.

Wickersham, James Pyle, "An Era of Growth." *A History of Education in Pennsylvania.* Lancaster: Inquirer Publishing Company, 1886: 551-585.

———, "Historical Sketch of Education in Pennsylvania." *The Pennsylvania School Journal* 16, no. 7 (January 1868): 209-212.

———, "The Rise of the Teachers' Profession." *A History of Education in Pennsylvania.* Lancaster: Inquirer Publishing Company, 1886: 642-661.

William S. McCaskey to John Piersol McCaskey, 24 December 1863. Rick Abel collection.

William S. McCaskey to John P. McCaskey, 26 July 1864. In author's collection.

William S. McCaskey to John Piersol McCaskey, 13 September 1864. In author's collection.

Winship, A. E., "Thaddeus Stevens." *The Pennsylvania School Journal.* 47, no. 7 (1899): 296-299.

Witmer, A. E., "Reminiscences of Paradise Township." *Journal of the Lancaster County Historical Society* 1, no. 5 (December 1896): 150-160.

"Woodman, Spare That Tree." *The Pennsylvania School Journal.* 34, no. 10 (1886): 424.

Young, Ronald C., *Lancaster County, Pennsylvania, in the Civil War.* Apollo PA: Closson Press, 2002.

Index

D

E

F

G

H

J

K

L

M

N

O

P

R

S

T

U

V

W

Y